Ôdakassin'a nspi Sôgemô Ôibgui Kôabi

ta Kedag Ô'banaki Ôtlokôganal

—A Visit with Chief Grey Lock

and Other Abenaki Stories—

Nôbi'taôlaui Alitemghil'ua Medaulinno 'Asokw Mgezo' ta agma Lakamiguezo

—Including Adventures of Medicine Man "Cloud Eagle" and his Family—

By E. George "Peskunck" Larrabee

Book I

HERITAGE BOOKS
2019

HERITAGE BOOKS
AN IMPRINT OF HERITAGE BOOKS, INC.

Books, CDs, and more—Worldwide

For our listing of thousands of titles see our website
at
www.HeritageBooks.com

Published 2019 by
HERITAGE BOOKS, INC.
Publishing Division
5810 Ruatan Street
Berwyn Heights, Md. 20740

Copyright © 2019 E. George "Peskunck" Larrabee

Original artwork by the author.

All rights reserved. No part of this book may be reproduced or transmitted in any form or by any means, electronic or mechanical, including photocopying, recording or by any information storage and retrieval system without written permission from the author, except for the inclusion of brief quotations in a review.

International Standard Book Number
Paperbound: 978-0-7884-5870-5

Chapters for *A Visit With Chief Grey Lock* & Adventures of Medicine Man Cloud Eagle and his Family, Book I

	Preface	v.
	Dramatis Personae	xiii.
1.	A 'Diving Hawk' Hat	1.
2.	Welcoming Song	22.
3.	The Prayer of Cloud Eagle	27.
4.	Handsome One's Medicine Garden	44.
5.	Handsome One and the Slow Ones	51.
6.	Wise Woman Remembers	56.
7.	Cloud Eagle acquires a Dog-Lock, Red-Colored Fusil	77.
8.	Cloud Eagle climbs the Hemlock Tree	87.
9.	Medicine Roots, Wild Tubers, and Fresh Greens	101.
10.	"Man from Nothing" Creates (Living) Human Beings	111.
11.	A Good Several-Together Persons Hunt	121.
12.	Cow Ringer Instruments and Turkey Harvesting	124.
13.	Mohicans Warriors to the Rescue	127.
14.	Why the Ash Tree is Good Medicine against Rattlesnakes	136.
15.	Lavish Praise for Grandmother Juliette	152.
16.	The Playful, Friendly Bear	155.
17.	"Firelock," the Shawnee Warrior, Asks about a Certain Name	163.
18.	A Ceremony with Spiritually-Powerful Turtles	168.

19.	The Return of the Good Hunting and Fishing Family	169.
20.	Different Views of Grandfather Rattlesnake	173.
	Addendum	179.
	Bibliography	183.
	Index	185.

Author's Preface

Considering that it has been the ambition of the author to imbue the present work with as much historical authenticity as possible, it occurred to him… that such authenticity should include his rendering of dialogue, of *language,* equally authentic. Especially in view of the fact that the narratives' main protagonists, Abenaki Indian people (whose activities were --at least somewhat-- recorded in colonial documents) necessarily spoke their own language. Ergo, said protagonists, whether quite real, such as Chief Grey Lock, his family and associates, or whether conjectural, such as the medaulinno --spiritually powerful person -- (usually translated as 'shaman' or 'medicine man'), Cloud Eagle, and his family… therefore speak their own tongue as they would have in actuality. Others are also involved in the narration, namely Iroquoians and Osôgenak (Algonkins-proper). Not that, in the colonial period, they wouldn't have known some French and English; and likely minor snatches of other European speech, such as Basque and Dutch. They certainly did, out of necessary interaction with the colonists over the years, with the result that Alnôbaiui [the] Common People's Way, the Abenaki language, is today permeated with words that have French and English sources… necessarily so, in the instance of names for domestic animals (for example) brought from Europe, non-existent here in pre-Columbian times.

    The author is quite conversational in Western Abenaki but is not fluent, and therefore many words used in this story are taken from Odanak Reserve (Québec) Chief Joseph Laurent's *Abenakis and English Dialogues,* 1884, the *Western Abenaki Dictionary,* Gordon Day, Ph.D, 1994, and such language guides …and from personal experience in seeking correct pronunciations that textbooks may not fully convey; such as for "my friend," spelled in textbooks as nidôba, but which is, according to the late Walter Wadso, Odanak Chief (1990s), pronounced nidô*mb*a (my emphasis)… with an awareness that the **old** language was spoken (except for shouting or loud singing) in ***non-labial frecktle*** mode; i.e., minimal movement of the mouth. An indication given by Sébastian Râle, missionary to the Norridgewock, 1691-1724, is: "They have several letters that are sounded wholly from the throat, without any motion of the lips: *ou* for example, is one of their number."[*]

    The author, aware of such minimalism (reflecting their *very quiet* world) regards 19th and 20th century language texts as having unconsciously absorbed Europe's louder accents. Therefore he declines to copy the modern texts exactly, here and there substituting a 'u' or ô for today's protruding-lips **w**, &c. An example: citing the Abenaki for female, his more respectful, softly voweled skua rather than the crass European - accented "squaw," the latter *loaded,* reeking, with colonialist male chauvinism.

[*] Volume IV, **Language of the Abenaquies,** Collections of the Maine Historical Society, 1856.

Author's Preface

The more loudly enunciated 'squaw' (there's that emphasized *'aw'* suffix), in "Indian Country" today, is, in some quarters, not even recognized at all, is *rejected* as a Native American term. Even thought to be something dreamed up by the white man, and with derogatory intention. It is true, indeed, that skua is not Iroquoian, is not Lakota, &c. Each Native nation, and supra-national language family, has its own term for the same thing.

At times, in the following narrative, the reader will also come across Abenaki words ending in skw, which the reader might take to be a shortened form of skua. But, as the saying goes, "t'ain't necessarily so." Especially if skw is the suffix on the name of a *male* animal (for example), it can't be true. 'Skw' may be used as the suffix for a female creature, but still doesn't indicate female. For example, an adult female beaver is skuamiskw, p. 30, *Western Abenaki Dictionary,* Volume II. The equivalent of female is in the prefix. Quite logically, there was no reason to indicate same in the suffix as well, except (apparently), in the case of a female bear. The suffix (in the instance of skw) may be a truncation of guaskw, among the definitions for which are "to a finish, enough, exactly," a way of indicating not just singular but mature, complete. Reference *List of Selected Roots,* Volume II, p. XXXVIII, Dr. Day's *Western Abenaki Dictionary.* An example: for an "arrow plant," a cattail, the word is pakuaaskw. The plural for same is pakuaaskol, and location is pakuaaskok, p. 65, *Ibid.* In Alnôbaiui, 'the Common Peoples' Way,' the Abenaki language, pakuaaskw actually indicates the arrow **shaft** plant, the word for an arrow shaft being pakua, "arrow shaft or blunt arrow," p. 16, *Ibid.* A complete arrow, "with a head and feathers," is tiskuôdi (plural tiskuôdial, location tiskuôdik), p. 16, *Ibid.* An arrowhead by itself is oziguôn (or oziguaôn), p. 16, *Ibid.* The shorter word, this author avers, is (very likely) the older, *original* term because it is easier to pronounce with less mouth movement, reflecting the Peoples' very quiet way of speaking, which, left undisturbed for many centuries, is how the People would have (ordinarily) spoken. The intrusion of the colonists, when there inevitably occurred instances, such as in the port cities, or noisy European encampments inland (squealing axels, lowing cattle, sergeants shouting, people talking at once)… which compelled visiting Ô'banakiak -- Abenaki people -- if they were to be heard, to speak more forcefully. The more the Auanock (the Strangers) noisily intruded, the more the People had to adapt their utterances until their own speech patterns became infected.

If readers will avail themselves of the language sources cited by the author, such as Chief Joseph Laurent's *Dialogues,* Chief Masta's *Grammar,* Dr. Day's *Dictionary,* etc. (cited in this work's bibliography), they will see some differences between spellings in those texts and, concerning a few words, the author's spellings.

Author's Preface

For example, Dr. Day's spelling for the cattail is pakwaaskw. To reflect the old, original non-labial frecktle mode, the author has modified this to pakuaaskw, replacing the first w with a u, and, while retaining the word-final w, reducing said w to a smaller point size and in the regular 'Tempest Sans ITC' typeface available in his PC type font. While the majority of his text is written in the 'Times New Roman' typeface (commonplace in English-language books and periodicals) he has chosen the Tempest Sans ITC font to express words and phrases in Native American languages (at least initially) because (1.) it is a more 'natural-looking' typeface, somewhat uneven, resembling hand-printing, therefore akin to pictographs (even though absolutely employing the "Latin" alphabet ("Latin" in quotes, as if casting doubt on the veracity of that term; see footnote below).* (2.) Another convenience of Tempest Sans ITC is that, in its main, or regular, font, it is, especially compared to 'regular' Times New Roman, a thin, *weak* typeface. This works out well -- in the sense of the author's purposes, -- because it compels him, in giving the typeface parity, or 'equal weight' to Times New Roman, to employ Tempest Sans ITC in *boldface*. He reserves, for most native words, the regular, "weaker" font to express consonants or vowels that were more softly spoken... more softly spoken, the merest breath, even within the context of yesteryear's quietly spoken languages. To emphasize this, the author often *further* shrinks such letters from a given sentences' 14-point size (in his original ms.) to 12 or 11 point size (occasionally in TNR also). The word-final w in his pakuaaskw is a case in point, that word-final w indicating the merest puff of breath, almost inaudible.

*Though the native peoples of the Americas didn't have alphabetical writing in the late (colonial-era) European sense... there are a few letters, however, extant in Mesoamerica (viewed by 20th century archeologists as mere decorations) that *do* coincide with the 'Latin' alphabet. Namely, to wit: G, L, O, and T, plain to see on pre-Columbian (*very* pre-Columbian) Mexica and Mayan temples and stelae. These are depicted in Hunbatz Men's 1990 *Secrets of Mayan Science / Religion*. The G, L, and T were often employed as borders on temples, the letters (as capitals of course) unrecognized (by modern, Western archeologists) as the same letters in European alphabets, understandably when *as temple borders,* because they are engraved *alternately* rightside up and upside down, especially the Gs and Ts. Sacred symbols, yes, but having meanings absolutely coinciding with today's 'European' alphabet.

For example the sacred T signifies the dependence of all animal life on air, oxygen, derived from trees, from plants in general... which the Europeans, on their side, incorporated into the present-day words '**t**ree' and '**t**ea,' obviously derived from a world-encompassing common language. G, originally a completely circular spiral, signifies the Great Spirit as the source of All Movement and Measure, emanating from our galactic center. A square G being easier to carve into stone, the middle cross-bar signifies life - generating power launched from the center, spiraling vastly outward. L and O are likewise symbols of great material and spiritual significance, O also used to indicate zero. The Mayans saw the center, where the Great Spirits' power emanates from as merely galactic (due to their lack of telescopes) because they could see the Milky Way. Today,

Author's Preface

On Syntax: Though it would be "truly authentic" for the author to have his protagonists speak in their olden, traditional *word-flow* rhythms, such vernacular, exactly translated, can be expected to be confusing to the average reader. As an example of how confusing it would be, consider the following explanation by author Lawrence Millman in his *Wolverine Creates the World,* 1993, in a note on the Innu peoples' language (which has Algonquian affinity with Alnôbaiui) accompanying his Introduction:

"Like other macro-Algonquian languages, Inueimun leans heavily on verbs and verb constructions. Whereas an English speaker might say "It's lousy weather," a speaker of Inueimun would say "It-lousy-weathers." That sort of tortured syntax is fine in the original, but not much fun to read in translation. It has the additional drawback of making one's Indian friends sound demented." Millman continues: "So I've chosen a more or less standard vernacular for my renderings of Innu stories." Kedalighinéna Natural, -- or Native -- peoples today, after centuries of genocidical oppression by the aggrandizing colonialist powers… are understandably sensitive toward phrases, in any European tongue (such as his 'tortured' and 'demented'), that can be taken as derogatory toward themselves. What Millman means is how a typical *Anglo-American* or *Anglo-Canadian* reader would view a sentence in Inueimun if said reader were to try to comprehend Inueimun in the languages' everyday *colloquial* grammatical structure. The Inueimun sentence structure doesn't easily match up with its equivalent in colloquial English. An English speaker with no linguistic training will quickly become confused.

Accomplished linguist John McWhorter, in his 2011 *What Language Is,* gives even more convoluted examples of sentence structure in his translations of examples of speech in many other non-European tongues, some even less well known than Algonquian and Iroqouian. Therefore the present author has, also, rendered conversations (and private thoughts) largely into familiar Anglo-American syntax or vernacular, though all the Abenaki, Iroquois, and Osôgena (Algonkin) words, *by themselves,* are as absolutely authentic as he can make them. *Primarily* translated into familiar Anglo-American vernacular, *occasionally* rendering a translation much as in the original Alnôbaiui… when not too convoluted compared to modern English. He trusts that it shouldn't be confusing to his readers, who he doesn't expect, in their majority, to be degrees-holding professional linguists.

The author has rendered the initial Abenaki (or Iroquois) sentence structures, as spoken by his protagonists, -- in the order that the words would be arranged in if they were speaking in colloquial English -- so that the reader can conveniently match the following translation in English with their foregoing Alnôbaiui equivalents.

having telescopes (including outer-space traveling telescopes such as the Hubble) we understand that the Great Creator's vast power emanates from the center of… the entire universe.

Author's Preface

There is no point in burdening the reader with the task of unraveling the decidedly unfamiliar native vernacular while they are trying to familiarize themselves with the simple meanings of native words, of nouns, verbs, adjectives, &c. While Americans and Canadians are already familiar with *some* Native American words and expressions -- for example, fully half of the names of the states of the U.S. have Native American names and many, if not most, of the country's major rivers (and five of the Canadian provinces) have native names. Canada and Mexico (from Mexica) themselves are native names, and the names of various American birds, animals, and fish also are known from their native roots (most of which are *Abenaki-related* Algonquian). The above is of scant help in understanding whole conversations in Abenaki (or in Iroqouian, etc.). Especially when one takes into consideration that the average American, by and large, though having lived all his/her life in said states, and alongside said rivers... *doesn't know what the names mean.* How many citizens of Massachusetts today know that the name, originally Mäsa'dzosek (or Mạssa'dzosek) indicates "Place of the Great Hills"..? The reference is to heights south of Boston, Milton area, encompassed by the Blue Hills Reservation. Compounding the problem is that some of the native names given to states are actually applied to a distant region from their place of origin. Wyoming, for example, is a Lenapéuk term (of the Algonquian language family, and therefore Abenaki related) derived from the Wyoming Valley of eastern Pennsylvania. The author attaches *uk* to Lenapé to indicate the animate plural, *people.*

Now and then in the following narrative, the reader will come across an Alnôbaiui term that seems quite familiar... for example, mkezen. Does that mean *moccasin?* It *does* -- it's the root of the modern, open-mouth-pronounced "moccasin." The next step up the reader's 'learning curve' at that point is to grasp the plural for moccasins... mkezenal. Abandoning the English S plural for the Alnôbaiui *inanimate* plural 'al.' A final note: The following quotation is from an observation on the Algonquian language and, by extension, on all tribal languages by the author of the 1980 *The Indian Crafts of William & Mary Commanda.* It is too delicious not to cite.

"If it is true that any culture is best reflected in its language, it is unfortunate that the Indian languages are so inaccessible to non-natives. *The Algonquian language, for one, is a splendorous thing.* To begin to study the Algonquian language is to realize immediately the stupidity of the portrayals on television, which have the Indians uttering little more than "ugh." *The white student of the Algonquian language would take a long time before he progressed beyond the Indian equivalent of "ugh."*

Author's Preface

This language lesson preface could extend much further, but, as the reader, perhaps waxing impatient, is presumably interested in visiting Chief Grey Lock and his people, the author has provided additional linguistic explanations, insights, in footnotes (occasionally quite copious ones) as his narrative moves along from chapter to chapter. Naua --Therefore, -- pônônsw citôiui… - without further ado…--

Nôuiponakisos -- Mid-Winter Moon -- January, 2019

Nspi Kedalamihiken --With Gratitude --

When an author's book (or books), are finally going to press, especially after a lifetime of effort (said effort including not only work, but *dreaming,* as well)… whom does he thank..? In this instance, *especially,* the native people of the Americas. In fact the native, the *natural* people of the whole world, victimized horribly by the colonizing European imperial powers, the tribal peoples whose story, whose resistance to generations of self-aggrandizing genocide is finally being told, not by merely this author, by many, an epic narration only now just beginning. He thanks those close to him, family members, his friends (collaborators to one degree or another), Msalkik pemôuzouinnoak ôadsi oliônimek -- Many people to thank.--

In making possible the present work, we thank not only those described within its pages, Chief Grey Lock and his people, but those shown in the work's 20th and 21st century photographs, those who donned their Abenaki or *Canadien,* &c., regalia, making history come alive, such as lyrical poet Phyllis R. Larrabee, wielding 'dibble stick,' &c. Also Chief Spirit Water, Gail Ruggles, secretary to the chief, present-day fellow tribal members, so many. He additionally thanks, for their editing of the present work, Gail I. Johnson and Brian Long, the latter a Public School English teacher of Eden, VT. Ms. Johnson was a professional Naturalist, for 33 years, at the Roaring Brook Nature Center, Canton, CT, presently of E. Montpelier, VT, and my Abenaki language student for the past ten years… who worked **very hard** with me in perfecting the complicated grammatical nuances in the language, *and* greatly assisted in completing the Index. He thanks ac'hi *mezi* abaziak -- also *all* trees,-- mezi auaasak ta 'lidooak' -- all animals and "those that fly,"-- namasak, fish, mezi minigha, all vegetation, mezi pemôuzouôgan tebeskôdiganak -- all life forms -- *in general,* auan, air, the very air that we breathe, so generously provided by those aforementioned trees and plants. Mother Earth herself, *the universe **itself***… Ktsi Manitou… The Higher Power that animates us, motivating our better natures. Not forgotten, all to be thanked.

E. George 'Peskunck' Larrabee   Woodbury, Vermont

E. George Larrabee

MY DEAR FRIEND, GEORGE "Flintlock," 'Peskunck' Larrabee, is truly one of the founding fathers and catalysts of French and Indian war reenacting, historical research, and the author of many muzzle loading / black powder-shooting and hunting magazine articles.

'Peskunck' started writing historical articles back in 1966 for the NMLRA organ *Muzzle Blasts*. He continues with *Muzzle Blasts* to the present day, illustrating its "Junior Blasts" feature, and (due to the excellence of his work for *Muzzle Blasts*) in 1979 was invited to join the staffs of the newborn *Muzzleloader* magazine and the *Black Powder Times,* and, thanks to his artistic and photographic talents, contributed original drawings and photos, including full-color front covers to the above, contributing also to the *Black Powder Annual,* to *Make It With Leather* magazine, to *Massachusetts Out-of-Doors,* the *Vermont Sportsman*, the *New England Homestead* magazine and various other journals and newspapers.

He started shooting flintlock muzzle-loaders in 1966 and was a founding member, and the first president, of the Honorable Company of Konekticutt Valley Firelock Marksmen (the Black Powder Division of the Westfield, MA Sportsmen's Club), a chartered NMLRA club. He was a qualified member of the trekking group The Partisans in the 1980s, which specialized in 18th century survival techniques. Developing an increasing interest in Native American history and culture, collaborating with tribal members, he has long since furthered the Native American communities with his writings and seminars. He was officially adopted by the Abenaki / Sokokiiak Nation of Missisquoi in a sweat lodge ceremony in 1990, serving today as a Tribal Council member of the (Missisquoi - allied) Clan of the Hawk.

Currently retired after nearly 23 years of work on the railroad as a Trackman, Machine Operator and Foreman (ConRail, Inc.), he has adopted a new career as a full-time writer / illustrator and works with youth, having served as an Americorps Volunteer, an Education and Prevention Specialist of the Dawnland Center, 1999-2002. He today continues to work independently against addictive substances, mingling 'prevention messages' among his elaborate presentations of Abenaki culture and language in schools, libraries, museums, and the like. Having served in the U.S. Army as a paratrooper, 1951 - 53, he has made a couple of sky-diving jumps in the 21st century and as of this writing is planning another one.

--Bob Bearor, Author of Heritage Books' *Battle on Snowshoes* and *Leading by Example* series

Dramatis Personae

"Grey Lock," warrior chief of 'Grey Lock's Castle,' the early 18th century fortified Abenaki town formerly on the Missisquoi River in the extreme northwest Vermont of today. He was known among his people as Ôauanoleuo, meaning "He Who Fools Them," eluding Anglo-American scalp hunters… baptized Pial-Azôn, *Pierre-Jean*.

A'lôn, baptized *Saint Hélène*, wife of the chief and leading matron among the Abenaki people. Hélène, spoken with an Abenaki accent, is rendered A'lôn.

Azôn-Badise, young son of Sôgemô -- Chief -- Grey Lock (Ôauanoleuo), christened *Jean-Baptise*. Has the nickname of "Migakadso -- Little Fighting Man."-- Also "Ôski Nikola --Young Nicholas,"-- after his godfather, Colonel du Milice, *le Sieur* Nicholas de Saint Ours.

Mali-Sallot, young daughter of A'lôn and the chief, christened after saints *Marie* and *Charlotte*. Also called (especially by the chief) Ktsi Sôgemôsku'sizo, Alnôbaiui for "Grand Chief, female, small;" the Abenaki equivalent of Princess.

Georges La Bluetté, French-Canadian tenant-farmer and *Ensign du Milice* and guest of Chief 'He Who Fools Them.' An aspiring *truchement* (interpreter), and *artiste* - chronicler.

Cæsar Besogne, French-Canadian *locataire-fermier* -- tenant-farmer, -- *Sergent du Milice*, aspiring *truchement*, friend of and assistant to La Bluetté.

Asokw Mgezo -- Cloud Eagle. -- An important Medaulinno and defender of N'd'akinna -- Our Land. -- Father of Oligouôgasku'sizo -- Beautiful Girl, -- and the boy Olôbao -- Handsome One. --

Ôeoandamsko -- Wise Woman, -- prominent Medaulinnoskua at Missisquoi and the mother of two teens, daughter Oligouôgasku'sizo and son Olôbao.

Oligouôgasku'sizo -- Beautiful Girl. -- Daughter of Ôeoandamsko and Cloud Eagle.

Olôbao -- Handsome One, -- young son of Asokw Mgezo and Wise Woman.

Pmauikho -- He Who Goes Ahead, -- war captain and chief of scouts of Alnôbak (Ordinary People, or 'Indians') allied with vanguard detachment of French soldiers and militiamen shadowing retreating British and Anglo-American army.

Lieutenant Louis La Mercier, commander of *troupes de la Marine* and co-commander of French-Canadian militia.

Dramatis Personae Continued

Jonas T'songeba, expatriate Mohican warrior (now considered Abenaki), a member of Pmauikho's band of fighting men / scouts.

Pepôkuan -- 'Firelock,' -- (Gun) in the Shawnee dialect, expatriate Suanni (Shawnee) warrior, member of Pmauikho's band associated with T'songeba.

Kisikauo -- meaning, in Alnôbaiui, 'He Produces' (or He Makes). The paramount Medaulinno -- Spiritually Powerful Person -- ('Medicine Man') of Grey Lock's town.

Nbizonhouo M'Sadokues -- 'Medicine Provider from Big River Forbears.' In Grey Lock's 'Castle' the paramount Medaulinnoskua ('Medicine Woman').

Nikola M'Sadokues, fighting man from Odanak Christian mission in Québec, brother of Llobal (Robert) M'Sadokues, another warrior with the band.

Kyâs'hútâ, 'Fire on the Mountain,' in Kaanauagihnono Iroquoian… from the Caugnawaga Mission near Montreal, co-chief with Pmauikho, uncle of the young Kaanaugi scout Sken'nenhahson'a dsi'ile -- He Who Walks Softly. --

Nespokusino -- 'He Dreams of Someone.' -- Romantic young Abenaki warrior / bow hunter who has not yet acquired his own paskhigan -- firelock. --

Olitôguezo -- 'He Sounds Nice.' -- Melodiously voiced fisherman / warrior / gatherer of Grey Lock's Castle.

Salom -- 'St. Jerome.' -- Baptismal name of the part-Abenaki, part-Algonkin hunter, a first cousin to Maigamo, a member of Pmauikho's war band.

Maigamo -- He is Wolf. -- Cousin of Salom, also part-Algonkin and part-Abenaki fighter… like Salom a grandson of Soliôn and Kuôgunas.

Soliôn -- 'Juliette.' Vivacious Abenaki daughter of Odanak's Head Chief Llobal, and an excellent hunter and resourceful wife… grandmother of Salom and Maigamo.

Kuôgunas, also called C'hila, Algonkin Nation husband of Soliôn, grandfather of Maigamo and Salom. His name Kuôgunas, indicating "Prickly One," reflects his bristly, ill-tempered nature, as does the nickname 'C'hila,' indicating one who is perennially cross, dissatisfied.

Ôualôba -- Pretty One, -- infant son of Soliôn and Kuôgunas… the father of Salom as an adult.

Ôdakassin'a nspi Sôgemô Ôibgui Kôabi ta Kedag Ô'banaki Ôtlokôganal
--A Visit with Chief Grey Lock and Other Abenaki Stories --

1. "Panihlamek Siômo" Asolkuôn'a -- A "Diving Hawk" Hat --

THE Abenaki chief that the English colonists had taken to calling "Grey Lock" -- because of his scalp roach of prematurely gray hair-- emerged from the snowy forest on this fine day in 1724. He entered the encampment of his family -- his "extended family," one might say, as there were six lodges here on the upper reaches of the Missisquoi River. As he came to the more level ground of the camp, preparatory to taking off his snowshoes, he doffed his raccoon-tailed hat and dropped the **pakesso**, the ruffed grouse he had gotten in his morning sojourn away from the encampment. The **osuadagen asolkuôn** -- fur hat -- had kept his head toasty warm as he had hunted, his flintlock **paskhigan** held at the ready for anything that he might encounter. Fortunately, in the interest of saving powder and shot, he had not found it necessary to shoot in order to bag the pakcsso.

As he looked down at the hat and the bird, kneeling to remove his **ô'gemak** -- snowshoes, -- he could see flecks of snow still clinging to the hat and to the partridge. They reflected the arrow-less, missile-less way he had gotten it… a clever method that was, most likely, many thousands of years old. Making his way over hillocks and crossing down timber, ever alert, he had been sharp-eyed enough to spot the grouse silently perched on a low evergreen bough. Rather than thumb the hammer of his firelock back to full cock and take aim, he had slowly taken off his asolkuôn. Then he had thrown it, as hard as he could, at the unsuspecting bird. As the hat hurtled toward it, seemingly coming out of nowhere, the grouse had panicked.

Siômo'a -- *A hawk,* -- swooping down to grab it in its talons?

Instinctively it had dived into a snowdrift to hide. The "hawk" wouldn't know where it had gone. But the chief did. He was able to see the hole in the snow that pakesso had made. Moving forward, he removed his mittens, and, bending over, quickly grabbed the partridge. Extracting it from the drift, with a deft twist of its neck the succulent bird was his. Picking up the snow-flecked hat, he put it back on, ready to turn toward home. He had done enough hunting for one day (though there was yet a chance of encountering something on the way back).

But first, one more thing. He reached into his hunting pouch and took out a still smaller buckskin pouch -- his odamôinoda, tobacco's pouch. Extracting a small amount of odamô, tobacco, he murmured words of apology to mollify the spirit of the pakesso, lowering the shreds into the hole in the drift that the bird had made. He had planted, cultivated, and sun-cured the tobacco himself (of the original, "primitive" *Nicotiana rustica* variety), as was the time-honored custom among native Eastern Woodland men. It isn't a task expected of the women, who, cultivating such food staples as maize, beans, and squash, have enough to do. The men, also, don't sow large fields of it, having, likewise, many other things to engage them. Odamô is useful, mainly, as a sacrificial offering, as on the present occasion, for burning in a ritualistic "smudging bowl," and for puffing on, briefly, in a circulated pipe in ceremony or in council.

Author's photo of "Chief Grey Lock's" raccoon - tailed fur hat and grouse, its neck broken, lying forward of snowshoes "ta pazeguen'ua agma meldzasak -- and one of his mittens."-- On right is well tanned buckskin odamôinoda, tobacco's pouch, decorated with seed beads, from which the chief extracted odamô, planted, tended and cured (largely by himself)… as an offering denoting his appreciation.

Those who had gotten into the habit of smoking (having become addicted) usually didn't prefer their own home-grown N. rustica. Their season's harvest would soon be used up if they did. They preferred to trade for tobacco, raised by African captives, brought up from the Caribbean Islands. The leaves of such, *Nicotiana tabacum,* were much larger, enabling a more abundant supply, and also made for a milder, tastier smoke. Some were lured into smoking for less than healthy, completely non-spiritual reasons.

He hurried a bit on the return to camp, as he had important guests waiting for him there, *Canadiens* from up along the Pitaubaguizibo ("Between Lakes River," which the French call the "Rivière Richelieu"). One visitor's name was Georges La Bluetté, and, in addition to making his living as a husbandman (dabbling somewhat in the fur trade) farming along the Richelieu, he was also what the Plac'môniak -- Frenchmen -- call an *artiste*. He was, in addition, unlike the average Canadien *habitant,* quite literate, at least in Plac'môniui, "[the] Whiteman's Way." He could be frequently seen writing with a lead stick or quill pen on parchment …or on one of those thin, white sheets that the People had come to term a pilaskw.[1] It was a brand-new Ô'banaki word, literally meaning "new leaf," from pili, new, combined with ôanibagw, leaf.

Approaching his family's wigwam, snowshoes under an arm, his firelock slung over one shoulder, and the pakesso in the other hand, Grey Lock saw that the nodsi-sezouigad, the artist, was up. La Bluetté had arrived quite tired from his trek upriver the day before, so, when the chief had risen in the dawn with a bit of hunting in mind, he had not awakened him to invite him to come along with his own firelock. Nor did he disturb La Bluetté's two companions, equally exhausted, who yet slept in another wigwam. One was another Canadien and the other their Missisquoi Abenaki guide, Tomô, from "Grey Lock's Castle," the fortified Abenaki town at the mouth of the Rivière Missisquoi. 'Nodsi-sezouigad' is the term the Ô'banakiak apply to the European idea of 'artist;' nodsi indicating expertise or professionalism, sezoui from sezohiga, paint, and gad having to do with personhood, an individual.[2] "Skillfully He (or She) Paints" might be a way of interpreting the term.

La Bluetté was sitting on a bundle of fresh hides by the fire. An outside fire: the customary fires inside lodges could be left until later. During the day, when it isn't madsekisegad -- bad weather, -- an outside fire, used in common by the inhabitants of the circle of wigwams, is preferred for the convenience of the wider space around it. The chief appreciated the warmth of the crackling fire as he drew near. He saw that La

---

[1] Rev. Joseph Aubery's c. 1690-1700 *French Abenaki Dictionary,* p. 389, Chief Joseph Laurent's *Abenakis & English Dialogues*, p. 32 (leaf), p. 62 (paper), Chief Henry Lorne Masta's 1932 *Abenaki Grammar*, p. 56, and, p. 280, Dr. Gordon Day's 1994 *Western Abenaki Dictionary*, Volume II.

[2] Chief Joseph Laurent's *Abenakis & English Dialogues*, 1884, p. 34.

Bluetté had one of his painting-boards in hand. It was about the same size as a small artist's canvas, but was made of very smooth wood. He was, the chief could see, gôa'gôa'daôikhimek -- sketching -- with variously colored *craions*. On another pile of furs and hides (in turn loaded onto a toboggan), opposite him, sat his spouse A'lôn. Her European saint's name was Abenaki accented. The French missionaries christened their converts, or intended converts, after the saints of the Church: Saint Hélène in this instance. As an emblem of her faith a silver crucifix hung from around her neck. Next to A'lôn stood the chief's young son Azôn-Badise -- Jean-Baptiste -- who beamed when he saw his father approach. La Bluetté had been drawing their posed likenesses on his paint-board. A'lôn smiled and broke her pose, standing up to take the pakesso her husband carried. She would (more thoroughly) gut it and strip the feathers away preparatory for roasting it as part of the day's repast. The chief had already, on his return, opened the bird and deposited the entrails on a handy boulder, -- none of his company were likely to want them -- but there were doubtless ravens and other forest creatures who would appreciate the largess.

La Bluetté turned, noticed the chief, and broke into a broad smile. "Bon Jour Nidômba! " he exclaimed. He then further tested his grasp of Alnôbaiui -- the Common (Native) People's Way, -- saying 'Paakuinôguzian'...which can mean Good Morning, if the time is before noon. If it is after noon-time it means "I'm glad to see you."[3]

The *Artiste* was nothing if not versatile in his interests. In addition to traveling to Indian villages and distant encampments to paint the People's portraits, activities, and material culture artifacts, La Bluetté sought to learn their various languages. Such would make his understanding of their culture, before it withered away from the impact of European colonialism, all the deeper. In this he had found a kindred spirit in Chief Grey Lock, who was originally from western Massa'dzosek in what the Iglismôniak were calling "New England." When young he had also lived among the Muheconnuck in the Hudson Valley, absorbing a substantial knowledge of English and Dutch... and also the Mohican dialect of Algonquian speech. As well as some Iroquoian from Mohawk who traded at Fort Orange/Albany. Here in the Abenakis' "N'd'akinna -- Our Land," -- considered by the French as part of Kanada, he had quickly learned the Abenakis' Alnôbaiui. Along the Richelieu and St. Lawrence Rivers he had encountered Huron and Kaanauagihnono (Caughnawaga) *voyageurs,* thereby broadening his understanding of their Iroquoian dialects.

The chief replied to La Bluetté, saying;"N'uigôdamô ôadsi namihômek d'kia spigui -- I'm glad to see [that] you're up." -- "N'namihô k'oladialôôb -- I see that you

---

[3] Chief Joseph Laurent's 1884 *Abenakis and English Dialogues*, p. 116.

[have] hunted well,"-- La Bluetté observed. The chief shrugged slightly, replying "Kisi ônda nôdami -- It's not much, -- pakesso'a, oguaskuô -- a grouse, merely.-- Minaguiba -- Though," -- he added, and went on to describe how he had gotten the bird without shooting it. La Bluetté was duly impressed, and at that moment conceived the idea of painting a scene showing the chief throwing his asolkuôn at a partridge. "N' ônda ibi ziguenôôb peza ta sisahlôgil -- I not only saved powder and shot-- ali lakamek n'asolkuôn -- by throwing my hat, -- kaneua ac'hi -- but also,-- nikuôbi n'olitosi uadsônô ôadsi pekenamek aguetsagak paskhigan-zôbôlagezo'a -- now I won't have to clean a dirty gun-barrel,"-- the chief couldn't help but boast. At the same time, he was looking with curiosity at several household articles lying on a nearby snow bank. La Bluetté followed his gaze. Usually such items were kept inside A'lôn's wigwam[4] or close to it, to preserve them from harm when small children and dogs ran furiously about in their play, especially on such a fine day as this. In cold weather birch bark containers and clay pots are especially vulnerable. "O, yalil -- Oh, those,"-- the artist said, referring to a roots-stitched birch bark container, a basket made from spiraling, brightly dyed reed stalks, and a crenellated pot that had traditional designs impressed into it while the clay was still damp. Metal pots being now available, few such pots were being made any more. Plus a smaller basket of woven sweet-grass. Below them was a scoop-shaped scrap of bone. La Bluetté explained that he had been using the items as props, asking A'lôn and Azôn-Badise to hold one or another of them while he rendered their likenesses. A'lôn had been, earlier, scraping bits of remnant fat and flesh off the frame-stretched hide of a woodland caribou that the chief had recently brought down a league or two upriver, to the east.

"Niona uadsônôbena olikadaôgan ôadsi kia -- We have a treat for you,"-- La Bluetté announced, having put down his paint board. The *Canadien* wrapped a piece of moose-hide around the handle of a steaming tea-pot that had been placed close to the fire. He poured for the chief, into a large ceramic mug, a generous amount of kapi. However, the coffee was more than simply coffee… it had been mixed with chunks of trail-frozen chocolate, making it into mocha. It could also be sweetened with ômuaimelases,* honey.[5] Indeed a luxury this far into the bush during the winter.

*Ôauilômua is Alnôbaiui for the wasp, *Polistes spp.*, order *Apocrita.*

---

[4] A time-honored Eastern Woodland custom was that, though the men helped build them, the women owned the wigwams that their families lived in.

[5] Ômuaimelases: Abenaki for "Wasp's (bee's) molasses," i.e., honey. Wawilômwaizogal, literally "Wasp's sugar (bee's sugar") also came to be used. *Western Abenaki Dictionary,* Volume II, p. 192.

When La Bluetté had asked his fellow tenant-farmer, Cæsar Besogne, to accompany him, as a toboggan-hauling partner and all-around assistant, recruiting Tomô once they had reached the chief's downriver "castle," he knew that, as a matter of simple courtesy, since they would be rather unexpected visitors, they should bring presents. Especially since he didn't want to merely trade with them for fresh hides and furs (ahead of the usual *coureurs des bois),* but wished to paint their images. He also wanted to talk to them at length, recording their answers to his queries by jotting down copious notes on his sheets of pilaskol.[6] He and Cæsar had not only brought coffee beans and hard chocolate (the chocolate stiff from winter's cold) …but also containers of honey, maple sugar, molasses, and a loaf of cane sugar. Not that the chief and his people didn't have their own supplies of same, or some of them. But by this time of year they would be running short.

When Grey Lock took the proffered mug, La Bluetté held out a wooden spoon, unplugging the large cork of a jar of honey, offering the option of sweetening the mocha as much as one might like. "N'uadsônôbena senômoziimlases ta *canne* zogal, ac'hi
--We have maple sugar and cane sugar, also, -- tsaga k' dassidaldamô -- if you wish,"--he said. "Ônda oliôni -- No thank you,-- yo aig oguaskuô oligen -- this is just fine,"--the chief replied, well pleased. He scooped some of the honey from the jar and mixed it in, blowing on the steaming mocha to keep from burning his mouth.

Taking a cautious but appreciative sip, his weathered face crinkled as he chuckled a bit to himself. "Ta n'lidahôziô n' uadsônôba padôzigô *kia* kagôi nekuitsiôi

Articles belonging to A'lôn lying nearby, from left clockwise: Oskan pelagakhigan, Bone hide-scraper, maskua dautigan, birch-bark container, pedeguigek abazenoda, round basket (of dyed reeds), mazalôpskw kuat, clay pot, and a basket woven of mskikoiz, sweet grass.

Author's photo.

---

[6] The suffix 'ol' denotes inanimate plural. Paper**s**. *Western Abenaki Dictionary,* Volume II, p. 280.

pamegizegak --And I thought I would bring *you* something special today," -- he remarked. Reaching down, he untied a buckskin pouch that had been attached to the leather belt hidden under his woolen waist sash. From it he extracted a handful of large red berries, saying "N' aleua ôanaldôôb pabômiui yolil --I [had] almost forgotten about these,"-- handing them to La Bluetté. The handful did not constitute the entire contents of the pouch. It bulged with still more.

    The harvest of berries was something else the chief had obtained during his morning hunt. When abroad on such a sojourn, the resourceful hunter not only keeps his eyes open to detect four-footed game (and two-footed, namely grouse and nahamak, wild turkeys) …but also looks for vegetative bounty. *O'hôô, Yes,* it is possible to gather yet-edible wild berries, even in freezing cold mid-winter -- if you know where to look. Certain kinds, of course. Before he had encountered the partridge, the chief had come to a small clearing that was, careful scrutiny revealed, nibimenek, a place of nibimenal --high bush cranberries.[7]-- Coming upon the clearing, he had studied the ground (it looked somewhat familiar), thinking that he may have been there before, and therefore it might be a place where flourished gô'gô'gouizak, "little sawtoothed (dentate) ones," leaves of wintergreen, *Gaultheria procumbens*. The red berries of wintergreen are able to continue, without withering, under the deepest snow, all winter long, remaining quite edible into the spring. Partridgeberry, *Mitchella repens,* called by the Ô'banakiak pabedeguibagasigil, is another evergreen whose red berries can be found under the snow.[8] The trick is to remember the locations of such low-lying berry plants before the snow falls. Returning during the winter, you use one of your snowshoes as a shovel to expose the plants. Carefully eyeing the clearing to see if he definitely recognized some feature, Grey Lock had refrained, on mere speculation, from taking off one of his ô'gemak and proceeding to dig. Not only might he be wasting time and energy, but such vigorous activity, throwing snow aside, might alert a nearby game animal, hitherto unaware of his presence, and scare it off. However, "lahi!" he *did* see a nibimenakuam bush, an excellent development. Many of the plump nibimen "cranberries," glittering ruby-red, hung within reach. Higher ones he gathered by using his alni-tmahigan, ordinary transverse-cutting instrument -- 'tomahawk,' habitually carried wedged at the small of the back. The chief used it to hook down higher branches to within reach. He could have stripped all the berries from the entire small tree by bending it over. But he didn't want all of them. Some should be left for the sustenance of other creatures and to seed future nibimenakuamak.

---

[7] High bush cranberry, *Viburnum trilobum*, p. 62, Chief Joseph Laurent's *Abenakis & English Dialogues*.
[8] Called partridgeberry, because, like wintergreen it is a ground hugging plant, grouse being a ground-feeding species. Pabedeguibagasigil means "Little round leaves," *Western Abenaki Dictionary*, Volume II, p. 221, from pedeguigen, round, ôanibagw, leaf, 'si' from the diminutive siz, and pluralized as 'gil.'

"Oliôni, oliôni, n'sôgemô --Thank you, thank you, my chief,"-- La Bluetté exclaimed with great appreciation, accepting the berries. "Yolil d' oligen ôadsi kelahamônmek... --These are good for preventing..."-- He paused, searching for the Abenaki word. He couldn't think of it, and concluded "...scorbut," French for scurvy. "O'hôô, acoui --Yes, certainly,"-- the chief agreed. Especially now, they concurred, in the depth of winter, far into the bush, when fresh greens had long been used up.

Tomô and Besogne then joined them, Grey Lock gesturing toward the coffee pot, inviting them to pour themselves some of... he struggled to think what it should be called. It was kapi, yes, but with the chocolate added... how about... he tried to get his tongue around *"chocolat."* Though 'chocolate' is from a native word, *chocolatl*, it is Mesoamerican, not Algonquian. Due to the Abenaki difficulty in pronouncing "ch" or "sh" in word-initial position, what he said came out as "tsôkoulat"... tsôkoulat-kapi.

Besogne and Tomô had also risen too late to join the chief on his morning sojourn. They instead made themselves useful by examining their two toboggans, and their equipment in general, for travel damage, making repairs as necessary. Breakfasting on bacon and chicken's eggs, they used their cast-iron 'spider'[9] frying pan to fry more bacon and eggs for A'lôn, her children, and others of the chief's company.

"Many of the plump nibimen "cranberries," glittering ruby-red, hung within reach. Higher ones he gathered by taking out his tomahawk to hook down higher boughs." Photo shows author using one of his pipe – tomahawks to hook down loftier branches.
Taken during Piaôdagos -- Moon of Falling Boughs -- (February), Woodbury, VT

"Ôitzauigw ta midsigw!! -- Come and eat!!"-- Tomô had called out to all who were within hearing.

Standard rules of hospitality of the Native American people, in general, are

---

[9] Called a "spider" because such pans are mounted on three iron legs, each 3½" long, enabling the long-handled pan to be placed directly on a campfire for faster frying.

expressed in such aphorisms as: "Pmi nôdodahid pitiga uigiuôm'a p'hanem couito uaidsimi ida 'Ôitzauigw midsigw.' -- When a visitor enters a lodge the woman must always say "Come eat."-- Kisi ônda maôigen tazaham kaguesa nesip'hamasi -- It is not right [to] refuse what is offered.-- Pmi auôsizak bapiak pasodaui --When children play nearby,-- agma couito uikuimô agemôuô alômi -- she must call them in -- ta nadona agemôuô ôadsi midsigw -- and ask them to eat."[10]--

When Tomô and Cæsar joined La Bluetté and the chief around the fire, they dumped armloads of firewood on the (steadily shrinking) pile that was already there. Another thing they had busied themselves with that morning was taking up their hatchets and going out to collect firewood. Though this might be a task normally left to women and children, rather than to warriors, to grown men, they had arrived as guests and it behooved them, especially Besogne, who was something of a stranger, to demonstrate appreciation for their hosts' hospitality by making themselves useful. They had also replenished the woodpiles of every lodge in the encampment, including that of the wigwam they were overnight guests in. This was the lodge of the young couple Sakso Sackett and his new bride Lowiz (Abenaki for *Louisa*). Sackett was, as his surname indicated, *métis,* though not the offspring of a liaison between a Canadian *coureur de bois* and an Indian woman ...but between a Pastoni captive and a warrior of Grey Lock's 'castle.' Sakso's mother, Elizabeth Sackett, had been taken, as a small girl, during "King Philip's War," 1675-76, and eventually brought to Mazipskoik, 'Place of Flint' (*Missisquoi* to the French). This was before Grey Lock himself had arrived at Mazipskoik, joining fellow exiles from the western reaches of Massa'dzosek, or "Massachusetts-Bay Colony," to use what the English called the area.* It turned out that the chief and Elizabeth had come from the same place. One of the first things Grey Lock would have learned as a child was his town's old Algonquian name, Ôauanokoo. The English had given it the name "Westfield," it being the furthest westward settlement in the province. The chief felt a special affinity for the young man, thanks to their mutual Ôauanokoo / Westfield connection. Sackett was usually invited to join the chief when he established a multi-family encampment for the purpose of trapping, hunting, or maple sugar-making. And of course Grey Lock wanted him as part of his band when he struck the war post, gathering willing warriors around him -- to strike

*The original Massa'dzosek is further east, the "Place of the Great Hills" near Massachusetts Bay, today the Blue Hills Preserve south of Boston. Settling westward, the colonists applied the name to the entire commonwealth. Appropriately, especially with 'Bay' dropped. Western Massachusetts *is* the more mountainous part of the state. For an Abenaki etymology, see p. 91, Chief Henry L. Masta's *Abenaki Legends, Grammar & Place Names*.

---

[10] Quotation is from Seneca spiritual revivalist Handsome Lake. "Odsi Kidôia'ua Ôalgid Nebeso, From the Code of Handsome Lake." Said 'Code' is today often called "the Longhouse Religion."

"Returning during the winter, you use one of your snowshoes as a shovel to expose the plants." Author's photo of wintergreen sprigs, previously noted during a snowless season, gôgô-guizak uncovered with toe of snowshoe in upper left section of photo.

Powder horn (and horn powder measure) included for size comparison.
  Photo by the author.

against the heretical enemy to the south, the ever-encroaching Pastoniak, the offspring of *les Anglais*. The fire leaping up with renewed vigor as more wood was added, Besogne endured the fierce heat momentarily as he poured himself a mug of mocha. Unlike La Bluetté and the chief, however, he preferred to sweeten the concoction with molasses. Though the blackish treacle might not be as sweet as honey or maple or cane sugar, he thought it was healthier. He picked up a spoon, the nearby container of molasses, and his mug and retreated to sit on another pile of toboggan-borne hides. Everyone around the fire leaned back a bit as smoke billowed out. La Bluetté, concerned that flakes of ash swirling up with the smoke would get on his fresh art work, placed the square within the protective confines of a caribou-hide *valise* he had made.

Though he had never doubted it, Cæsar's association with the multi-talented and high-minded La Bluetté made him more aware that, the more you knew, the more you strove to learn, the better off you are. When he accompanied the artist/chronicler among the *naturels,* he was just as interested in learning about their customs, methods, mythic stories, and languages as was La Bluetté himself. As a *sergent* in their mutual company of militia, he was, like the roving artist, rapidly becoming known as a useful interpreter in relation to the *langues maternelle* of their native allies.

The chief had emptied his deerskin containing the nibimen berries into the colorful basket made from reed stems, inviting everyone to take some. They should eat, build up their strength, he advised, because tomorrow they would be stripping the sheets of birch bark from the lodges, pack everything onto the toboggans, and take the riverside trail downstream to the next campsite. It was a considerable number of 'looks' to the west, a fatiguing journey on snowshoes.

Québecois habitants the *artistique fermier* Georges La Bluetté and *ouvrier agricole* -- farmhand -- assistant Cæsar Besogne, blanket coats taken off for hauling their loaded toboggans, take a break on the way to (or from) Chief Grey Lock's upriver encampment …apparently discussing something seen in the distance. *Fusil* --firelock-- resting against cedar tree behind them presumably belongs to Mazipskoik guide Tomô. The author is "La Bluetté" and Frank Maione is "Besogne."

Photo: Bob Bearor.

They might be weary when they arrived, but would still have to take their rolls of maskua, birch bark, and mount them on the wigwam poles that everyone knew (or hoped) were still there, from the previous year, still upright and sturdy. Firewood would have to be collected -- hopefully, again, there might be still some left from the previous year, -- though, of course, it would be covered by snow, and fresh fires kindled in the renewed lodges.

The objective of making another camp further down the valley was because it was getting to that time of year, the time of maple sugar-making. The cold was not quite as severe, daylight was lasting longer… "Mozokas, the Moon of Moose Hunting,"[11] would soon be upon them. Makuônikas, the Red - Boiling (Maple Sugar-Making) Moon (April) would follow. Though it would be only Mozokas soon, if the People were to make a sufficient amount of maple sugar, enough to last into the following winter, they had to prepare. There would be much cutting, collecting, and stacking of firewood. A great amount of fuel would be needed to heat rocks to a high enough degree sufficient for dropping into the trough (fashioned from a hollowed-out tree), into which copious, seemingly endless, amounts of maple sap would be poured. And everyone couldn't be doing nothing but collecting firewood. The nadialuinnoak, hunters, would still have to be going out after fresh meat. The women might have to stitch together new birch bark

---

[11] So called, not because it was the best time for hunting moose -- as long as there were moose, they could be hunted at any time,-- but because you could venture, for the first time since the previous autumn, to *EAT* moziya, moose meat (especially of the bulls) once more. As of the previous year's first frost (or September's full moon) the bulls have gone into "the rut," *stopped eating,* and their flesh becomes permeated with adrenalin and hormones… making their meat taste terrible. By November they have become raw-boned and stringy… not much better. But, by March, *starting* with the mid-winter thaw of **January**… sap rises in trees again, making the diet of moose more nutritious and therefore their flesh fatter and more palatable, "quite delicious."

sap - collecting containers if the old ones, left at the site from last year's sugar-making, had deteriorated too much. Some of the bark for covering the lodges might have to be sacrificed for this purpose. It was too early to strip fresh bark from the "canoe birch" trees. To remove large sheets, sap would have to be rising under the bark first, and that required warmer weather -- quite a bit warmer. Fortunately the hunters had harvested sufficient numbers of whitetail deer, moose, and caribou at the headwaters of the Missisquoi, in the dense, swampy wilderness where herds of placid magôliboak --shovel - antlered ones -- (woodland caribou), roamed. Their hides would serve to replace wigwam bark until maskuamozi ôskidakuam -- birch tree sap -- was rising again. To mention just one of the tasks that band members would have to deal with in addition to collecting sufficient firewood.

Consuming the tart nibimen berries, between sips from his own mug of mocha, a question concerning language occurred to La Bluetté.

"Niak minôbeski, n'sôgemô -- I am curious, my chief, -- odsikaui abazi yolil alnimenal odosa -- why the tree these berries come from, -- liuitamôb *nibimenakuam?* -- [is] named *nibimenakuam?*-- Pskaôdnkuenal'ua abazi môdzagiak olôgiadiganôpetaui aki --The branches of the tree grow well above the ground.-- Kaguesa uadsônôzik kisito nspi *nepi?* -- What has it to do with **water?**"--

As he spoke, A'lôn rejoined the party seated around the fire. She had plucked and cleaned the pakesso, skewering it on a green-striped moosewood spit so as to roast it over the skueda -- the fire.--

Ôauanoleuo pondered the question for a moment. (Grey Lock's Abenaki name was from Ôauanoleuad, meaning "He Who Fools Them," thanks to his adroit tricking of pursuing enemies. The suffix 'o' replaces 'ad' to show it's his personal name).

"Ah," he replied. "Kia oliha palalokôôb'a nspi ntami'ua kelozôugan --You made a mistake with the first part of the word. -- *Nibi* gôgizi ônda idamoo *nepi*[12] -- *Nibi* does not mean *water*. -- K'd alaldag'ua 'nebi' --You are thinking of 'nebi,'-- kelozôugan ôadsi nepi -- the word for [fresh] water. -- Kisi ôdoka nibizi -- It relates to my switch." -- "Nibizi? -- My switch?" -- queried Cæsar. His curiosity was also piqued. "Kaguesa uadsônôzik ni abazi uadsônem kisito nspi nibizial? -- What has that tree have to do with switches? -- Kaguesa nibizial? -- What switches? -- N' ualdamôbena Alnôbak ônda'dagamak auôsizak -- We know the Ordinary (i.e., Native) People don't hit children -- nspi nibizial -- with switches, -- olidebiui agemôgik, ali... -- to correct them, as...-- -- ah -- *les Anglais* kisito -- ah, -- the English do." -- With a

---

[12] Sometimes pronounced, and often spelled, **nebi**. The Nipmuk Nation of the central Massachusetts area have **Nip**, from *nepi*, for water, in their name. The name indicates "Inland People," because nepi, *fresh* water, in contrast to briny coastal ocean water, must come from inland. The suffix 'uk' is the animate plural, here indicating people.

twinkle in his eye, the chief nodded toward A'lôn. She had been listening, and now her round face broke into a mischievous grin. "Ôskebi -- Perhaps, -- ôskebi," she said, hesitatingly, indicating that she wasn't entirely certain of what she was going to propose. "…kisi uadsônôzik kisito nspi bapimek pabaskuhamaldo --…it has to do with playing the ball game."-- 'Pabaskuhamaldo' indicates the game called *lacrosse*. La Bluetté and Besogne raised their eyebrows at this, but refrained from interrupting with an obvious "Tôhné kassi? -- How so?" --

"K' ualdamô tôhné pemôuzouinnoak ômkak akuôbi --You know how people wager so much-- pmi agemôuô sanôbak bapiak papuôgan -- when their men play the game,"-- she went on. "O'hôô -- Oui,"-- chorused Cæsar and *le Artiste* as Sackett and Tomô nodded knowingly (the latter two were already vaguely familiar with the story).

"Matsimi agemôuô cousoudelak ômkak pita, **pitta** guinatta papuôgan --Always their women wager very, ***very*** much on the game. -- Ali k'ualdamô --As you know. -- Zaui niona -- Sometimes we, -- she corrected herself, -- Zaui **agemôgik** ômka aleghikôk agemôgik uadsôna! -- Sometimes *they* gamble everything they have!"-- …implying that she herself wouldn't be so heedless.

When she said "cousoudelak" she had used an old word for women, instead of the newer, Gallic-inspired 'p'hanemak,' derived from the French *femmes*. She paused, and, -- to build up suspense? -- turned the mkuetsazem pakesso -- roasting grouse -- over on its stick. Of course, it needed to be done anyway. "Kassi -- So," -- and here she switched to the modern "p'hanemak" in the event that the Canadiens were not familiar with the old term; "p'hanemak d'odamiuaskatta na agemôuô alnôbak gahouameg -- [the] women become very anxious that their men win. -- **PITTA** odamiuasko! -- *VERY* anxious!" -- she emphasized. "Guani pazegw papuôgan -- During one game,"-- …she now placed some birch bark, and a few pieces of wood, on the fire to more thoroughly roast the bird, the oily bark sizzling… "kuena yanegi, n' delaldamô -- long ago, I imagine, -- dotsi atsagema nibimenakuam'a -- there was a nibimen bush -- ôtsigen kuahliui bapimek kikas -- growing near the playing field. -- Ônda pazego oualdamen kaguesa kisi asma liuitamôb pmi -- No one knows what it was called then." -- She paused again, turning the partridge once more… took her time, carefully scrutinizing the pakessoiya. Was it ready? The oios, meat, to her practiced eye, still looked a trifle undone.

At last, as La Bluetté and Caesar shifted with impatience, she continued decisively and emphatically: "***Pazego*** p'hanem -- ***One*** woman, -- ladaôbi agma sanôba ao zautosamek -- seeing her man is flagging, -- alitasimek odaok -- falling behind, -- piayab zagezoatta agma môuakinnoak uadsônôba ôaniadon… became so afraid that her team would lose…" O'hôô -- Yes, -- they were staring at her; she had their full attention… were regarding her with baited breath. "…agma ôdosab li abazi -- …she went to the tree -- ta boskuezen peskaôdkuen'a --and cut a branch off. -- Melikenmek --Holding [it] strongly,-- agma ôdosab anegi nisuiididsi -- she went after her spouse-- ta môdzaiui za' zamhô agma!-- and started whipping!

Aueskapola! To wake him up!" -- She laughed, everyone joining in her mirth. "Ato kedagik p'hanemak kisi dadebad -- Probably other women did the same. -- Niona ualdamôbena agemôgik kisito pamegizegak -- We know they do today,"-- she concluded, her face wreathed in smiles, as with everyone listening. "Ta yanmô tôni nibimenakuam ato olintonab kisi liuizuôgan --And that's how the nibimen bush may [have] received its name. -- Kassi nokemes hliab -- So my grandmother told me. -- Ônda pazego ualdam ôadsi acoui -- No one knows for sure."--

"Tôniyo --Whatever, --" La Bluetté remarked, his wide smile, as with everyone else, brightening their otherwise snow-bound, forested environment. "Kisi maôuito oligen ôtlokôgan'a, yanmô ôadsi pakaldam -- It makes a good story, that's for certain,"-- he encouraged, jotting down notations with his pencil-stick. Everyone began looking at the hotly dripping pakessoiya.

"N' idôba minauitôzo -- I would say [it's] done,"-- A'lôn remarked, testing the pakessoiya with one of those new-fangled French utensils, a twisted-wire nimatguahigan -- fork. --

"Cigitaua'i moua! Let's eat!" she called out. Everyone brought out their eating utensils. La Bluetté produced wooden trenchers for himself and Besogne, mouth watering. He loved freshly baked or roasted pakessoiya.

Ôigapuôgan! -- Bon appétit!--

Azôn-Badise elbowed his way through the eager diners, carrying a large steak of magôliboiia -- caribou meat. --"Ya ônda dabi! -- That's not enough!"-- he said, thrusting his chin at the pakessoiya. With a happy shout he threw the steak onto the still-hot spider frying pan. The fresh meat sizzled almost immediately. A'lôn lifted the moosewood spit and worked the pakessoiya off the stick with her knife, sliding it down onto a thick piece of birch bark at her feet. With the knife in one hand and the fork in the other, she carved up the bird, handing the breast to Ôauanoleuo. Since he had bagged the bird, he should be served first. Also, he was the oldest of the present company, and ktsiiak -- elders[13]-- are always served first (even if he wasn't the oldest, with his gray scalp roach he seemed to be. In the present relatively small party, though, he actually was). She next gave the legs to La Bluetté and to Besogne, knowing, from previous visits -- in the case of La Bluetté at least,-- that he considered the tastiest part of any bird, whether chicken, grouse, turkey, or pelaz -- pigeon -- to be the leg, "the drumstick." The two were favored with this choice serving because they were honored guests. It was definitely cheering and encouraging to have such interested and accomplished visitors in the depths of the snow-choked forest. Tomô was most welcome too, and had not joined the band originally, to begin with, because he had other business back at the "castle"… one of them being to keep watch as part of the fortified town's defense force. You never knew when renewed warfare might break out between the British and French crowns. The English might urge on a Maguak war party against the town. As it was, the chief had been leading war parties himself southward into his old Massachusetts homeland for the last few years. To the east, in Maine, treaties had been broken and war had erupted. This was not a conflict between the British and French, but between the Pastoniak, Bostonians, and the French-allied, but essentially independent native nations to the north of the established New England colonies. The French were *officially* staying out of it, but Québec Governor Vaudreuil surreptitiously encouraged warriors to carry out raids. He hoped to stall the northward, Canada-threatening aggrandizement of the ever-ambitious *Anglais*.

Ôauanoleuo's primary purpose, in discouraging further English expansionism, was to seize captives: to obtain the release of hostages, for possible adoption, for ransom, or for selling or gifting to the French. Living prisoners were far more valuable to him than mere scalps. This didn't mean there weren't fatal clashes; there inevitably were, and the colonists who were stung by the raids ardently wished to retaliate. An expedition of scalp-bounty rangers dispatched against his stronghold the previous year had failed to reach its goal… but it was almost certain they would try again. Therefore

---

[13] Though "ktsiiak" indicates tribal elders, definitely, linguistic analysis indicates that it means more than merely being chronologically older. A translation of the Old Anglo-Saxon "elder" (originally *yldra* or *eldra*) indeed indicates older. In Abenaki this would translate as negônia, from 'negôni, old.' 'kts' being a contraction of ktsi (or kici), "great," with the suffix iia, *inside*, -- an example being pakesso*iya*, the "iya" indicating the *interior* of the grouse,-- we see… **"Those Great Inside"** …ak being the animate plural.

the stockaded "castle" needed a contingent of fighters present to defend the place at all times.

When his son had nudged his way through the adults around the fire to throw the steak of magôliboiia into the frying pan, indignantly observing that the proffered pakessoiya was not enough, he was not reprimanded for rudeness by his parents or anyone else. To begin with, he had, unnoticed, extracted a sharp knife that was hanging in its buckskin sheath from a pole-stub of the door-frame of A'lôn's wigwam. He had then marched over to the carcass of the latest caribou that his father had bagged, --its hide freshly removed -- and, hacking vigorously, chopped off a large piece of one of the haunches.

Far from reprimanding him for his cheeky attitude in cutting out the steak, without any permission, brashly bringing it to the fire, his parents had smiled with almost delighted indulgence, approving his initiative. Such self-reliant, self-starting "willful" behavior was something that they cultivated in their offspring. If Azôn-Badise was to grow up to be an effective hunter, trapper, and warrior, a good provider for his own someday-family and a courageous defender of his people... he had to be able to think for himself. He had to show initiative, had to have backbone, and not allow the shackles of unnecessary shame, of unwarranted timidity, hold him back. He was at times called "Ôski Nikola -- Young Nicholas " -- in honor of his French godfather, the chief's good friend *le Cavalier* and militia colonel Nicholas Saint Ours. *Le Colonel* was the proprietor of a blockhouses-guarded *seigneury* along the Riviére Richelieu, where La Bluetté and Cæsar were tenant-farmers. The Christian name of the prestigious, stalwart Saint Ours was something to live up to, as well as Azôn-Badise's own Alnôbaiui nick-name of "Migakadso... Little Fighting Man"...!

When he had brought the steak forward his cousin Deniz (after St. Denis), who, joining the adults at the fire, had laughed, saying "Ola ôadsi kia! -- Good for you!"-- He had noticed Azôn-Badise knifing the carcass and understood. If the younger boy had not gotten there first, Deniz would have done it himself. The same could be said for Mali-Sallot, baptized 'Marie-Charlotte,' the young daughter of He Who Fools Them, who had come over to hear her mother's story about the etymology of nibimenakuam. Mali-Sallot's nickname was formidable in Abenaki; Kinjamesizkuo,[14] which, in English, boils down to simply "Princess." And in French just as simple: *Princesse*. Ironically her Alnôbaiui nickname was part English to begin with, Kinjames, from "King James." *Kinjames* is the Ô'banakiak term for the title of any European monarch, reflecting that some of the Peoples' forebears were originally from Massachusetts, many from the region the Pastoniak now called the "District of Maine." They had heard it from the first *Anglais* themselves, either on the coast of Massachusetts-proper or on the Maine coast,

---

[14] *Abenakis & English Dialogues,* Chief Joseph Laurent, p. 49.

most likely from factors at George Popham's short-lived fur-trading station[15]…that the English were the subjects of King James I. Realizing that there were queens in Europe, to name them, "Kinjames" was feminized to Kinjamesizkuo… Not understanding that the consonant ending *James* could be used as a possessive, the Ô'banakiak added their own possessive 'i', adding the i to make *siz,* a diminutive, because a queen was usually the consort of a king, and therefore subordinate, women (unless an unmarried queen such as Elizabeth I), being subordinate to men in the European social hierarchy --even among the aristocracy, -- 'belonging' to their husbands or fathers, etc. Skua, denoting female, had to be added as well, and, to indicate that it is a particular person's *name,* the suffix skua modified to 'zkuo.'

He Who Fools Them often found it more convenient to call her "Princess," given his background in the English-occupied territories to the south, though it came out as *Plincess,* due to his natural propensity to speak with an Algonquian accent. Alnôbaiui's lack of the consonants F, Q, R, V and X are due to the non-labial freckle way of speaking, i.e., minimal movement of the lips, which also militates against the clear pronunciation of H in word-initial position, and "th," as in *think,* also "sh" as in *should,* and J in word-initial position. The unwieldy R is usually replaced by an L and the equally unwieldy F by such devices as 'p'h,' as in 'p'hanem,' from the French *femme.* To mention a few differences dictated by the non-labial freckle mode.

At other times, however, when he was in a reflective mood, thinking bitterly about the various transgressions that the domineering, land-hungry English had inflicted on his people, driving him into the arms of the French, he didn't want to refer to his daughter with any name smacking of Iglismôniui, the Englishmen's Way, and preferred the completely Algonquianized version of princess, which is 'Ktsi Sôgemôsku'sizo.' This designation is made up of the following: Ktsi for Great, Sôgemô for Chief, sku[a] for female, and siz as the diminutive… which, taken as a whole, spells out: "Great female chief, small." Ktsi Sôgemô, "Grand Chief," would be the Abenaki equivalent of King. At times, especially if the sky was greyly overcast, or confined to their lodge by an endless rainfall, his thoughts turned to *les Anglais* and he became so deeply depressed and morose… that he didn't want to even refer to her as "Plincess" (let alone invoke Kin' James) even if he imagined he was using the French 'Princesse.' It was too close (really the same). At such a time he was glad to employ 'Ktsi Sôgemôsku'sizo,' lengthy as it was. She completely understood him, no question about it. Her first language was Alnôbaiui, the mother tongue of the People of the Dawn Land.

---

[15] Popham and Raleigh Gilbert, of the Plymouth Company, attempted a colony at the mouth of the Kennebec River as early as 1607. Pages 39 and 106, *The Indian and the White Man in New England*, Chandler Whipple, 1976.

On a knoll overlooking la Riviére Richelieu, is "Ôauanoleuo -- He Who Fools Them," -- also known as Chief Grey Lock, in earnest conversation with "*le Sieur* Nicholas de Saint Ours, *Colonel du Milice,*" the proprietor of a wilderness estate, a *seigneury,* fronting on the waterway. Such seigneuries were typically fortified as outposts established to defend the territory of Québec against Maguak - *Anglais* incursions. Le Colonel and the chief are -- quite likely,-- discussing ways and means of safe - guarding Kanada, of thwarting Anglais *agression.*

Author's (retouched) photo was taken at the Fort George Historic Site, Lake George, New York.

The pakessoiya was quickly consumed, the chief generously sharing the breast part with others, actually eating only a little of it himself. He had tasted pakessoiya many times before... At times, having come far and hunting alone, he had consumed an entire grouse by himself -- sometimes two or three, -- being famished (barely scorching them over a small fire), there being no one to share with. But at present, in his wintry extended-family situation, he was more interested in his role as a Good Provider. He viewed the pakesso as a mere appetizer, the magôliboiia that A'zôn - Badise was frying up as the main course. And there was more where that came from. He poked fresh splinters of wood under the frying pan to keep it hot enough for that "more." The caribou steak tasted particularly good because there had been a residue of that morning's bacon grease in the pan, adding to the steak's flavor.

His feisty spouse, when she had finished licking pakessoiya and magôliboiia juice off her fingers, had an announcement to make. Prefacing her remarks with the observation that the arrival of their guests was to be celebrated, was an occasion for joyous feasting, she said, "N'uadsônô olikadaua ôadsi meziuitta! -- I have a treat for all!"-- She gestured toward the large iron kettle that had been hanging over the fire, suspended from a moosewood tripod, all this time. A fetching smell had been emanating from it, but none except A'lôn and Mali-Sallot knew what the contents were. "Yanegi mezi uadsônôbanik dabi pegigeda -- After all have had enough roast meat, -- niona uadsônôbenadzi uigatôzo uôbimen pagasôbôkôn! -- we'll have delicious chestnut stew!"-- Upon the arrival of their guests the previous evening, A'lôn had dipped into her *caché* of treasured chestnuts. At first she had intended to make uôbimen abônak -- chestnut cakes (patties),-- which would not consist of simply peeled and pulverized old chestnuts from the previous autumn, but, the granulation mixed with water and then baked, would have corn meal and chopped onion as part of the ingredients.[16] In addition, since the Canadiens had brought sea salt as well as various sweeteners, such as maple sugar from trees tapped by *les Canadiens,* cane sugar, etc. (their own onions, too), the patties would be baked with such sweeteners added. However, in preparing the rare treat, it dawned on the compassionate woman that in making the delicacies for Tomô, their guests, and her immediate family members …she might be inflicting a sense of deprivation on everybody else in the hunting band. Their mouths would surely water when they smelled the cakes roasting. There was only one outside fire here. The others constantly used the fire for their own needs. At the same time, she didn't want to use up most of her hoard of the savory nuts all at once. There would be hardly any left over for the sugaring camp. While sugaring camps involve a great deal of work, the time was also a festive one, everyone cheered by the prospect of another season's abundance of delicious maple sugar. By Skamonkas, Maize Harvesting Moon, some maple cakes would be boiled down to senômoziimlases[17] and the syrup dripped onto freshly popped corn kernels (popped in oil from fat).[18] *Another* treat to look forward to, come harvest-time. The new season's resulting supply also made an excellent trade item, much valued by prosperous *messieurs* in the French towns. It occurred to her, since she knew there were uôbimiziak abaziak[19] -- chestnut trees -- nearby, she could take the camp's moosehorn-blade shovel -- it would be the ideal instrument,-- and dig into the snow and the forest duff beneath and find more chestnuts. Hope sprang up in her breast… and then died. Doubtless there *had been* plenty but such auaasak -- [wild] animals -- as gray squirrels would have harvested many as winter approached. Large animals, deer and bears, whose strong teeth could easily crack the husks, would have scuffed up as many as they could to add on enough fat to survive winter's scarce pickings and freezing cold. She sighed, discouraged. Sitting by the fire, the chestnuts-filled reed basket in her lap, she fingered the beads of the rosary from which her crucifix hung. Should she pray to the Virgin? Could Sazos -- Jesus -- tell her anything?

---

[16] Pp. 100 - 101, *Native New England Cooking,* by Dale Carson, Pennacook Abenaki culinary expert, 1980, Peregrine Press, Old Saybrook, CT.
[17] *Western Abenaki Dictionary,* Volume II, p. 394. Source: "rock maple molasses." Asen or sen is the word for stone, or rock, p. 16, *Abenakis & English Dialogues,* Chief Joseph Laurent.
[18] Dale Carson, *Native New England Cooking.* See her recipe for traditional Native American popcorn, p. 95. The above reference to maple syrup-dripped popcorn invokes the origin of the "crackerjacks" confection.
[19] The Abenaki for chestnut tree, *Castanea dentata,* uôbimizi, indicates "white woody plant" for its whitish heartwood. *Western Abenaki Dictionary,* Volume II, p. 70.

She tried to think of what the revered Mkazaui Pitkôzonak -- Black Robes, -- the missionaries, would advise. She strove to remember their harangues -- *"sermons,"* they call them. There was one episode in the life of Sazos in particular that had to do with food... What was it? *Enni!* Now she remembered... the story of the abônak ta namasak! -- loaves and fishes! -- He was haranguing a great crowd, his donnéak having set out a basket of fish and loaves of bread with which to nourish the hungry while he spoke. Though it was a large basket, there would surely not be enough for everyone there... for the -- what did the fathers call such a mesailen -- crowd --? *La multitude;* that was it. And yet, *miraculeux!* -- there was a miracle! No matter how many loaves and how many fish were taken, the basket never emptied. There was always more. Ah, an *oligen* parable, but she, herself, was no miracle-worker. She was but a humble nizuiididzi ta igaues -- wife and mother. -- Staring into the crackling fire, she continued to finger her rosary. Then it came to her. Their guests would provide the solution! After La Bluetté had mentioned all the sweeteners and other foodstuffs that he, Besogne and Tomô had hauled such a long way on their toboggans, not only for themselves but as gifts for the chief and his people, she had planned to use a bit of those sugars in baking the chestnut cakes. But why limit herself to La Bluetté's sugar and salt? What about the bacon, the glazed ham, the kaoziia -- beef, -- the wheat flour, and so on that they had brought?

Why not use some of those ingredients **also?** Of course, if all those elements are included, it will make each patty pretty dense and heavy. What is something else the French like? Ah... *lasob.* "La soupe." They enjoy making rather watery stews called *soupe.* Kassi --So, -- if the chestnuts are first roasted, then cut up and thrown into the large kettle with water and other ingredients, there should be plenty! Delighted, she fairly laughed out loud. Maskaulohôzik Dodabi! -- Praise Be! -- She had remembered the loaves and fishes story. Sazos was probably much too busy with far weightier concerns to pay heed to such a mundane matter as how to multiply the roasted chestnuts treat. She was certainly glad she had found a solution! Could her own personal Guardian Angel have whispered into her mind?

Enni, she reflected, Spirit worked in such mysterious ways. In that respect, she mused, the doctrines of the friars weren't all that different from what the medaulinnoak believed. Saki gôdaukiui! -- Quite similar! -- She and the chief couldn't understand some of the finer points of what the Black Robes' so forcefully exhorted... it was baffling. But it didn't seem to matter. They nodded respectfully in agreement, receiving benefits thereby, such as food from the Whitemen during hungry times. That is, if the French could spare the provisions. When necessary everyone shared short rations.

Having gotten everyone's rapt attention with the chestnut stew announcement, and seeing the strong, tall hunter Pabasôgizo -- Half Moon -- and nephew Alsanid

Toboggan-hauled zogelozuôgan -- cooking, -- mohômek -- eating, -- ta odzesmimek auakôganal -- and drinking utensils -- that could have been used in Chief Grey Lock's winter hunting encampments. From left to right, clockwise: 1. pewter plate, 2. coffee beans-grinder made of wooden box and ironwork mechanism (the image of mkui-oleguan kogeleskua --a red-winged blackbird-- painted on one side). Coffee mill is also useful for pulverizing corn kernels and medicinal ingredients such as slippery elm bark. 3. Heavy iron akogw --kettle, -- 4. kokuiz'a --a small pot-- of brass, 5. a three-legged "spider" frying pan with, 6., an amkuôn --wooden spoon.-- 7. Rolled tin cup with thong attached for suspending from waistband, and, 8. copper tea pot with porcelain handle-grip. Author's collection of colonial-era Eastern Woodlands trade goods on snow.

Pskaôdkueno -- Strong Bough -- approaching with a moose-hide drum, A'lôn went on: "Kaneua ntami -- But first,"-- she qualified, fulfilling her office as the leading matron present; "Niona olintônôbena n' odoui[20] nôdodahidak! -- We [have to] welcome our distinguished visitors! -- Niona acouiba lintôbena Kolibiyôn[21] Lintóuôgan --We should sing the Welcoming Song."-- Hardly had "Lintouôgan" fallen from her lips than Ôauanoleuo, extending a hand toward the Québecois, exclaimed *"Pahakuinôguezi, nidômbak! -- **Greetings,** my friends!"*-- 'Pahakuinôguezi' is a salutation used to welcome those you haven't seen for some time. As others gathered, they brought out their gourd ceremonial si'zi'uanak -- rattles. -- This opportunity to sing, drum, and use their musical instruments (always light-weight ones in the winter, where the trails, both deep in snow and lengthy, had to be traversed)… cheered everyone's appreciation of

---

[20] Odoui means "of high quality," *Western Abenaki Dictionary*, Volume II, p. 113.

[21] The **K** of Kolibiyôn is a contraction of "Kiouô --You're -- welcome," welcome in the sense of *into our home* (or camp, etc.) Kolibiyôn is not used when responding to someone who thanks you. Instead the benefactor modestly replies Indakaué, indicating the sense of "It's not much," or "Think nothing of it."

the brightening day. Among the assemblage eyes were shining and faces glowed.

When the Canadiens had arrived the previous evening, Tomô briskly snow-shoeing ahead to alert the encampment to their arrival, it had been too late (and "too early," also, because some hunters had not yet come in)… to organize a proper welcoming ceremony. The first concern was to see to it that their weary guests were given refreshment and allowed to unwind and rest. Room had to be made in various lodges for their bedrolls of wool blankets and fleecy sheepskins. For all that, despite their fatigue, the generous La Bluette and Besogne insisted that they distribute their cargo of sheepskins brought as gifts. And that their hosts should try them out, then and there. The items were just what people need, when bedding down in the winter (rendering blankets and furs even warmer, much warmer). Azibaua'al odsi azibak -- Sheepskins from sheep -- agemôuô môtsagenabanik agemôuô'nihlôdziui -- they [had] raised themselves. -- The pair had also brought presents from their patron, *le Sieur de Saint Ours*. But the presentation of *le Colonel's* gifts could wait until the morrow.--

2. Kolibiyôn Lintouôgan --Welcoming Song--
(Also known as Makagamoldimek Lintouôgan -- [the] Gathering Song) --

Scarcely had the chief completed his 'pahakuinôguezi' greeting than Pabasôgizo lifted his drumstick and pounded hard on the pagholigan, beginning the welcoming song. Those who had taken out their rattles began to shake them to the beat of the drum and the rhythmic chanting of the assembly. This was a joyous occasion and all sang lustily, abandoning their usual quiet, minimal mouth-movement manner of speaking, smiling broadly as they melodiously chanted:

Wic'h qui de ge gung ge gameh
Kola dit ni gey-yeh,
Mah weh o me wiska wa zay
Gwelda swel do daym da way!

Some had also, thinking ahead, joined the assembly facing their guests carrying short but stout sticks of rock maple or other hard wood. In the environment of a hunting camp, hauling toboggans over rough trails, it was a risky proposition to bring drums along, the taut hide drumheads of which could be easily broken in transit. They were rather bulky as well. The sticks were a far less problematical substitute, enabling their owners to clack them loudly together in rhythm with Pabasôgizo's drum, adding substantially to the ebullient din: *Wic'h gwi da d' sig nis gamic'h*
Kola dit ne gay-ya,
Nen emay dic'h na del da day   a kak may dey do dowt de *wo!*

As their voices rose in enthusiastic pitch, the singers' entire bodies began to sway in tune with the chanting, drumming, and rattle-shaking, moccasined feet tipping heel-and-toe rhythmically. Even the older Alnôbak, such as the chief and A'lôn, who had stepped back, making more room, swayed in tune with the drumming and singing, toes tapping lightly up and down.

Wic'h gwi da d'sig-no kuma
Kola dit ne gey-ya,
Cep gwids a day ma de nok dik ba
Way hi ah o way!

Then the repetitive chorus, *Way ha, way ha, way ha ya,* came even more enthusiastically. The boys and girls, the younger men and women, edged away from their original positions and danced in front of the Canadiens and around the fire, stamping the now bare earth with uninhibited zeal, shaking their si'zi'uanak or rapping their sticks as they did so. *L'Artiste* and Cæsar, grinning joyously, felt their feet begin to move also in tune with the chanting. The music, *"sauvage"* though it was, proved to be infectious. They couldn't resist.

Way ha, way ha ya, Way ha ya yo a!
Way ha, way ha, way ha ya,
Way ha, way ha ya, Way ha ya yo a!

Soon the two were so affected by the pounding, sonorously chanting rhythm that they were vigorously foot-stamping and rocking in an arabesque, repetitive manner along with everyone else, voicing the chorus of *way ha, way ha ya, way ha ya yo a!* with as much gusto as the most *"sauvage"* (so-called) of them all. The cultural differences between Alnôba and Frenchman evaporated as the two abandoned themselves to the dance, emitting periodic cries of **'YIP!'** and **'AHOO-O!'** as they bobbed joyously around the fire. With *seeming* abandonment... the dance, so wild to an uninitiated observer, was actually well structured, imbued with a disciplined harmony derived from the participants' inner consciousness of reverence for Nigaues Aki -- Our Mother, the Earth, -- and profound gratitude for the blessings of Ktsi Manitou, Great Spirit / Great Mystery (the same Power called by the French *Dieu, les Anglais'* God, or by that word the Black Gowns preferred for their converts, Ktsi Niuaskw).[22] The rhythmic beating of the drum and sonorous shaking of the rattles is said to be a reflection of the heartbeat of the Earth Mother herself, harmonizing the seemingly

---

[22] Presumably to displace, in Woodland Algonquian language-family terms, manitou, 'god,' or 'spirit,' apparently intending to demonize 'manitou' and thereby undermine the native peoples' indigenous, so-called *'païen'* spirituality. Niuaskw is from niuaskouôgan, "deity," *Western Abenaki Dictionary*, Volume II, p.107.

spontaneous singers and dancers with Creation.

When Pabasôgizo had been getting ready for the welcoming ceremony he had held his drum level, like a servant carrying a tray of wine goblets into the salon of *un bourgeois* in Québec City. Balancing the drum from underneath, holding it where the thongs keeping the drumhead tight converged, he sprinkled an offering of odamô onto the drumhead. The others didn't begin to chant or shake their rattles until he had powerfully!-struck the drum, his vigorous beating vibrating the scattering of tobacco until the last crumb had bounced off. Then the assembly erupted into enthusiastic song.

On one level La Bluetté and Besogne were glad, even elated, to be so honored with the Welcoming Song. On another level they vaguely, dimly knew that they should be frowning with inward disapproval. The ceremony that they were (in effect) participating in was not a Christian one. The black-robed friars regarded the Peoples' drums, si'zi'uanak, and chanting as *païen* -- pagan, -- as *"du Diable."* The French themselves, though, played drums and other musical instruments. The militia *compagnie* that the two were members of had its own martial drum. These instruments had been blessed by the Bishop of Montreal or one or another of the lesser clergy, conferring upon them churchly legitimacy. The songs said instruments enhanced were also sung in French, the tongue of "His Most Catholic Majesty," or, better yet, were hymns choraled in Latin, that presumably divine language.

The two Québecois were also *donneuers,* laymen of the Church who voluntarily contributed -- donated -- time and energy to the work of the missionaries, hopefully facilitating the conversion of *les sauvages.* When the pair had hauled their heavily loaded toboggans over wintry trails, fraught with danger, to reach Grey Lock's hunting encampment, one commodity that they had deliberately excluded was akubi, hard liquor. There were prohibitions against trading or gifting spirituous liquors to *les naturels,* inspired by bitter experience. One reason why the two were visiting Ôauanoleuo's hunting group was to see if any blandi was being circulated at that distant location "in the bush." Such donnéak -- as the Ô'banakiak called *les donneuers* -- were the eyes and ears of the Black Gowns in keeping destructive akubi away from their charges. In the 17th century fearless *missionnaires* had periodically risked the torture scaffold when they had trekked southward to missionize among those nominal allies of the English heretics, -- historically hostile toward the French, the Five Nations Iroquois. A selling point, favorably impressing alcohol-alienated adherents who agreed to remove to Kanada, was their solemn pledge to rigorously enforce sobriety in the consequent mission towns. The fathers had made the same pledge to *les Abnaquies* upon forging into northern New England regions, attracting them also to new villages constructed along the southern shores of the Fleuve St. Laurent. At the present moment, however, as the two Canadiens basked in the love that the chief's people were embracing them with, *literally* with song and dance, such a concern with aboriginal paganism was the last thing they had in mind. It was one thing to worry about when on the farm along the

Richelieu, where priestly parishes, churches, chapels, shrines, and crossroads crucifixes were encountered between the farmstead and Montreal (and to the east) …but it was another thing entirely… when deep in the wilderness and enjoying the hospitality and protection of Ôauanoleuo and his family and friends. To bring up such an issue now would be ungrateful… churlish.

L' Artiste and Cæsar, without having to actually discuss the matter, were in agreement that, in carrying out their obligations as donnéak, it was quite sufficient to keep an eye out for akubi and, if any were discovered, to enlist the chief in getting rid of same. They knew that the chief and A'lôn and (as far as they could tell) all of his family were adamantly against inebriation. Ôauanoleuo especially, when he had been among the Pastoniak and the Dutch, had suffered painfully from it. The Mkazaui Pitkôzonak'i --Black Robes'-- effectiveness in keeping brandy away from their converts became a major factor in motivating him to remove north into the forests along Lac Champlain. He had gained his reputation as One Who Fools Them by his prowess as a French-allied war captain. This had been during the frontier conflict known as "Queen Anne's War," winning him the chieftainship at Mazipskoik. It was a responsibility he took seriously. He knew that strict sobriety was a fundamental element in the cohesive well-being of his people and the effectiveness of his warriors. Though the independent-minded chief didn't necessarily agree with all the doctrines of the missionaries' theology, he did heartily agree that alcoholic addiction was a terrible thing. He was as determined as any of the Black Robes to keep Mazipskoik free of the curse. Nor was he content with merely keeping liquor out of his "castle" (and radiating outward camp sites). When he visited encampments further up the lake such as at Scodoquek,[23] at the mouth of the Rivière Lamoille, and, further south, at the mouth of the Winooski River, he inveigled against inebriation. These were among the places where he expected to recruit additional warriors for his expeditions southward into New England. He didn't want his war party to be encumbered by any imbibers who would be taking nips from a flask along the way. Such sots would definitely endanger the sober warriors, and their own lives could be forfeit, when, upon reaching a settlement -- akubi long gone, -- they would surely attempt to ransack an outlying "likely looking" house to find English rum:

---

[23] The lower stretch of western Vermont's Lamoille River, where the rocky, down-rushing river levels off as it joins Lake Champlain was historically called Scodoqua, from the Abenaki Mskitegua, meaning "it is dead water, it is a reach," *Western Abenaki Dictionary,* Volume II, p. 218. Because of the calming of the water as a mountains-originating stream enters the level water of a lake, larger river, or the ocean, in the Abenaki worldview a river can have two names… one for the turbulent upper river; another for the "dead" or still water of the lower river. Another example is Scatacôok (or 'Schagticoke') for the lower Hoosic River where it levels off as it enters Hudson's River. There is the hamlet of **Still Water** near the present-day town of Schagticoke, New York. "Still Water" is simply an English translation of the Mohican "Scatacôok." The Saco River in Maine also. *Saco* is an obvious truncation of the Abenaki Msoaku'tegw, "showing-wood river *** river of standing dead trees, p. 329, *Ibid.*" Inundation-drowned trees are found in still waters. Beaver dams originally added to the depth and thereby the calmness of the lower Saco --"Dry wood river (trees dead by beaver)" *Ibid*, p. 329.

inviting an unexpected musket blast or a blow from an axe.

When among the Mskiteguak or the Ôinoz′kiak (the latter designation indicates 'Leeks-Land People')… *or* in the other direction, north, among Alnôbak along the Richelieu (those who frequented the French forts, finding employment as voyageurs), he not only made it clear he wanted no drunks as warriors… but also closely scrutinized those who claimed to be sober. He didn't accept such claims until he was absolutely certain they were true. In this he not only had the help of the Black Gowns and their donnéak, but was sometimes accompanied by his own spies, beginning with his own immediate family. A'lôn, Strong Bough, Deniz, Mali-Sallot, and even Azôn-Badise were enjoined to be warm and accepting toward this or that recruit, but at the same time keep a suspicious eye open for the slightest sign of inebriation. Supplementary "Ôauanoleuo donnéak" was cousin Half Moon and other relatives. Even included was his brother Malalamet, who usually lived among the Muheconnuck. Or back in old Ôauanokoo, at times visiting Mazipskoik with trade goods from Albany.

3. Aiyamihauôgan'ua Asokw Mgezo --**The Prayer of Cloud Eagle** --

As everyone sang and danced enthusiastically their energy was boundless -- or *apparently* boundless. After awhile their ebullience began to slacken, the older celebrants tiring first, the youngsters last of all. Mali-Sallot and 'Nikola' felt that they could dance and sing forever, it was so much fun. But all things must end, and presently the music faded away, everyone chuckling and bright-eyed with merriment as they returned to their original places. They put away the drum, their rattles or clacking sticks and looked for bowls and spoons for the proffered chestnut stew.

Again, A'lôn raised her hand to give everyone pause, announcing "Kaneua ntami! --But first!" -- once more. Before ladling out the steaming pagasôabôkôn, stew, the feast should receive its blessing. It was time to give thanks. Everyone calmed down and faced the fire and each other reverently, eyes downcast as A'lôn offered up thanks to Ktsi Niuaskw, expressing gratitude for the food, for everyone's good health and their being together with splendid friends on such a fine day. As she finished her invocation someone else was heard. It was the deep voice of a tall, well-built older Alnôba (though not as old as Ôauanoleuo), whom L'Artiste and Cæsar had hardly noticed until now. His presence had become more obvious when he had joined the celebration with a si'zi'uan, on a long stick, that was not a gourd rattle. It was fashioned of hide membrane. Opposing pieces of thin membrane had been cut into the shape of mikinakw'a, a turtle, and skillfully stitched together with fine sinew.[24]

La Bluetté and Besogne felt something of a chill as they recognized the voice as belonging to Asokw Mgezo... *Cloud Eagle.* They reacted with a bit of a start, a slight apprehension because the solemn-faced *"sauvage"* was a Mazipskoik tribal "Medauinno -- Person of Spiritual Power,"--...a 'Medicine Man.' Of course, in the next instant they knew, especially La Bluetté, that there was nothing to fear. Asokw Mgezo was a firm ally of the French, though emphatically not a convert, decidedly a practioner of the old ways. He and his spouse Ôeoandamsko, Wise Woman, were personally quite friendly toward the two Québecois. That they were not Christians and were the spiritual advisors for, and often the healers of, acolytes who clung to the old *païen* beliefs... was not, necessarily, a problem. The important thing to keep in mind was that they were *potential* converts. Therefore it behooved an earnest *donneur* to be as friendly and helpful toward them as possible. To, in a word, demonstrate Christian charity. One could contribute to their acceptance of the One True Faith by force of example. The

---

[24] Before the thin handle is inserted into the (damp) membrane, pour sand through the hole intended for the stick. When the membrane dries, having been placed close to a source of heat, pour the sand out. Replace the sand with small pebbles or corn kernels. The rattle will now keep its bulbous turtle shape (or the shape of whatever it has been cut to). Final step: There should be two flaps extending downward from the bulb; enclose these around the inserted handle and bind fast with sinew or string. You may want to add a dab of glue.

Canadiens rather instinctively knew that they should refrain from attempting to engage "medaulinnoak, spiritual-medicine people," in convoluted theological argumentation. Evangelism should be left to the friars, who were trained in such matters.

Hardly had A'lôn finished her invocation than Cloud Eagle stepped forward and, as if continuing her prayer, as if picking up from where she had left off, said *"O'hôô! --Yes!"* -- indicating that he agreed with what she had said ...was merely expanding upon her blessing. *"Cigitaua niona mildôbena oliôni Ktsi Maneniuiô!* -- Let us give thanks to the Great Mystery!" -- the shaman intoned more loudly in a confident voice that might be described as richly baritone. Lifting his hands midriff high, palm upward with the hand that wasn't holding the handle of the turtle - shaped si'zi'uan, his dark eyes came sparkling alive as he looked upon the patiently waiting assembly.

"Nidômbak n'alôgomômak! -- My friends, my relatives! -- *Noda nia!* -- Hear me!" -- He said, ascertaining that all were paying close attention, and, his intonation more heartfelt and richer yet: *"N'd oliôni niona d'yodali adouiui!* -- We are thankful [that] we are here together! -- *N'mildôbena oliôni n' augôuôuzôbena ôali sôgelamalsouôgan!* -- We give thanks that we enjoy good health!" -- Paraphrasing A'lôn's blessings on the viands they were about to consume, and having just returned, with Wise Woman and their two youngsters, from the south, a successful hunt, he raised his arms higher, saying *"Cigitaua n' mildôbena oliôni* -- Let us give thanks -- *ôadsi ôligen auaasak auani mildôbena agemôgik ôios ta kizagenol li niona* -- for the good animals who give their meat and hides to us, -- *...kassi nii niona kisi zibkôuzi ta ôlaimegôn!* -- ...so that we may live long and prosper! -- *Cigitaua n' mildôbena oliôni ôadsi Oligo Aki!* -- Let us give thanks for the Good Earth! -- *Cigitaua n' mildôbena oliôni Nigaues, Aki* -- Let us give thanks to Our Mother, the Earth -- *auani mildôbena niona akuôbi!* -- who gives us so much!" -- The encampment was located on level ground where the forest sloped down to the bank of the Missisquoi, where snow-covered ice floes were caught on boulders. Cloud Eagle inclined his head toward the nearby rushing stream: *"Cigitaua n' mildôbena oliôni ôadsi namasak alômi sibo!* -- Let us give thanks for the fish in the river! -- *N' acouiba mildôbena oliôni ôadsi namasak alômi meziôitta nebesal, siboal!* -- We should give thanks for the fish in **all** the lakes, the rivers! -- *Cigitaua n' mildôbena oliôni ôadsi ôeleguanoak* -- Let us give thanks for the winged ones, -- *ôadsi mezi nagik na lidooak!*[25] -- for all those that fly! --

---

[25] Lidooak, "Those that fly," the ak pluralizing Lidoo, "He (a bird) flies," *Western Abenaki Dictionary,* Volume II, p. 152, would also encompass madagenihlasak --**bats**,-- which, in the language, are seen as *featherless birds*, are "leather birds (leather fliers)." This can be understood if we break down the name into its several components: Mada indicates negativity, **not always** in the sense of bad, and here in the sense of *without: absence of.* The word for leather is madageniya, *Ibid,* p. 222, indicating substance, skin, hide, without hair or fur. Hla, isolated, indicates "go," *Ibid,* p. 167, and in the context of bats can be understood as indicating flight.

Cigitaua n' mildôbena oliôni ôadsi olakuika! Let us give thanks for the good forest! Abasikôk mildo niona *akuôbi!* --The forest gives us *so much!*"-- This last invocation was especially inspired by the warmth of the crackling campfire. He was standing in close enough proximity to appreciate its heat. He was adequately dressed for the season, for the present winter month, wearing clothing made out of moose, elk, and caribou hide with a woolen blanket coat over the buckskin raiment, a hood-like fur hat on his head (not unlike the chief's fur hat thrown at the grouse). But he knew that, even so, he would be feeling the cold without the fire. The heat emanating from the leaping flames would not be possible without auazonal -- fuel wood. -- He was grateful too, when Strong Bough stepped forward to add more wood and pieces of bark. And where does firewood come from? Odsi Olakuika! --From [the] Good Forest! -- When their wise forebears, fashioning the People's language untold ages ago, had named the moon of the present time of year, they had honored the trees, which, at this juncture, release an abundance of auazonal -- firewood.-- Piaôdagos indicates Moon of Falling Branches, February. A time when millions of trees release so many dead (and therefore nicely dried out) branches that enough firewood is available to last right through to the following Piaôdagos. Life-sustaining firewood scattered, hither and yon… lying on the ground! Who could ask for more? Cloud Eagle concluded his invocation with a reference to Dabaldak'ua Pmôuzouôgan, the Master of Life, the One Source of Movement and Measure. Dabaldak "Mildo niona azittauôgan n' coualda! -- Gives us everything we need! -- Niona oliôni Nônguic'hi-Ntatôgw! -- We thank [that] All-Mighty Power -- ôadsi Azittauôgan! -- for Everything!"-- With this he lowered his hands and bowed his head in humility. He fairly whispered "Na Ho," a phrase indicating that one is finished. His listeners murmured "*Ah* Ho," in effect saying "We have heard you, we agree with you." Then he looked up, smiling, and couldn't resist giving the si'zi'uan a bit of a shake, his smile widening into a grin, conveying "Kizi olidebimiciseda -- It's good eating [time],"-- namely that bountifully enriched chestnut stew, as well as some fresh venison from those two deer that he and his teen-aged son Olôbao had gotten, earlier in the day, when their family had returned to the camp.

When they had trekked south, carrying rolled birch bark sheets from their present lodge (as part of their overnight shelter) on their toboggan, they had as their objective a certain wetland that had once been the habitat of abagôloak -- flat-tails,-- i.e., beaver. Abagôloak hunters no longer went there (unless for such aquatic fur-bearers as muskrats or mink) the beaver having been long gone. Which was a shame, as it was said the tmakuak -- (tree cutters[26]-- another Ô'banaki word for beaver) that had once lived there had been gigantic, three or four times as large as the present-day animals.

The suffix ak provides the animate plural.
[26] P. 28, *Ibid.*

Recent hunters reported that the once-extensive lake there, hardly a trace of an ancient beaver dam at the outlet, had shrunken to mud and grassy tussocks with a cattails-choked pond in the middle. The place was now moskuasek …the home of muskrats; with a few moskuasak[27] lodges and feeding stations among the expanse of reeds. Evacuated tmakuak lodges advertise their abandoned state by sprouting --in the spring, -- wild flowers and grasses while they gradually deteriorate and diminish. Trappers intent on catching muskrats, or whatever other furbearers they might find there, hadn't seen, about a year ago, even so much as a hint of an old beaver lodge. Before setting out on their hunt, agreeing to return the next day so as to be ready for the band's move to the downriver sugaring camp, Cloud Eagle and family had engaged in a ceremony to implore the aid of the mystic Nanaualdad'ua Auaasak, the Keeper of the Game (said to roam about mounted "on a stag," that is, on aiyôba nolka, a buck deer). Ôauanoleuo, Half Moon, Strong Bough, Deniz, and Mali-Sallot had been invited to join them in the rite. Though the baptized, ostensibly Christian participants in the ceremony had been taught to think in terms of Ktsi Niuaskw, in rejection of the traditional "Ktsi Manitou," they assumed that everyone was actually thinking… of the same Great Spirit, the same mysterious, ineffable Power, no matter which particular language was employed. They participated as if the Black Gowns and their entire Church didn't exist. Where they were, "alômi pizaga -- in the bush,"-- forging westward from their extensive easterly winter hunt… there weren't any friars to harangue them with doctrine… with the intention of changing them into tithe-paying subjects of *le Roi Louis*. Here they were utterly dependent on the good will of Manitouak'ua Olakuika -- the Spirits of the Good Forest. -- And were acting accordingly.

Author's photo of fallen branch in "clearing of maple – sugaring camp" during Piaôdagos, Moon of Falling Boughs. Parts of poles, upper right, left corners, are putative wigwam shafts. Poles will be covered with bark once the chief's party arrives.

Note scampering mikoa, [red] squirrel, in background.

---

[27] Moskuasak: muskrat*s*. *Western Abenaki Dictionary*, Volume II, p. 260.

Authors' photo of iced-over moskuasek --muskrat habitat,-- within the town boundaries of Hardwick, Vermont.

The men and boys passed Cloud Eagle's soapstone-bowl pipe from hand to hand, taking puffs and solemnly saluting the cardinal directions. Their low-toned words, or silent thoughts, were in praise of Ktsi Manitou and in propitiation of the Forest Spirits.

Wise Woman, Mali-Sallot, and Ôligouôgasku'sizo,[28] were not offered the pipe when it was circulated. Their participation was important, but it didn't include smoking the pipe. The ceremony took place in a small clearing off to the side, surrounded by a screen of young evergreens and a few stately ôadsoimiziak,[29] "mountain trees," i.e., beeches, their lower branches featuring stubbornly clinging autumn leaves. Cloud Eagle's family had worked hard to clear a circle of snow away, using their ô'gemak as shovels as well as the camp's moose horn - bladed shovel. Then, prayerfully putting down offerings of killinick,[30] they cut small branches and sprigs from cedar trees. The môlôdagw[31] twigs (from a particularly venerated tree species) had been placed in a circle around the area where everyone was to sit or stand. More twigs and small boughs were spread out where people were going to sit. Such skins as from caribou, bear, wolves and raccoons, belonging to the participants, were also put down to avoid sitting directly on the chilly ground.

---

[28] Ôligouôgasku'sizo is a contraction of Ôligouôganui Nokskuasiz, meaning Beautiful Girl (much as Olôbao means Handsome One). She was (for short) Ôubi Mamidzôlo, White Moth, her more frequently used nickname, often shortened to simply Mamidzôlo. "Mamidzôla" can mean butterfly, but here indicates moth, white butterflies being rare. Mamidzôlo refers to *differentiation,* the designs on their wings which both species share. *Western Abenaki Dictionary,* Volume II, p. 56. To indicate it's her *name,* 'o' is added to the suffix.

[29] Also may be perceived as "highland trees." *Fagus grandifolia,* p. 31, *Ibid.*

[30] A mixture of dried basswood flower petals and fragrant dried autumn leaves --such as staghorn sumac, -- mixed with tobacco. Killinick is a New England region version of the more familiar, more widely known Algonquian kinniknick, "It is mixed."

[31] Môlôdagw, "low branch," northern white cedar, *Thuja occidentalis,* P. 66, *Ibid.* Môlô is a root designation also meaning deep, as in Môlôkipiui: *deep in the woods,* p. 332, *Western Abenaki Dictionary,* Volume I.

"To cite her proper name, Oligouôgasku'sizo, Beautiful Girl," rather than just her nick-name. Young Jade Elizabeth Kiang, grand-niece of the author, poses as Oligouôgasku'sizo.

Cloud Eagle or Ôeoandamsko often did the smudging, wafting the smoke upon the entrant with a feather fan, the acolyte also "gathering" the smoke to himself or herself with agma'i -- his [or her's] -- own cupped hands. This sacrament is intended to help the participants purify themselves, inside as well as out, leaving any negative thoughts or feelings outside of the sacred circle.

Later, at the sugaring encampment, an already existing sweat lodge, located in a secluded place, would be repaired and used. Fresh protective môlôdagw twigs would be put down. Circles of fragrant cedar sprigs are put down to help keep out negativities that might interfere with the ceremony. Cloud Eagle, Ôeoandamsko, and all concerned wanted Spirit to be happy with their devotional effort. Though Ôauanoleuo had been duly baptized as *Pierre-Jean* (pronounced Pial-Azôn) he remained basically *un païen*... believed that any spiritual endeavor, in whatever language, was good if positively motivated, if done sincerely, done well.

Though the women and girls involved didn't partake of the pipe as it was circulated, they nonetheless had an important function in the ceremony... similar to the protecting circle of cedar twigs surrounding the supplicants. In order for Spirit to hearken to their prayers, women don't need to smoke the pipe. The purpose of the odamôgan[32] -- the pipe -- is to carry the thoughts of the men, their prayers "visible" in the form of the wafting smoke, to the Spirit World. The women, however, by their very nature, being the nurturing givers of life, who produce new life, children... are considered so spiritually powerful, *as they are*, that they have no need of the extra "reach" of paôlaôbai odamôgan -- the ceremonial pipe. -- It is quite enough for them to be "smudged" with killinick smoke, -- the killinick, or unmixed odamô, pegedadamek alômi ôauasi "pegadadamek kuat'a"-- smoldering in a sacred "smudging bowl,"--

---

[32] An interesting word: like many others, it does "double duty," describing more than one thing. Odamôgan defines not only the tobacco-smoking pipe, but what in English is called the dragonfly, p. 117, *Western Abenaki Dictionary,* Volume II, "from its shape." A *spiritual* role is attributed to the **ceremonial** pipe. Like medauihla, the loon, -- [the] spiritually-powerful flier, -- the hovering, flitting dragonfly travels back and forth between the material and spirit worlds.

along with the men, upon entering the ceremonial circle. Sitting on mats or skins in the ceremonial circle (or standing, as the case might be), the women usually form an outside circle. They are invited, by virtue of their spiritual power, to form a barrier against negative influences reaching the men. The men, not being as spiritually powerful, need the aid of the pipe, of the fragrant odamô, as well as the protective presence of the women. In fact, ever since the arrival of the Auanock, the Strangers, irrespective of whether they were Plac'môniak, Iglismôniak, or Dutsmôniak... one catastrophe after another had afflicted the People. Such as the onslaught of previously unknown, pandemic diseases... being one. In forming an adequately protective shield around the men as they prayed with the aid of the pipe, despite the absence of a sufficient number of females, Cloud Eagle decided on a compromise. One reason why he had chosen that particular clearing was because of the sheltering screen of evergreens. It was basically kôkskisek, a place of cedars. The majority of the conifers were ôski nebizon abaziak, young medicine trees, *cedars,* môlôdagok -- *deep* cedars -- (called 'white' cedars in modern lexicon). The communicants would form half-moons facing each other... Sanôbak, the men, would face the women, the thickest part of the cedars behind the men. A spiritual advantage of cedars, especially the young trees, is precisely their molôgen, their "deep" nature. Their low-hanging boughs, almost touching the ground, make it difficult for bad influences to get through. Older cedars have higher branches and therefore offer much less of a barrier. In the case of the present small ceremony there were not enough females to completely encircle the men and boys. Not everyone in the encampment took part. Convinced converts had, to an extent, been alienated by the missionaries. Also, there was much work to be done. Some were away hunting. Women and girls were cooking, processing carcasses, taking care of the smaller children... there was always much to do. At the same time, Cloud Eagle included such youngsters as Deniz and Strong Bough, and of course, his own offspring. Years ago such youngsters would have been allowed to observe, but would not have been inveigled to directly participate in such ceremonies. Now, however, with the alienating advent of the missionaries, Asokw Mgezo and Wise Woman considered it imperative to include children at an early age. They wanted to start their feet on the path to spiritual power, onto the Good Red Road ...were determined that their youngsters take to heart all the old 'medicine' practices. The friars, obviously, were absolutely intent on undermining the Peoples' indigenous culture. They wanted to transform the Alnôbak into subservient, tithe-paying Frenchmen. The Alnôbak, as self - sufficient, sovereign people ...would be no more. Long winters ago, the famous Sieur de Champlain had said it, addressing his native allies along the St. Laurent: "We shall become one people." What he really meant was that the Alnôbak would become *French* people. But if the world of the Alnôbak, the Ordinary People, was to remain in balance, if the fish and the animals, the winged ones, the fecundity of the earth itself... was to continue to flourish, the old ways could not be abandoned. To neglect the Ôligo

Mkui Ô'udi would be to court disaster. Fortunately the medicine trees here, for the most part, were young and therefore low-limbed… exactly what was needed. The feminine half-circle faced the sanôbak, their backs to the more vulnerable side, where bare - branches hardwoods mingled among the conifers.

Upon the completion of their early morning ceremony, Asokw Mgezo had called their three dogs -- which were so well behaved that some called them medaulemosak -- spiritual - medicine dogs.-- He and his family, on snowshoes and hauling their loaded toboggan, set off for the muskrat-place once renowned for its giant tmakuak. Chief Grey Lock, who had participated in the ritual with the same positive attitude with which he attended the rites of the Church, wished them well, A'lôn seeing them off with Christian blessings.

When Cloud Eagle's family arrived at the wetland later in the day, they found that Nanaualdad, the Keeper, indeed seemed to favor their enterprise. Approaching the "muskrat place" with great caution, their canines so well trained that they refrained from unnecessary barking and scurrying about, they were delighted to find that the place was no longer a shrinking muskrat marsh… The flat-tails had returned! A considerable body of water had drowned out the p'hanemôdebal,[33] grassy tussocks, impounded by an extensive dam of mud and sticks. The dam (and associated coffer dams) was a construction that conferred upon the tree-cutters yet another Abenaki name, auadnakuazidsik,[34] meaning "wood carriers." Out upon the iced-over, snow-covered expanse they could see a freshly - built beaver lodge.

It resembled a wigwam, a quite conical one in shape, though of course snow covered. The morning had brightened as they had pushed along the obscure trail to the pond, the sun shining through filmy clouds. And, as they stealthily approached ever

---

[33] "Women's heads," p. 178, *Ibid*, indicating the grassy tussocks found in swamps, due to the long blades of grass, reminiscent of the long length of the odôb'kuan -- head - hair, -- of women.

[34] *Western Abenaki Dictionary*, Volume II, p. 29.

closer along the margin of the wetland, Cloud Eagle whispered for Olôbao and Mamidzôlo to step ahead of Wise Woman and himself (at the same time, he and Olôbao had to glare sternly at the dogs, who were becoming increasingly excited, to keep them from barking). Asokw Mgezo, taller than the youngsters, had glimpsed a rare sight that he wanted them to witness. There was a bit of a snowless area on the south side of the lodge, and there, sitting on its haunches, was makuabid: a "red one who sits!"[35] It was sitting on its lodge, soaking up the warm late-February noonday sun... "Enni! (Well!)" warm to a beaver, at least.

Despite the area's reputation as a long-bereft adalamiskuid[36]-- place of beavers, -- Cloud Eagle's intuition had been to bring along the amiskuôganal --ice chisels for breaking into beaver houses -- that he and his children had made. Each amiskuôgan was of a different size... a longer one for himself, shorter ones for son and daughter.

As they crept closer the makuabid ceased to be a makuabid, getting down on all fours. He (or she) slipped off the lodge and into a small, almost invisible area of open water. The dogs quivered and whined as they saw this, fairly bursting in their desire to bark and charge after the tmakua. The hunters restrained them, urgently hissing *"Taboot!* -- Quiet!" -- and *"Zôgenauigi!* -- Be Still!" -- However, it wouldn't be long before the adiak would be able to yelp, howl, and dash about all they pleased. Wise Woman and Asokw Mgezo preferred the old Alnôbaiui word for dogs,[37] 'Adiak'... for *their* dogs, at least. For the moment, however, they continued their stealthy course somewhat inland from the swampy margin of the pond. They had the concealment of snow-hung trees and snow-capped boulders of various sizes.

Cloud Eagle and his family wanted to keep the beaver house in sight, but at the same time wanted to remain unseen, especially since the slight breeze was favorably in their faces. They wanted to be able to spot any auaasak venturing into the open terrain of the wetland's margin. Some of the boulders were so enormous, being glacial erratics that it was necessary to skirt wide around them. In so doing they came across a game trail. They could tell it from a mere thready indentation in the snow because they saw msalkil lômptok -- many tracks -- in it. Older, wider tracks had probably been made by moose or uôbozak -- white-rumped ones.[38]-- Fresh tracks were those of wolves, of uôkusesak -- foxes, -- and some kind of large, *quite* large, cat. Possibly pittôlo, that

---

[35] P. 29, *Ibid.*

[36] *Ibid*, p. 29.

[37] *Western Abenaki Dictionary,* Volume II, p. 114.

[38] More commonly called "elk," *Cervus Canadensis*, p. 127, *Ibid*. While giving wôboz for the elk (animate plural wôbozak), Dr. Day omitted the *precise* Abenaki definition. If we extrapolate from the Shawnee wapiti --that peoples' name for the elk, "white rumped,"-- we very likely also have the Ô'banaki definition, thanks to Eastern Woodland Algonquian affinity. The Shawnee 'wapi' or ôapi, "white," corresponds to the Abenaki wôbi (p. 447, *Ibid.*), or uôbi, for white (the latter spelling being the author's preference).

tawny cat of "very much tail," or of the gray, taller species of the uigôdiak, "no tails." Wise Woman and Asokw Mgezo had become aware, recently, that some of the Québecois were demonizing that gray cat as *"lucifee"*-- a sobriquet apparently drawn from another French name for their evil spirit, *le Diable* (or did they mean the even larger one of very much tail?) There was no time to carefully examine which was which at the moment, however. If they kept a sharp eye out they might see the animal itself, not just its tracks.

Something else the family had brought with them, in addition to the long-handled metal amiskuôgan chisels, was a weapon specifically intended for nailing tree-cutters and moskuasak. The prototype had been made from a straight sapling with two limbs branching from the main trunk. Three altogether, cut shorter and sharpened, formed a trident. French blacksmiths had improved on this by fabricating metal socket - hafted tridents that could be fitted onto a wooden handle. It was something of a grim irony that the long handle of the tmakua-astahigan, beaver-stabbing instrument, had been made from a drifting kaskamaakw,[39] a 'beaver stick.' The stick had been used for food, a flat-tail having eaten the bark off. What was interesting about this particular kaskamaakw was, to Olôbao and Mamidzôlo's incredulity, their father's claim that the stick he had found had its bark eaten off by skuamiskw, an adult *female* beaver.[40] The siblings were astonished. To simply *look* at a beaver, an active, living one, it's impossible to tell its gender -- except, possibly, in regard to a pregnant one… and then only if she's out of the water. The gnawer of this stick he had not witnessed in the act of peeling off the bark. He had found it days, perhaps weeks, later. How can you tell the animal's *gender* from the tooth marks? Age, yes, from their size, whether mature or an aualsiz, "carried on back little one." But *gender?* Was their father bapimek? -- joking? -- Aig agma bapimek nspi agemôuô? -- Is he playing with them? -- Brother and sister had grinned at each other in wide-eyed wonder. He had to be kidding!! On the other hand, he is medaulinnoid -- a person of spiritual power -- …isn't he? Indeed he is. No question about it… he was able to discern things by means as yet unknown to them. Such insight, such rare knowledge, was something they wished to acquire themselves, so they routinely harkened to whatever their parents told them with great attention. And, yes, to Ôeoandamsko as much as to their father, for she was powerfully *medaului*
-- spiritual -- also. She was equally as much a medaulinnoskua -- spiritually powerful woman -- as he was medauinno, a 'medicine man.' She had not been given the name, in solemn ceremony, of Ôeoandamsko, Wise Woman, for nothing.

As the family crept closer to the beaver house Asokw Mgezo urged Handsome One in front, who stepped forward cautiously with tiskuôdi, an arrow, notched to the

---

[39] Stick peeled by female beaver in (beaver's) house and allowed to float to surface of the water, *Western Abenaki Dictionary*, Volume I, p. 251. Term is related to kaska, "It is wide" (the surface of beaver pond), *Ibid*, p. 251.

[40] *Western Abenaki Dictionary*, Volume II, p. 379.

cord of his kuena tôbi -- long bow,-- Cloud Eagle close behind, trade-gun at the ready.

"As they crept closer the makuabid ceased to be a makuabid, getting down on all fours. He (or she) slipped off the lodge and into an area of open water." Author's photo, taken near home, Woodbury, VT, in late February.

It had been primed and loaded all along, and now he thumbed the flint-gripping hammer back to full cock. The paskhigan was not yet as potent as it looked, for, as a safety precaution, he had left the frizzen's buckskin pitahlaguôgan[41] -- steel-sheathing cover -- fixed onto the striking steel. The average warrior/hunter usually didn't bother with the device, having enough self-confidence to assume that they knew how to handle a firelock safely. However, Asokw Mgezo frequently hunted with his family, being especially intent on teaching both Olôbao and, to cite her proper name (rather than just her nickname) Oligouôgasku'sizo, Beautiful Girl… everything he knew about hunting and his wildwood wisdom in general. At such close quarters a devoted parent didn't want any one of his family members to be unexpectedly endangered by such a volatile, dangerous alokataôgan, machine, as his paskhigan -- explosion instrument. -- When Cloud Eagle had acquired his first fusil there was something that resembled a knife sheath on it. The sheath was "up-side down" when in use. He had seen such sheaths on the fusils of others and, finding one on what was now his own, instantly understood what an excellent thing it was. He termed it "tsegelaz-tsanniguôgan'a, a sparks-stopper." Something similar that Cloud Eagle added to his firelock, soon after he had

---

[41] *Western Abenaki Dictionary,* Volume II, p. 344. Dr. Day cites 'Bidahlagwôgan' as describing a knife sheath. This term should serve as well for what the firelock - shooting colonials called a "hammer stall" or "frizzen boot." It is a leathern cover sheathed over a flintlock firearm's striking steel to prevent accidental discharges when the arm is loaded, primed, and the hammer brought back to full cock. The leather barrier will prevent the hammer's flint from making sparks should the hammer inadvertently fall forward, striking the frizzen. 'Pitah' relates to "into"…something is inserted *into* a pouch, a sheath, etc. Other examples of *put into* articles are pit'halôn for an arrow quiver and pitôgan for a pouch. "What something is put in and covered up," *Ibid,* p. 300. Oskanahlaguôgan --Steel-sheathing cover-- from oskanahlagw, "bone metal," (includes alnahlagw, *Ibid,* p. 205, "ordinary metal," iron). Alna from alni, ordinary. Lagw denotes metal. Steel equates to oskan for bone, *Ibid,* 378.

obtained it, was a greased leather *asenapanes*,[42] **stone**-a'pan, gebahigan, cover, which protected the fusil's ignition system from rain or excessively wet conditions. Needing an upward bulge in the middle to accommodate frizzen and hammer, the covers are routinely made out of the knee sections of deer legs. Some of the Canadien habitants, *fermiers* such as La Bluetté, made theirs out of cows' knees. The covers are oblong in shape, holes being punched through the edges to accommodate thongs with which to tie on the cover over the ignition system. The frizzen "boots" also serve to keep the striking steels dry in wet weather... or wet conditions. La Artiste, having business in Québec City, was fortuitously present once when a fresh company of La Marine *troupes,* direct from France, were disembarking at the Lower Town.

He had been astute enough to notice the hammer stalls on their muskets as they filed ashore. When opportunity offered, he had inquired about them, being told that they were not only a safety measure but helped keep the frizzens dry at sea and on the St. Laurent, including when it wasn't raining. The *fusiliers* had to sometimes muster on deck where they were subject to sea spray. Like the native hunters, the average Québecois seldom bothered with the device. However the artistic, but at the same time practical, La Bluetté immediately resolved to make one, once he returned home, for his *fusil de chasse*. And also minute ones for his *pistolets*.

At the present moment Asokw Mgezo kept the frizzen boot in place. He wanted to be ready to shoot, having brought the hammer back to full cock while yet some distance from the tmakua lodge so that the abagôlo --flat-tail, -- wouldn't hear the slight click. Though the *click!* of thumbing the hammer back to full cock was scarcely audible, Cloud Eagle knew that animals have acute hearing. The makuabid -- or former makuabid, the once and future "red one who sits,"-- might detect it nonetheless, and take alarm. The sound was definitely metallic and therefore strange to a wild animal's ears. When the tree-cutter had slipped out of sight it had not slapped its tail against the water as a warning that danger was approaching. So far, so good. If Asokw Mgezo saw it again, within much closer range, he could slip the hammer stall off the frizzen and be able to shoot immediately. The tsegelaz-tsanniguôgan, "sparks-stopper," was made of sinew-stitched leather. It made no sound when you removed it.

The tmakua had probably dived into the water because it was "dinner time." It was most likely out in the middle of the pond now, under the snow - opaqued pkuami --ice, -- pulling up a branch from the rocks-anchored store of green saplings and boughs that had been deposited there the previous year for pebon midzouôgan, winter food.

---

[42] Asen -- [the] stone -- being of course the gunflint. Original gunflints (from nodules of *true* flint, in general) were mined from the vast chalk deposits on either side of the English Channel... and still are, today. The native people's own comparable stone, pieces of chert ("A flint-like stone," *Webster's Dictionary*) can also be used in the jaws of a firelock. Whether European flint or American chert, when such a stone is fixed into the jaws of a flintlock, the name changes from merely mazipskw, flint/chert, to padôgiapskw, "thunder-stone." *Western Abenaki Dictionary,* Volume II, p. 150.

There was, perhaps, another flat-tail out there, doing the same thing. The beaver they had glimpsed was, very likely, one of a pair, nôbamiskw ta skuamiskw -- an adult male beaver and (an equally mature) female, -- who were living in the lodge, who had built it and the dam. Though… there might be another lodge further upstream, as yet unseen, perhaps just beyond the yonder jutting peninsula.

When the family had finally approached the lodge to within easy range of Olôbao's arrow and Asokw Mgezo's paskhigan, they paused, Ôeoandamsko and Oligou ôgasku'sizo laying hands on the increasingly tense dogs to soothe them, to calm them down. Now to wait. "N' askauôbôbena --We wait, we watch, -- nikuônmbi -- now"-- Cloud Eagle whispered. Looking carefully all around and seeing no immediate target, he silently resheathed the frizzen boot over the striking steel. The tsegelaz-tsanniguôgan in the meanwhile had been dangling by a thong from the trigger guard. Olôbao relaxed the cord of his tôbi. In the far distance, beyond the undulating, trees-bristling line of hills, mkazasak,[43] crows, called. Harkening to the cawing, they couldn't hear anything that indicated that the charcoal-colored ones had any concern with them. The family remained crouched down, immobile as possible, Olôbao, Ôligouôgasku'sizo, and Wise Woman gathering their adiak to them, both to control them and for their furry warmth. Once you stop moving, on a wintry day, the cold penetrates.

Li ôskinnos ta nôkskua askauôbimek naskôdahômeguad -- To [the] boy and maid the watching / waiting seemed endless.-- When it seemed that they were about to begin shivering uncontrollably in spite of clinging tightly to the dogs, Cloud Eagle quietly eased the hammer on his fusil forward to half-cock and carefully laid it down. He eased it down horizontally, sideplate down, lockplate (ignition-side) up, and whispered: "Niona acouiba tmihlôbena kuenakuamal -- We should cut poles -- ôadsi boleua-adelimek pmelodigan -- for the escape-blocking fence."-- Stepping out of his snowshoes, he drew his large steel-bladed knife from the thick leather sheath he had made for it, carved and painted with decorations honoring how the blade enabled him to blaze trail through the woods. Sister and brother also undid their ô'gemak, extracting

---

[43] Mkazasak, crows, from mkaza, charcoal, *Western Abenaki Dictionary,* Volume II, p. 68, and mkazaui, black (charcoal-*like*). "Mkazas, literally charcoal person, a crow," *Ibid,* p. 94. The 'ui' for like, similar to, is eliminated in defining the bird in favor of the suffix za(s), a second '**caw**.' The Abenaki definition for the crow cleverly combines **both** its color and its familiar call. Other Algonquian dialects and Native American languages (known to the author) employ variations of only "caw caw" for the crow. Incidentally, the "English" word… is *also* descended from the call of the crow… likely beginning in the ancient Near East and segueing northwest through the ancient Mediterranean. The ubiquitous European R was injected as the term evolved through such stages as **kron** and **korn** to, eventually, meld with the Anglo-Saxon *crawan*. Whether the Anglo-Saxons *pronounced* the R is another question. They may have actually *said* "ca'wan" (meaning "cawer"). C*r*awan may have been written in, unnecessarily, by scribes who, back then, -- had to deal with various dialects and styles in vocabulary, lacking codified standards such as *Webster's Dictionary* or the *Encyclopedia Britannica.*

their alni'tmahiganal, i.e., tomahawks.[44] Leaving Ôeoandamsko to control the dogs, they made their way back to the toboggan. They had not brought it further for fear that hauling it closer would alarm the flat-tails. Saplings grew nearby and the closest were cut and trimmed to provide fence poles. Asokw Mgezo used his strong bladed knife. It had been an expensive item, but was well worth it because the extremely hard steel, once sharpened, kept the edge razor keen. He cut through each sapling with but one stroke. Cloud Eagle also carried his own iron-headed hatchet.

The blacksmith who had made this also had not left the poll (the part of the head opposite the blade) rounded as on most hatchets fabricated for the Indian trade. He had added extra iron and had squared and beveled the poll so that the reversed tomahawk head could serve as a hammer. And that was how Asokw Mgezo was going to use it now. The cut saplings in hand, Cloud Eagle and his children advanced toward the tree-cutters' lodge, also carrying their ice-chisels and the tmakua-astahigan trident. They walked, as quietly as they could, on the snow-covered ice of the pond to the beaver house. Wise Woman continued to hold onto the straining dogs. Though the tree-cutters might be able to hear the slight sounds they were making, presumably they were gnawing nutritious bark from the kaskamaakuak they had hauled up from the bottom of the pond. Hopefully they were fully preoccupied with the succulent taste of tender maple-sapling or poplar bark (Kaskamaakuak: *Wide*-pond branches used for food).

The three rounded the lodge on two sides, stepping to the edge of the open water on the south side, where the submerged exit of the beaver house ought to be. With his children on one side, and himself on the other of the wine-dark nepi, Asokw Mgezo pointed a fence pole into the water, extracting his hammer-polled hatchet. Thick leather covered the blade which was also tightly wrapped to the haft with thongs. Another safety measure… if the hatchet is used as a hammer, the head left uncovered, the sharp hatchet blade might bounce back and hurt him. No one wants their nose cut in half! Olôbao wielded a similar hammer-hatchet, though not as large as his father's. Beautiful Girl, not wanting to damage her smaller tomahawk by attempting to use it as a hammer, instead was using a rock-maple gualôm -- club[45]-- as a rude mallet. As quickly and as quietly as they could the trio inserted a line of sticks, firmly hammering them down, Cloud Eagle using his longer arms to finish the barrier in the middle. Pounding the last pole into place, the medauinno put away the hatchet and quickly snatched up his tmakua-astahigan. Staring intently down into the water, he held it at the ready. Ôligouôgasku'sizo and her brother at the same time jumped up onto the beaver house. Seizing their ice chisels, they shouted for their mother to come forward. Now

---

[44] *Abenakis & English Dialogues*, Chief Joseph Laurent, p. 63. A hatchet, smaller than the (less common) full-sized axe, is an **alni-tmahigan**. "Alni, ordinary," because *more common* than the full-sized axe. Also axe, hatchet, "instrument for cutting transversely," *Western Abenaki Dictionary,* Volume II, p. 182.

[45] Gualôm, a club, a word that can also be used to indicate a *bat*, as in baseball bat, p. 77, *Western Abenaki Dictionary,* Volume II.

enthusiastic energy exploded, the released adiak charging forward wildly, barking sharply as they bounded onto the lodge. Idzia ta itsakaso, Brother and sister, alemamtahiga agemôuô amiskuôganal -- drove their beaver-hunting chisels -- ali zôgelak ali agemôuô tônega -- as hard as they could -- alômsanon tmakua'i uigiuôm --into the tree-cutter's lodge, -- twisting, hacking, to loosen the sticks and frozen mud of the dome. Their mother joined them, using Asokw Mgezo's larger amiskuôgan to stab into the top of the lodge, adding her might to the effort. The three weren't really trying to break all the way through into the flat-tails' chamber... the lodge was too strongly built with interlocking sticks for that. It was tightly constructed not only to shut out talon-clawed predators but also winter's below-zero freezing cold. Tree-cutters have no fire with which to warm their dens; they depend on the warmth of each others' bodies. Actually breaking through would take too much time ta ozômi saagalokôn -- and too much fatiguing effort.-- Ôeoandamsko and her youngsters were merely giving the *impression* of attempting to break through, to panic the denizen, or inmate<u>s</u>,-- of the lodge. If indeed, there was anyone at home. The dogs were doing their part, frantically barking for the sheer joy of it and enthusiastically scratching at the roof of the lodge. Suddenly Cloud Eagle stabbed down into the water on the inside side of the 'fence.'

Oligouôgasku'sizo and Handsome One immediately jumped down to their former positions on the opposite end of the pmelodigan, just in time help their father haul up the flat-tail he had skewered. As he brought it up into view, the teenagers thrust their amisuôganal under the tmakua from their side of the open water to lift it onto the ice. Wise Woman also joined them with her longer ice-chisel... though she didn't descend as quickly, not wanting to sprain an ankle jumping down, or slip and fall into the nepi. Between them they manhandled the tmakua up onto the ice shelf. They could see, in an instant, it was kamiskw -- a fully adult beaver.[46]-- But of which gender?

As she helped pull the inert carcass further along onto the ice, Wise Woman directed a questioning look at her husband. When she had been climbing down to help, she had seen the water swell up slightly next to the pinioned kamiskw while two of the fence-poles wavered.

"O'hôô! -- Yes!" -- Asokw Mgezo responded, grinning. "Adodzi 'aobanik nisak'ua agemôuô! -- There were two of them!"-- While he had been thrusting hard downward, pinning the flat - tail as it paused before the unexpected barrier of the pmelodigan, he had glimpsed another shape follow the first through the dark, tannic acid-stained water. That one too had been brought up short by the fence, but then, panicked by what was happening to its mate, pushed powerfully through the sticks, knocking two somewhat askew.

---

[46] *Western Abenaki Dictionary,* Volume II, "Beaver of parent generation," p. 29. Plural and location are both kamiskok.

Displayed on a "primitively hooped" tmakua pelt (from a Walden, VT beaver pond), are replica 18th century instruments such as Cloud Eagle would have used. Most of the leather safety accoutrements were made by the author. Shown, from top, are: 1. Lock cover (behind *fusil*) to shield flintlock firearm's ignition system from rain. 2. "Pitahlaguôgan -- steel-sheathing cover -- fixed onto striking steel (the *frizzen*)." 3. Hammer - poll tomahawk with leather cover over blade (tied to haft). 4. Trade knife next to (5.) sheath decorated to "...honor how the blade enabled him to blaze trail through the woods." 6. "...the long handle of the tmakua-astahigan had been made from a drifting kaskamaakw, a beaver stick," a stick found floating on kaska, *wide* surface of pond.

As the family gathered around the body, Cloud Eagle having extracted his astahigan, their adiak converged, sniffing and growling at the carcass. The tree-cutter had been killed instantly when the middle prong of the trident penetrated just behind the head, the other two tines keeping it in place as Asokw Mgezo's thrust shoved it against the bottom. Nerves of its spinal column severed, the tmakua had perished instantly.

Asokw Mgezo, taking the inert form by the tail, lifted it up to examine the tree-cutter's genital area. Ôeoandamsko looked closely also. "Iahi!" she hurrahed. Cloud Eagle exclaimed "Ahaa!" exclamations expressing success and satisfaction.[47] They could have just as easily exclaimed "Ôligen! -- Good, it is!" -- Their victim was of the gender they were hoping for. He was nôbamskw, -- an adult male. -- Not that they had anything against the nôbamskuok of the flat - tailed nation in particular, pakalmeguad ônda -- certainly not.-- Their joy was based on the fact that it was not skuamiskw (an adult) female beaver. Or palmeskua, a young, about two years old female. The other flat-tail that had darted from the lodge, that had been glimpsed before vanishing under the ice… had been the skuamiskw. The good thing about that female was that she was probably already pregnant. It was the time of year for such. Dali 'aoba baami

---

[47] "Interjections," *Abenakis & English Dialogues*, Chief Joseph Laurent, Odanak Reserve, p. 90.

tademakuak[48] -- There would be more tree-cutters. -- "Kisi nôbamskw -- It's (a mature) male beaver, -- dôniua kagui niona linkauadsôbenoob, which is what we hoped for," Asokw Mgezo explained to Beautiful Girl. "Kagui niona ayamihôbenoob ôadsi, What we had been praying for," Ôeoandamsko pointed out, and Oligouôgasku'sizo recalled that, while the family had waited, keeping a lookout before advancing upon the flat tails' lodge, Cloud Eagle, while holding onto his paskhigan with one hand, with the other had extracted a bit of odamô from the odamôinoda -- tobacco's pouch -- inside his general - purpose couidebak pitôgan -- necessaries pouch. -- Looking over at his son, he had nodded. Without a word being exchanged, Olôbao also dug into his odamôinoda. They quietly put tobacco down (grown and cured by themselves), focusing on catching nôbamiskw, and absolutely not a skuamiskw. Handsome One felt a bit of pride in doing this, as it had been only the previous spring when he had dug up a plot and started his own odamô nebizonkikôn, tobacco medicine - garden. In previous years he had been much "too busy" hunting, fishing, and playing games. His maternal uncles had hinted that he should start, but he had procrastinated until the preceding year. As the buds on the trees were appearing, the flowers of skotam uizôuataual[49] -- trout lilies -- already blossoming, Handsome One's uncle Managuôn Mskuamago, Rainbow Salmon,[50] had rather forcefully suggested that Olôbao begin his own odamô nebizonkikôn. He had underlined his suggestion by handing Handsome One a packet of odamôkikaimenal[51] -- tobacco seeds -- he had saved from his previous autumn's harvest. Cloud Eagle also contributed some of his odamôkikamenal, as did other uncles.

Handsome One was... a bit shocked by all the outpouring of generosity, and was *definitely* motivated. If he wanted to keep the esteem of his father, in fact of everyone, -- he had better get busy! With such an embarrassment of riches in hand, he had gotten to

---

[48] Tademakuak: "Beavers in general." *Western Abenaki Dictionary,* Volume II, p. 30.

[49] While skotam is the legitimate word for trout, specifically speckled trout or brook trout, p. 422, *Ibid.*, uizôuataua, plural uizôuataual, the **uizôu** translates as *yellow,* and the suffix ataw from peskuataua, flower, literally "it is open" (a blossom), p. 151 *Ibid.* Thus, in Alnôbaiui the English designation translates into "trout yellow-flower," "lily" being a strictly European word. Extrapolating from Day's "wizôwatawa," yellow flower, for the **yellow water lily**, *nymphaca advena*, p. 228, there is no reason why "yellow flower" can't be applied to the blossom of the trout lily also. In Abenaki the plant, *particularly* the leaf, is mozilalo, "moose's tongue," *Ibid,* Volume I, p. 327.

[50] A particularly colorful name, as mskuamagw, salmon, translates as "red fish," p. 330, *Western Abenaki Dictionary,* Volume II. The name of a *person* called Salmon is distinguished from the actual fish by replacing the w in word-final position with o, the o indicating that *He is (or She is)* Mskuamago -- Salmon.-- The "mskw" in the term indicates red, as well as complete, whole.

[51] Kikamenal specifies "seeds for sowing," in contrast to the more abstract oskanimenal or skanimenal for seeds. Oskanimen is derived from "a seed, literally **bone-berry**," p. 338, *Ibid.* Oskan indicates bone, with "skanimen" being a shortened form. 'Men' (or min) indicates seed or berry. Is there an *extremely* **ancient** Abenaki connection between the English "men," (singular *man*) and **Adam** (*the* Man), etymologically descended from ancient Hebrew, who *gave his* **seed**, i.e., impregnated Eve? And what do we make of se*men*?

Author, in green blanket coat and insulated *pebon mkezenal* -- winter moccasins,-- using tomahawk to trim stick being inserted as part of "tmakua pemelodigan, a beaver fence." Procedure was part of experiential exercise in northern Vermont pond. Hole in ice was made just outside the presumed exit of beaver house. First snow shoveled away with one of author's ô'gemak (background), then ice chopped through. Method is for setting an underwater trap on inside - side of "fence" for whenever beaver exits lodge (*if* the lodge is occupied). Catching beaver with trident is best done if there is already open water at exit, combined with element of surprise.   Photo: Francois Petoine.

work right away. He borrowed a moose's shoulder-bone bladed mattock to tear up turf and expose fertile soil. That done, what next? *Enni!* He needed a lakahigan! -- a hoe! -- The lad made his own hoe from the handy shoulder blade of aiyôba, a buck. The handle for the hoe-blade he made from a maple sapling, which, at a certain height, needed to have an almost horizontally-growing limb branching out. He had at first glibly assumed that finding such a sapling with the requisite limb would be easy…

4. Olôbao'i Nebizonkikôn --Handsome One's Medicine Garden--

It wasn't, he discovered, searching through woods swarming with tiny but severely biting gigue'ts'ze'gibsak. "Little no-neck ones"[52] to the People ("black flies" to the Pastoniak). To keep from being driven crazy, he had to repeatedly apply an oily substance that was a combination insect repellent / sunburn ointment. It was concocted from raccoon fat or bear oil, conifer sap, and certain herbs.

As he slathered it on, periodically swatting at the no-necks as they sang their war song in his ear, he profusely thanked ktsi nemahômak ta okemesak -- great - grandfathers and grandmothers -- who had devised the formula for the ointment long, long ago, saying *"Oliôni, oliôni, n'kitsiiak!"* There are plenty of saplings in the good forest, especially in such places as storm-blasted clearings, but one with the almost horizontal branch, at the right height, was much rarer than he had imagined.

Though they didn't grow odamô themselves, his mother and sister, as well as an

---

[52] Under Fly, p. 152, *Ibid.*

array of aunts and female cousins, were quite pleased that he was cultivating his own garden. Past masters at growing things, they were free with useful advice on how to best nurture his tobacco patch. He felt triumphant when, during niben, the summer, the leaves of the seedlings that had sprouted started filling out... topped by uizôuigen peskuasauônsizal -- small yellow flowers.-- It was pleasant to witness, when he arrived to hoe weeds or to harvest leaves that were large enough, the mamidzôlak, both the larger, black-striped, often yellow / orange ones, i.e., butterflies, and the white or dun-colored smaller ones -- moths, -- alight on the blossoms to collect their nectar. He was also pleased, at first a bit startled, to witness the advent of unusual flies that the elders said were rarely seen at Mazipskoik. Are they ôauilômuak? -- wasps? -- The plump wasps had small wings but nonetheless flew about with a menacing hum... were not silent, like the familiar mamidzôlak. They were freshly arriving "Plac'môniak'i odzauasak --Whitemens' flies."-- Questioning other cultivators, he learned that the Québecois call them *abeilles*. Relatives from the Odanak Mission, on the St. Lawrence, and other villages to the north, were familiar with them, noting that the French had brought them over many summers ago. When they built nests -- and apparently the Plac'môniak even -- how interesting! -- built nests *for* them, called *ruches,* delicious

Photo from Makuônikas --Red-Boiling Moon -- (April), of deer's shoulder blade hoe. "Made from the shoulder blade of a nolka, the handle from a maple sapling." Using construction found in nature, nearly horizontal branch from main stem, aligned with flange rising from shoulder bone, author secured handle to the blade. Flange was drilled with two holes for wrapping (initially wet) rawhide thongs to wood, the thongs then heated, making them iron-tight.

ômuaimelases, wasp's molasses, could be harvested. Though it might be painful to do so; the flies have a vicious sting. You seldom see even one deep in the forest, as *les abeilles* need places where there are blossoms. Not many flowers can flourish in the deep shade of the overarching forest canopy. They didn't seem to care if the blossoms were wild flowers or were in peoples' gardens. Like those hovering quiet ones, the nanatasizak -- hummingbirds,* -- it's the nectar they're after. Or the pollen. Both? The boy would observe closely.

*Nanatasiz, "Little mute one," hummingbird. *Western Abenaki Dictionary,* Volume II, p. 195.

There were soldiers over on Lac Champlain's Isle La Motte, who, even now, might be building *ruches* at their camp there, where the 1600s Fort Ste. Anne had once stood. The Mazipskoik bees were obviously feral migrants, doubtless from the hives on the *seigneuries* along the Rivière Richelieu. As more and more pabemaksig kitolagol --great sailing vessels -- arrived from France, disgorging new colonists on the docks at Sorel and Mont Royale, the numbers of tenant-farmers increased, enabling *les seigneurs'* estates to expand southward along the Richelieu… in turn fostering a greater demand for honey. However, some of the "domesticated" bees were proving "disloyal," and free ranging honey bees were multiplying, building their own nests in the forest, in secluded places not too far from where flowers were growing.

Bears took notice… that beehives are similar to the nests of insects -- especially those of "paper wasps" -- whose hives they had been pillaging for untold millennia. The bees' independent hives, usually built in the hollows of old trees, were becoming known to moôuinak. Some thought that the bears had, quite quickly, evolved a taste for the sweetness of honey as developed as that of human beings. The bruins intention, however, is to consume the grubs within *and* the wasps themselves, ***sleeping*** wasps… motivating them to make their raids in the night. To be rewarded with the additional boon of honey, a "midnight snack," involving an unexpectedly sweet 'dessert.'

Stitching freshly-plucked odamô leaves to sticks with strings of sinew, Olôbao at first raised the sticks on the stubs of poles to cure the leaves in the sun. Slowly drying leaves need no shelter from the rain as long as they remain green. A concern in curing is, once the leaves have begun to mellow into the desired stage of usefulness, their chlorophyll dried out, turning them a rich tan or brown color, the leaves… if left unprotected, can go bad if subjected to successive days of wet, rainy weather. Rather than deepening the richness of their brown coloration the leaves can become black with mould. This can be a rather sad development when one considers that the very word for "brownish" in Alnôbaiui is "odamôbameguezid -- he that is *tobacco-colored.*"[53] -- However, Olôbao needed the sun to continue drying his leaves, so he built a shelter for his harvest. A quite open one, facing mainly east and south-east to admit sufficient sunshine while at the same time shielding from the rain… understood to commonly drive from the west. Ali zibki niben -- As late summer -- gradually eased into taguôgw, autumn, the youth built a leaves-protecting shelter, following the example of his elders, who built what might be called "odamô uigiuômal -- tobacco wigwams" -- to protect the sticks - strung leaves from too much rain (and from morning's dew). These were not like residential lodges, uigiuômal ôadsi Alnôbak -- lodges for the People, -- which

---

[53] *Western Abenaki Dictionary,* Volume II, "--the one that is brownish, he that is tobacco colored," p. 52. The word can also be a "name for a brown bear." Chief Joseph Laurent, in his 1884 *Abenakis and English Dialogues,* under "Colours," p. 45, lists "It is brown" as wdamôôbamegua. (A shortened form is odamôui, tobacco - *like*).

Author's photo, Before and After, of a large paper wasp nest that hung, during a recent summer, from a maple tree near agma uigiuômo -- his home. -- On right, nest "Atsagema, Before, alômi mezi kisi ksalô --in all its glory,"-- wasps trafficking in and out, going about their business.

Photo on left demonstrates "Anegi, After," following ôazesa gadonala -- nest attack -- by a nocturnally visiting bear. Mere shreds of wasp nest scattered in grass the only evidence the once thriving ôauilômua community ever existed.

were closely covered with bark and reed mats to conserve the heat of the central fireplace in cold weather, made with openings only for the doorway and the smoke-hole above… the doorways covered with deerskins to retain the fire's heat in the winter.

The putative Handsome One's "first tobacco patch," planted "some distance from other gardens." The leaves of the seedlings that had sprouted started filling out, topped by yellow flowers." Picture shows one of author's annual odamô plots. Elfin yellow flowers, somewhat trumpet- shaped, can be seen, largely on the left. Author's photo

Nor did he need to extend the bark all the way to the ground. Which was just as well. When, in the early summer, he began searching through the forest looking for bark, -- especially the always preferable maskua -- birch bark,-- he was asked, in the event that he came across a yet-unsullied birch, to forgo stripping any bark from that tree. The Flint-Place People had utilized so much birch bark, for lodges, moose calls, rain ponchos, containers, &c., over the years that "virgin" canoe-birch trees of sufficient size were no longer easy to find. That is, within a few minutes' walk from the gardens around the chief's 'castle.' Since the bark necessary for a tobacco ôalaga uigiuôm --bark shelter -- doesn't have to be of the best quality, merely adequate, he was asked, especially by the women, who made so many articles out of fresh birch bark, to use pieces of maskua naighé naôat -- that are *passé* -- …from trees that had fallen numerous winters ago. Or from dead birches that might be still standing. Such bark is, surprisingly, often still quite good. In contrast to other trees, the bark of fallen birches is usually so enduring and resilient that it's the *last* part of the tree to rot away.

Msali kiuihla -- Many a wanderer, -- coualdam aguanitigan -- needing shelter-- odsi mamôtsa'ua zazalaki madzekizegad'pita -- from the onset of a sudden tempest,-- glancing quickly around, had spotted a large (sometimes enormous) birch trunk lying prostrate nearby. With a few swift knife cuts he or she availed themselves of a quite tough, but flexible, shelter. There had even been occasions when there had been no time to take up the bark (or perhaps ônda tsakuagw -- no blade -- for cutting it with).In such instances, because absolutely all of the tree's heartwood had rotted away, leaving only the bark (which yet maintained the shape of the former entire trunk)… the shelter-seeker had simply crawled into the now hollow tree -- or *former* tree, one could say.

Array of author's *Nicotiana rustica* variety tobacco leaves. Sewn to sticks-hung strings and hung out to cure in the sun, as Eastern Woodlands men (First Nations men as a whole) have done for countless centuries. Well dried out, quite odamô' ôbamegua --tobacco-colored -- (i.e, *brown*) leaves, picked earlier, hang from foremost stick. Leaves harvested later, still green, hang from stick in back.
Late summer photo.

Thinking about the durability of birch bark as he searched for maskua scraps through the forest, Handsome One recalled an old story. It was one of the atookuakun ôdsemouôganal -- wonder-tale stories. -- Its central character was one of the great creation-shaping heroes of Alnôbak history. Which one? Had it been Ôdzihózo, or Kullos'kahp? No matter. Somehow the Hero (who could be mischievous) had offended ktsi Padôgilidoo -- the great Thunderbird, -- who pursued him vengefully. Running for his life, in desperation the Hero had literally *dived* into a hollow birch. The tough, resilient bark saved him from the gigantic eagle's talons and beating wings. Since that day all (paper) birches have borne the marks of the Thunderbird's down-beating wings. Kina tali azi maskuamôzi pamgizegak -- Look at any birch tree, today -- ta k'namitôdzi -- and you will see. --

Discovering that the moôuinak were harvesting wild honey, Olôbao thought that perhaps he could do the same. When out hunting, and such hunts were not always after game animals; sometimes he searched for certain herbs, or a sapling or such of just the right configuration (such as for his hoe handle) …he kept an eye out for wild bees' nests. It seemed an exercise in futility, however, as he never seemed to come across one. He certainly noticed enough pitta negoni -- very old -- pitta guina odabazimak -- very large tree trunks. -- Such elder trees are usually pabasi macinauôgan -- half dead -- ala tagôaôiui macinauôgan -- or entirely dead, -- and often have suitable hollow cavities in them. He would stop, listening for the flies' humming, and look for them entering or leaving; but saw none. He developed an appreciation for cavities in tree trunks that he had not had before.

When Olôbao noticed a honey bee or two hovering about the flowers of his odamô crop -- or on any flowers, -- if he wasn't particularly intent upon some other purpose, he attempted to follow an *abeille* when it abandoned the blossoms and flew toward the woods. Apparently the ôauilômua had collected sufficient pollen and was heading back to its hive. Again these excursions seemed an exercise in futility, however, for in his attempts to "track" the bobbing, weaving insect among the trees, over ledges and hillocks, through muddy sloughs, over down-timber and what have you... he inevitably lost sight of it.

Eventually someone, who had spent a great deal of time further north, among the Québecois, informed him that the Plac'moniak had developed a method of tracking free-ranging abeilles. They would obtain some fine wheat flour, quite uôbi, and, when a bee had alighted on a blossom, would very gingerly sprinkle some of the flour onto the abeille. When the bee flew away, they were able to keep it in sight, discovering its nest.

"Odamô uigiuôm --Tobacco wigwam" -- built by the author, Skamonkas --Maize - Harvesting Moon (September) -- Made of sheets of "scrap" birch bark, the construction shelters strung - up odamô leaves from rain while at the same time admitting enough sun to continue curing leaves.

For size comparison, uadsoimahalakus ôigebi abazenoda -- brown - ash splint basket -- made by author, on ground, is six inches tall.

When Olôbao heard about this, it was too late in the season, flowers were fading, insects hiding from the increasingly cold temperatures. However, one of his tracking attempts had a positive outcome. His intent focusing on a bee had led him quite afar, and on his return he wasn't quite sure of his way. Climbing a hill to look around, he noticed, just above a highland pond, a long ledge sheltering an extensive kôgw den, apparently a winter retreat of the spiny ones... layered with a great amount of kôgw pakikôgan! -- porcupine manure! -- Telling others about it, mostly women and girls, later he led them to the place, where they filled containers with dung to use as fertilizer.

Two bees clinging to the seed-bearing center of a sun flower. To warm themselves? The season having become increasingly chilly, it made sense. "Kisi kizoskôgan'a, kisi - ônda? -- It's a *sun* flower, isn't it?"-- Author's photo of sunflower in his front yard garden, early autumn.

5. Olôbao ta Mandaôasak --Handsome One and the Slow Ones--

Noticing a hollow tree, "Nikuôbi, dali oligen-kinamek biguagen'a -- Now, there's a fine - looking hollow,"-- Olôbao would say to himself. "Madsiatta naodsi ôauilômuak d'ônda lauakak --Too bad some bees aren't using it."-- He felt mollified when he, upon closer inspection, ascertained that some of the hollows had been, in the winter, used, and by equally important creatures. By fur bearers such as apanakesak, martens, olaniguak, fisher 'cats,' azbanak, raccoons, and, if the cavities were sufficiently large, moôuinak, bears. At times he encountered a slow one, mandaôasw.[54] Accompanied by a dog, he was glad that the kôgw,[55] "prickly," was up in a tree, where the adia couldn't get swatted in the face with those sharp quills. Of the two names for the hedgehog, he preferred mandaôasw: -- slow one. -- It was less confusing, as kôgw sounds too much like 'akokw,' the word for a kettle, a cauldron.

---

[54] *French / Abenaki Dictionary,* Rev. Joseph Aubery, p. 408, circa 1700.
[55] *Western Abenaki Dictionary,* Volume II, p. 299. **Kôgw** is related to **kôuigen**: "rough, *prickly*," p. 326, *Ibid.* Author's emphasis.

Usually, when he encountered one, it was in a tree (though not very high up) and he and the animal gazed at each other in silence. At such times manni, slow, isn't the word for it. The auaas, animal, doesn't move *at all*. You know it's alive, however. It stares at you with eyes that are quite alert, as fascinated by the appearance of the strange creature below as you are by it. Once he had been astonished to look up and see one almost directly above him. Not that that was all that unusual, but what was holding it up there certainly was. It was clinging to what was -- what had to be -- a *network* of slim branches. *Pitta* biui bskaôdkuenal! -- *Very* thin branches! -- Boughs so slim and weak-looking that Olôbao was astonished that they held up such a large creature at all. The answer had to be that the ends of some of the branches, had, -- by the weight of the mandaôasw? -- caught on to each other and interlocked. It could happen. They were flexible, yet obviously tough branches, despite their size. Another question: *Kagui kisitomek nospiui dali?* -- **What is it doing up there?**-- If it ate into any one of those branches, hardly bigger than twigs, it would snap and down would come... well, **kôg**w, falling as hard as a cast iron kokw! Searching for something in particular, he didn't have time to linger... a mystery. He would uncover the reason later.

Another encounter featuring mandaôasw was in Midsouôgankas, one of the late summer "Eating Moons" -- Harvesting Moons, August and September,-- at the end of Tmezôuas -- Cutting Moon,[56]-- August,-- or the beginning of Skamonkas, Maize-Harvesting Moon. It had been very hot and dry lately, unusually dry. The women had been going to the river with ualaga dautiganal -- bark containers -- that had been made for collecting maple sap, and bringing up water for their wilting crops. He had wondered if he should do the same for his nebizonkikôn, but the growing odamô seemed to be doing just fine. Scouting molôkpiui -- deep in the woods, -- he had crossed the beds of bone-dry brooks and skirted sloughs that, normally quite watery, were now sun-baked depressions of hardened mud. Approaching another brook bed and intending to cross, he had looked over to where there was, in wetter weather, a small waterfall. At the bottom of the drop (only about a foot high) was matanaski! -- at last! -- a bit of nepi. Hardly a cupful, scarcely worth bothering with. He also saw, immediately, why he wouldn't want to bother. Gathered around the puddle, just about nose to nose and regarding each other fixedly, were three creatures you ordinarily don't see all in one view. Aligedaid'a, a jumper,[57] mandaôasw'a, a porcupine, ta segôgw'a! -- and a skunk!-- It was understandable that they would be thirsty, and had coincidentally happened to come upon the cupful at the same time. Although they weren't huge auaasak, there probably wasn't enough water for all three. Were they going to fight over it? Olôbao, fascinated by the prospect of witnessing such a struggle, inched closer. The three were

---

[56] Cutting in the sense of harvesting sweet grass; also separating ripe squashes, beans, etc., from their vines.
[57] A snapping turtle, *Western Abenaki Dictionary,* Volume II, p. 424

focused on each other, completely unaware of his presence. He was in no danger of being bitten by the snapper, or struck by the quills of mandaôasw.

However, he realized with a bit of a start, segôgw was another matter! He didn't know who would win if they started fighting, but one thing was certain, the skunk, win or lose, was going to unleash his awful smell! Not that aligedaid would care, and mandaôasw..? However, he himself *certainly* would... he absolutely didn't want to become tainted with that repulsive scent. Once unleashed, it permeates everywhere. Segôgw doesn't concern himself about whether you are an actual enemy or not. The youth was planning on visiting the attractive maiden Asauanlômso, Warm Breeze,[58] that very evening. He didn't want to arrive reeking of horrible segôgimôguezo! He departed from the scene as quietly as he could. As interesting as it was, the resolution of the trio's dilemma would have to proceed without him. Agma "agua poniadomek kuôgueniui agma asma nikôni -- He "was quitting while he was still ahead."--

Tabena -- Later, -- when he related what he had seen to his elders, they agreed that his story was extremely interesting. None of them had ever seen such an encounter between three such different auaasak themselves, though the ktsiiak had lived through many winters. Asokw Mgezo and Wise Woman, being medaulinnoak, spiritually astute persons, pondered the incident for its deeper meaning. Obviously the encounter had been prompted by pakusatagizegad -- the dry weather, -- but was there significance to it beyond that..? Inquiring around, a consensus of opinion agreed that an aligedaid, or any mikinakok -- turtles -- in general, wouldn't care very much about sufficient water at such a time. The hesitant ones, considering that they are not fish, have amazing abilities, such as to remain underwater for a long time. As winter comes on they burrow deep into the mud, where you might think nothing can breathe, and are equally unfazed by unusually dry conditions. Mandaôasak can also take drought in stride, chewing on green leaves for moisture. Segôgw, however, was another matter. Olôbao had, most likely, been wise to leave when he did.

On the other hand, could it be... that those whom the boy had seen were delegates to an emergency council..? Perhaps the three were grand chiefs of their respective nations, meeting to determine if anything could be done about the dry weather. And, though Sôgemôk -- the Chiefs -- Mikinakw and Mandaôasw might not care that much about water for themselves... they certainly, out of courtesy, would want to meet Sôgemô Segôgw at a place where there was at least a little water, for him. "Ala ôadsi skua -- Or for *her*,"-- Wise Woman had pointed out. How do they know that Segôgw is a male? "Kagui tônega'ônda Segôgw... -- Why couldn't Skunk...-- uadsônab saunks'a? -- be *a female chief?*"-- she wanted to know, providing an unexpected twist to the discussion. In fact, how did they know that *mezi nenhloak -- all*

---

[58] Can also, in fact quite commonly, mean south wind, as well, p. 449, *Ibid.*

three -- weren't female chiefs? Olôbao had said nothing about gender. The others nodded, conceding that it was possible.

Ôeoandamsko had not said woman chief as sôgemôskua, as per usual, but had used a more streamlined rendering from an Algonquian dialect to the southeast, of the territories that *les Anglais* were calling "Massachusetts-Bay Colony" and "Providence Plantations." Fifty summers previous there had been woman chiefs among the Wampanoag and Narragansett Nations who had been quite well known. They had figured prominently when Ktsi Sôgemô Metacom, christened "King Philip" by the Pilgrims, had led a war of liberation against the domineering, land-grabbing Iglismôniak. The famous female chiefs Ôu'itamw, called by the English "Weetamoo," and Euasaunks, dubbed by them "Awashonks," had figured prominently in the uprising. Ôu'itamw had died in the fighting, and Euasaunks had saved her people from destruction by switching sides from Metacom to the Pilgrims. That had not preserved her from puritanical persecution, however. Later she was punished for transgressing one of the "Bostonians'" many regulations. Theocratic English laws that were as harshly applied to the native allies of the Pastoniak as to the surviving subjugated "hostiles"… were among the grievances that had kept the grandparents and parents of both Wise Woman and Cloud Eagle moving westward and northward. Ôeoandamsko's ancestry was basically among the Nipmuck, the nation of central Massachusetts.[59] In moving periodically to get out from under the thumb of the Pastoniak (another word used in reference to their oppressors was 'T'sauguaqock,' meaning "Knife Men," or 'Cutthroats'), Wise Woman's forebears had fallen in with so-called "River Indians." These were the people of the Massachusetts section of the fertile Connecticut River valley, remnants who had once belonged to the Pocumtuck Confederation. Seeking freedom, attempting to live in their time-honored, traditional way, the associated exiles gradually moved northward up the Long River, the Connecticut. Meeting resident Sokuakiiak and, further north, the Koasak -- Little Pine Trees People, -- they mingled with Alnôbak who cheerfully traded with, but refused to be subjugated by, the Pastoniak. The exiles' experiences with the Anglocentric, draconically applied rules and regulations of the Puritans increased their distaste for the colonists' religion. This reinforced their traditional "medicine" practices, encouraging Ôeoandamsko and Asokw Mgezo to participate in ceremonies, walking the Good Red Road well before they took an intense interest in each other. In fact it had been while their ktsiiak had been introducing (what they recalled of) the south - eastern Nickommo[60] ceremony to the Koasak that they realized that they had so much in common. Cloud Eagle, falling in love, began to actively court the comely maiden. They had not been given the names of

---

[59] The Nipmuck territory encompassed, basically, what is today Worcester County, Massachusetts, extending a bit north into (what is now) New Hampshire and somewhat south into Connecticut.

[60] P. 192, *The Wampanoag Indian Federation*, Milton A. Travers, 1961. Also *One of the Keys*, 1975, p. 40.

"Wise Woman" and "Cloud Eagle" yet. That would come later. Ôski 'Olakamigesku'sizo' -- [The] young 'Courteous Girl,'-- that had been what she had been known as at the time, -- though she had other suitors, responded warmly to the youthful Asokw Mgezo's advances. He had been rather shy, but she encouraged his suit, however indirect it was. She had sensed that they were on the same trail, the good medicine path, quite early. He was going to be 'Eua Pazego --The One.'--

Having pointed out that nenhloak auaasak, [the] three creatures, could be female chiefs, Ôeoandamsko was trying to recall what Euasaunks' actual name had been. She knew the Iglismôniak called her "Awashonks," pronouncing it in their mobile-lipped, almost barking way of speaking. But Euasaunks had been her *title* ...composed of saunks, hereditary female leader, and eua, an Algonquian equivalent of the English "the" (or of the French *le* or *la*).[61] All but a more knowledgeable few of the English thought it was her name. An example of interpreters trying to express an Algonquian equivalent of *the* is the title of the Puritans' holy book when it had been translated into Massachusetts-area Algonquian. It had been interpreted, and so printed on the front cover, as *Up Biblum*. 'Up' is the equivalent of "the"... *The Bible*. Her elders recalled seeing copies of it when they had still lived in Massa'tzosek. The Reverend John Eliot and a handful of Puritan missionaries had used it to win converts. Eliot's believers were organized into "Praying Indian" towns. The new Christians were prevailed upon to abandon their indigenous culture entirely, adopting not only the Puritans' belief system, but also their jurisprudence and other appurtenances of Iglismôniui -- the Englishmen's Way -- ...including, even, the wearing of English-style clothing.

All of which had done the converts absolutely no good. When "King Philip's War" had broken out, the converts having nothing to do with Metacom's warriors, their towns had been assailed by mobs of hysterical Pastoniak. Hundreds of hapless, entirely innocent converts had been seized (those who couldn't manage to escape into the forest) and marooned on Nolka Menahan -- Deer Island -- in Boston Harbor ...where their "fellow Christians" hoped they would starve to death. The haters of "ye Salvages" had also nearly drowned the Reverend Eliot himself, ramming and capsizing his boat when he and the Reverend Mr. Gookin had attempted to bring provisions to the island.

Of course, what was at the bottom of it was that many of the Pastoniak, shillings, pounds, and pence in mind, saw a golden opportunity to seize the converts' property without paying for it. When the war was over the Praying Indian villages were gone

---

[61] In Algonquian dialects the equivalent of the European "the" is seldom spelled out. It is implicitly understood without having to be actually enunciated, except in more measured, more formal speech. For example, the M of Mhaga is the equivalent of *The* body, *Abenakis & English Dialogues,* p. 24. If referring to his or her own body, the speaker says nhaga, the n representing (in shortened form) *nia,* for *my* body. Speaking to another, the speaker says khaga, the k a truncated form for kia, *your* body. Even in English, "the" is a relatively new word (historically speaking), being a shortened form for "that."

(save a few, such as Natick toward the coast), the land taken over by those Pastoniak who had been neighbors. Friendly, caring neighbors, the converts had thought, bent on providing good examples of pious Christian behavior. Their "brethren" would show them the way to the New Jerusalem... to "ye Citie on a Hill."

6. Ôeoaṇḍamsko Mikualḍa --Wise Woman Remembers--

Wise Woman (and, if she asked him, probably her husband, as well) could remember a few other words and phrases of those southeastern dialects from when they had been children in Kueniṭegw pasahana -- [the] Long River valley. -- She smiled to herself as she recalled a phrase from the Agauam'uk dialect, a phrase that had been inspired by the weather and the time of year they were in at present. It was 'mic'h'een'neen-kisos'...(she couldn't help but put an Abenaki accent on the suffix, kisos, sun -- or the moon, the "night-sun,"-- here representing month). It meant "Moon of Everlasting Flies." The flies in question are what the English call "house flies," not the bees whose elusive hive Olôbao was seeking. The term is largely onomatopoetic ...you can sense the annoying buzzing of the flies in the repetitive syllables. Ô'auksuauni was another phrase,[62] for a later, and favorite, time of year, now approaching. It indicated that time following the autumn hunt, when an abundance of food from the game that the hunters had brought in was being prepared for the fall thanksgiving feast -- one of the periodic thanksgiving celebrations. -- A leisurely time of year... for the now relaxing hunters, at least -- one of wagering, playing games and relating accounts of adventures occasioned while hunting.

The Mazipskiak, so many being the descendants of migrants from the east, including the coast of Maine, used English-originated names to describe the Europeans' domestic animals, pluralizing them with Ô'banaki pluralizations. Their ancestors had probably first heard the names for these animals at Popham's early fur-trading station, encountering the French, around the same time, further north. Their forebears hadn't understood the European word - final 's' as a pluralization. Thus a cow, singular, is kaoz. "Cattle," plural, is kaozak.[63] The People didn't always copy the Strangers' words for those niḍazoak, tame beasts, however. Occasionally a descriptive, onomatopoetic word was devised, such as the southeastern, Wampanoag/Nipmuck nay'nay'yomiuôt for the horse, Ôeoandamsko remembered. The Ô'banakiak routinely employed ases for the horse (plural asesak), at first having bravely said *hases*. But, because H is difficult (for eastern Algonquian speakers) in word-initial position (the first letter in a word), the H was later dropped as being too difficult, slowing down what you are trying to say. She recalled some of her relatives mentioning another term used by their southeastern

---

[62] P. 50, *The Wampanoag Indian Federation,* 1961, Milton A. Travers, Christopher Publishing House, Boston.
[63] *Abenakis & English Dialogues,* Chief Joseph Laurent, p. 35.

forebears, miauene, a council, or counseling,[64] when she was growing up among the Sokuakiiak and the Koasak. The Sokuakiiak and the Little Pine Trees People, of course, had their own terms for the same ceremonies and gatherings. Their medaulinnoak were glad that the newcomers were mentioning these things, however. A Mkazaui Pitkôzon had arrived, with his assistants, and built a bark-roofed chapel almost in the middle of Koasok, the council-fire town of the Koasak.[65] The aiyamiha'uigamigw -- prayer house -- had been constructed within a stone's throw of the centrally located three pine trees. These were the koasizak -- little pines (pine saplings) -- that had been planted in honor of the ancestors who had bequeathed to the upper valley Alnôbak… the proud name of Little Pine Trees People. "People of the **Little** Pines" but often translated, by the English, as simply 'Pine Trees People.'

It was good that he had come, on the one hand, strengthening the Koasaks' ties to the French, facilitating access to French trade guns, ammunition, and other supplies. Such goods should enable them to more effectively resist the Pastoniak. They liked trading at such downstream centers as Deerfield and Northampton, but the exiles from the south had thoroughly informed them about the Iglismôniaks' land-grabbing inclination. As well as about their dislike of the Peoples' traditional beliefs… of their intolerant attitude toward the Alnôbak in general, calling them "tawney Imps," and "salvages."

Few could disagree with the Black Robe when he harangued them to be morally upright, warning against the rum of the English (and the blandi of the *coureurs de bois)*. His devotion to the sick, to the bereaved, to the less fortunate, was also most welcome. On the other hand …the Alnôbak spiritual leaders worried that his teachings were undermining the Peoples' traditional Medauliui -- Spiritual-Medicine Way. -- Wasn't *La Bible* the same as *les Anglais'* Up Biblum, the speaking new-leaves that had turned the heads of the southern Praying Indians? And which had been instrumental in leading most of them down the psalms-paved path to utter disaster..??

Another old, southern phrase that came to Ôeoandamsko was kôietta, an expression of tenderness…[66] it evoked thoughts of the old homeland, of the ancient Nipmuck heritage. The word caused her to think of her mother and of the wisdom of her elders. Of medicine ways that had almost been lost… but which she and Cloud Eagle were steadily regaining. Her eyes moistened with sentiment as she remembered.

Wise Woman sighed and came back to the present, realizing that she had become lost in reverie. What was Guelegueno saying? (from Gueleguenad, Flicker Person) one of Olôbao's uncles. He was asking the boy if he had ever seen a kôgw dance. Handsome One had to admit that he hadn't. "O'hôô --Yes,-- agemôgik pmegak zaui, k' ualdamô

---

[64] P. 40, *The Wampanoag Indian Federation*, Travers.
[65] At the "ox-bow" bend of the Connecticut River, where Newbury, Vermont, is now.
[66] Reference "Dedication," *The Wampanoag Indian Federation*, Travers.

-- they dance sometimes, you know."--- Asokw Mgezo allowed that this was true. Despite their glacially slow movements most of the time, on rare occasion mandaôasw can be quite playful. He -- or she -- will rise up on hind legs, almost like a human being, and rock back and forth. "O'hôô, pmegamek! --Yes, dancing!"-- For the joy of living, apparently, glad to be alive. Perhaps in appreciation of dining on so much good bark?

Olôbao and the others were reminded of the ceremony that they had engaged in only that morning. Appealing to the Spirit World for the relief of rain, Cloud Eagle had raised his pipe to the cardinal directions, passing the odamôgan clockwise, to Olôbao, Strong Bough and other male traditionalists, while the outer circle of women and girls murmured and shook their si'zi'uanak. They had not held the ceremony inside the palisade of the 'castle,' where the Black Gowns' chapel was, where his converts might frown on such an *infidèle* ritual. It was more fitting, in any case, to conduct it out among akikônal, the fields, where rain was most needed. The pipe put away in its beaded buckskin pipe-bag, Pabasôgizo -- Half Moon -- and others had taken up their odamô-blessed drums and started beating them, medauinno Asokw Mgezo and the rest of the men taking out their rattles. All began dancing solemnly in a clockwise circle, their thoughts, their chanting, focusing on zogelôn -- rain.--

They danced for a long time, the day growing hotter as the sun rose toward its zenith. At last, on the advice of his wife, Cloud Eagle called a halt, urging everyone to drink some refreshing tkebi -- spring water -- from the gourds brought over earlier. It wouldn't do to court dehydration… they didn't want anyone keeling over from the heat.

Asokw Mgezo, Wise Woman, Olôbao, and others who had participated in the rain dance were now resting in the shade of the ceremonial arbor that had been constructed outside of the town's palisade. This was no time to withdraw within the stockade, the stout walls of which blocked cooling breezes. The tall palings were appreciated during the winter, when they obstructed cold wind. Their bower had been built with poles forming a circle, with a few roof-beams meeting in the center. In warmer weather, as now, evergreen boughs were placed across the beams to provide gentle shade. As they sat and talked, everyone faced each other in a circle. No one's back was turned to anyone else. Some attempted to cool themselves with fans (usually made of the tail feathers of the larger wild birds), using them also to brush away annoying flies. Others sipped from their hollow gourds.

"Madsiatta k' kiziô'ônda askauôbiôôb --Too bad you couldn't have waited -- kueni dabi -- long enough -- ôadsi namito tsaga Mandaôasw nôdsi pmegaba -- to see if Slow One (was) going to dance,"-- idzia Ag'ebalamo -- cousin Bull Frog[67]-- remarked to Olôbao. He had taken care to say "kiziô'ônda -- couldn't,"-- and not "wouldn't," as the latter might infer cowardice, something that Ag'ebalamo didn't want

---

[67]Another onomatopoetic Abenaki term, "…name is imitation of his (bull frogs') voice," p. 54, *Western Abenaki Dictionary*, Volume II.

to imply. He wouldn't have remained looking on long enough to become tainted with Segôgw's awful spray, either.

"Kisito segôguak pmegak? -- Do skunks dance?" -- Azôn-Badise asked. His father, the chief, was absent that summer. He was over two hundred miles to the south, leading raiders who were dodging rangers hungry for the bounty on "Rebel" Indian scalps in the woods of western Massa'tzosek.

Nzasis Managuôn Mskuamago -- Uncle[68] Rainbow Salmon -- answered him: "Alamtod'a agemôgik kisito -- In a way they do. -- Kaguesa'ua -- Sort of,"-- he chuckled. "Migakaibmegauôgan'siz k' idô -- A bit of a war dance, you could say.-- Kaneua k' maui tsaga k' ladaôbiô -- But you better leave if you see that.-- Kinauitigan agma -- It means he,-- ala skua -- or she, -- kisi alosamek ôadsi lauakamek agma sônkusi -- is going to throw his weapon,-- agma maskimôguezi -- his stink.-- Mezena alemosô nanabi! -- Get away fast!"--

Uncle Managuôn Mskuamago elaborated on his theme, making it clear that he was describing something that he had seen himself. "Adodsigid Nmahom Si'si'kua --Like Our Grandfather Rattlesnake,"-- Segôgw gives fair warning before attacking. The warning, the bit of a war dance, consists of foot-stomping, teeth-clicking, hissing, and perhaps even growling.[69] The stamping of feet is reminiscent of somebody engaged in tikkakamaso, stamping on the ground with one's heels,[70] which young men elaborate into a courtship dance. Most animals really walk on their toes. Few walk on their heels, like human beings. "Nidzia, Moôuin, our Brother, the Bear," -- will do so, to stand upright. He warned that you should watch out for when Segôgw raises his tail... 'Mezena alemosô!' It's possible that Segôgw had danced too, after Olôbao had prudently quit the scene. Not in anger, not as a warning that she was going to "cut loose," but to do a rain-bringing dance. Along with Nidzia Kôgw -- Our Brother Porcupine. -- Everyone was beginning to talk themselves into believing that the three creatures were not only chiefs, but better yet, Medaulsôgemôk! -- Spiritually - Powerful Chiefs! --

"Kagui pamômiui Aligedaid? -- What about Jumper?"-- Half Moon asked. "'Aligedaid' ligeda ibi pmi zagamuamek apcikozid'a --'Jumper' jumps only when biting an enemy,"-- he pointed out. "Dôniua kisi'ônda pmegauôgan'a -- Which isn't a dance."-- ...so much for the medicine-chief theory...

Ta askua... -- And yet...-- the turtle might have had a role there anyway, thought Cloud Eagle, his brow knit in concentration. What gave him, and then others, something

---

[68] *Maternal* uncle, as opposed to Nnôdsikw, paternal uncle. *Abenakis & English Dialogues*, p. 22.
[69] P. 141, *New Hampshire Nature Notes*, Hilbert R. Siegler, 1962, Equity Publishing Corp., Orford, NH.
[70] *Western Abenaki Dictionary,* Volume II, p. 375.

of alômiladaôbi'ua, ôli'laldamuôgan -- an insight, of good thinking, -- in regard to the question was when, casting about for clues (ôadsi kinauitigan'a -- for a sign) -- he happened to look down at what lay next to him. It was his turtle-shaped membrane si'zi'uan. Wise Woman looked at it too. *Mikinakw-alôgihlôk! Turtle-shaped!* Then they looked over at Mahom Kasko -- Grandfather Heron, -- whose ceremonial rattle, secured in the woven sash around his waist, was not just turtle-shaped, but was fashioned out of the shell of a turtle itself. The unusual si'zi'uan had been gifted to him by Kaanauagihnono friends. It even appeared to be a whole mikinaukw, because they had, using a bone for the handle, extending the bone all the way through, carved the bone extension into the likeness of a turtle's head. *Aligedaid'i dup'a*, tali nii..! -- *A snapping turtles' head*, at that..! --

But... of course, Segôgw and Mandaôasw wouldn't have attempted to use Aligedaid for a si'zi'uan. Her shell was not hollow, she was all there.

Gazing beyond Mahom Kasko, the shaman noticed something else that might be significant, that might be kinauitigan'a -- a sign. -- It was the tail-feathers of a pakesso that Oliguôgasku'sizo was using for a fan.

"K'hli --Tell me,"-- he inquired of Handsome One. He asked if the lad had seen any pakessoak, -- or just one grouse, -- at about the same time he had come upon the three creatures in the stream bed. Olôbao lifted his eyebrows, pleasantly surprised. His father was on to something! "Alidebihla, o'hôô -- As it happens, yes," -- he replied. Just before intending to cross the brook bed, shortly before noticing the three, he had been startled by a pakesso that had exploded upward. He had no inkling that it was there as he approached, practically stepping on it. He had not mentioned it until now, had almost forgotten about it, as it was such a commonplace experience. A pakesso's coloring and feather markings blend so well with the carpet of autumn leaves on the forest floor that anyone going into the woods -- it doesn't matter why, -- frequently are startled by the suddenly thunderous flight of a pakesso, -- at times several of them -- who presume that they are escaping from an enemy.

Asokw Mgezo was silent, mediating on this new information. What Olôbao had said indicated ...hinted at the possibility ...that there had been *yauak -- four*[71] --

---

[71] Cardinal Numbers, *Abenakis & English Dialogues*, p. 73. The pluralizing of words in Alnôbaiui can be confusing because there are, in general, two distinct ways of expressing the plural. These are, as suffixes, 'ak,' ostensibly the animate plural, and 'al,' (or ol) denoting the inanimate plural. This is not a hard and fast rule, however. Some inanimate objects are pluralized as ak -- trees, abaziak, for example, even though trees can't move, are rooted to the spot. Ô'gemak -- snowshoes,-- are another example. This use of ak may be described as an *importance* plural. One might say outstanding. Numbers, also (except for pazegw, one) are pluralized, *as well as* the objects being numbered. Four, by itself, in the abstract, is simply iau (or yaw, *Western Abenaki Dictionary*, Volume II, p. 156). When enumerating four objects, however, it becomes iauak, as above, or iauol, p. 73, Chief Joseph Laurent's *Dialogues*. There are more ways of stating 'one,' also. Pazegw is one in the abstract. **Pazego** means one animate person or creature. **Pazeguen** indicates the inanimate (or *less* animate, less

Medicine Chiefs at the gathering. Handsome One may have come upon the grouse just as Pakesso was arriving on the scene. O'hôô, ali *agma,* nôbahla --Yes, as *he,* a *male* bird, -- had been arriving on the scene. The *nôbahlak* -- *males* -- of both the meskagôdagihlak ta pakessoak -- spruce partridges and [ruffed] grouse...-- d' *pakholidak...* -- are *drummers..!* --

It is well known that the nôbahlak partridges, using their wings, practice drumming... most frequently siguak -- in the springtime,-- to attract skuahlak -- female grouse.[72]-- Some think that they use hollow tree trunks to drum on. However, they use auan nihlôdziui -- [the] air itself. -- Akinna ao agemôgik pagholigan! -- The world is their drum! -- Though the nôbahla meskagôdagihla -- male black spruce-bough bird -- will sometimes drum on a standing, but leaning tree.[73]

Asokw Mgezo directed another question at Olôbao. "K'pazôbiôôb kôgagui dali...-- Did you see anything there...-- nada alinôguak nôbi pagholi'abasiz'a? -- that looked like a drumstick?" --

Ônda, No, he had not. The usual fallen branches and twigs lay about, of course. He hadn't noticed a particularly blunt-ended stick, much less one with its head wrapped in a hide covering.

At the center of the arbor was the tribal drum, the most important drum of the Mazipskiak. It was so large, over four feet across, that it was suspended from four wooden stands. As many as six drummers, sometimes as many as eight, if they crowded a bit, could beat on it at once. Later that day, after everyone was rested and had something to eat ...they would renew the rain-requesting ceremony, when it was not so stifling hot. A'lôn and other cousoudelak would be bringing a kettle of freshly cooked succotash. The leading traditionalist men would sprinkle odamô on the drumhead and then pound on it with their personal drumsticks. The others would circle them, shaking their si'zi'uanak and singing.

Mina, Again, Asokw Mgezo and Ôeoandamsko found themselves looking at the same thing. They were looking at the drum, especially at the top of the drum. Soon after it had been made the taut hide drumhead had been decorated with images. They were representations of Abenaki moieties -- of affinity groups, -- clans, -- if you will. They were somewhat faded, from the drumhead being pounded by so many drumsticks, so many times. There was the likeness of Ogauinno, the Sleeping Person (the Bear), for one. And... and... the image of Pelauinno, Hesitant, Delaying Person -- *the Turtle..!* *TA' UA -- AND OF...* -- Now the medicine couple were looking outside, at the sky.

---

outstanding) one.

[72] *Abenaki Indian Legends, Grammar, and Place Names,* Chief Henry L. Masta, for both nôbahla and skuahla for male and female birds, p. 59. Reference the separate genders of various animal species, p. 58 - 59. *Abenakis & English Dialogues,* also, pp. 36 -38.

[73] *New Hampshire Nature Notes,* Hilbert R. Siegler, 1962, p. 47.

Others noticed, and turned to look. *Ôhôô!* Yes! *O'hôô!* Yes! There they are -- and of *Zogelônihla,* the *Rain-Bird* (the Swallow)! Hardly had they seen the swift birds darting about, when they heard it... faint, distant, but discernable. *PADÔGI! --Thunder! --* The rumble of thunder coming from the west, thunder-clouds pushing the hot air before them. Air pressure was changing, stirring up flying insects, and zogelônihlak, the rain - bringing birds, know it is time to feast.

Agemôgik *Maôuigen* Sôgemôk! --**They *Are** Chiefs!** --

Everyone gazed at the acrobatically swooping and diving swallows in awe, straining to hear the distant thunder. Looking into the western sky, they could see the dark thunderheads piling up above the Adirondack Mountains on the other side of Pitaubagw, the Lake Between.[74] Not that they hadn't seen vast cumulus clouds piling up in the summer sky before during this dry spell. But those clouds had disappointed... they had brought no rain. But today would be different. Zogelôn is coming!

Cloud Eagle and Wise Woman rose, as did everyone else, smiling at each other. Everyone picked up a si'zi'uan, or one of their drumsticks. They needed to beat on the drum before the storm arrived. Though there were many evergreen boughs spread overhead, such a "roof" wouldn't keep out the hard-driving rain. The kettle or kettles of succotash might be on the way, but they should begin their gratitude ceremony, hungry or not. Rather than continue their appeal, the ceremony would now be one of thanksgiving. Padôgiak, the Thunderers, should know that their arrival is appreciated.

As he put a handful of his tobacco on the drumhead, Asokw Mgezo contemplated yauak Pisouakamigw Medualui Sôgemôk -- the four Wildwood Spiritually-Powerful Chiefs -- who, undoubtedly, had mounted their own ceremony to bring on the rain. Even now he could feel the air growing cooler, and powerful gusts kicked up clouds of dust all around them. Trees beyond the fields were showing the paler undersides of their leaves. The blowing dust would be, soon, turned to mud.

The four certainly had one drummer there -- Pakesso. Of course, Pakesso does his own kind of drumming... called **neguanapozin** to distinguish it from human drumming. And had one of the feathered lôbatahigasak -- pounders, -- been there? Pounding on a tree to make sound, not just to find grubs... is something that *nôbahlak* lôbatahigasak -- *male* woodpeckers -- do. It's their mating call. You can certainly call it drumming! They had at least one dancer there, Mandaôasw, -- and Segôgw too? He may have simply beaten on Aligedaid's shell with his forepaws, hind legs in place, moving "heel and toe."

Aligedaid could have served as a living drum, also bringing to the gathering the

---

[74] Lake Champlain.   *Maôuigen indicates 'are' in the sense of "it's correct, exact, right," *Western Abenaki Dictionary,* Volume II, p. 136.

wisdom of the many years of her -- or his -- long life.

As he slammed his drumstick down Asokw Mgezo realized that msaltoak auaasak -- many creatures -- could have been there! The four that Olôbao had seen might have been only the very first few of... msali pôbahami! -- many more! -- Such a rain-dance gathering, if it was similar to an Alnôbak ceremony, would have need of, in addition to drummers and dancers...? Would have need of singers! D' dali nodsintôkuak alômi Olakuika? -- Are there singers in [the] Good Forest? -- ...What a question!!! As if in answer to his thought everything was illuminated, brilliantly, by a searing flash of lightning. It was followed by a frighteningly loud crash of padôgi as a chill wind swept across the drum, blowing away the last shreds of tobacco that were being rapidly bounced off by the drummers. Tkalômsen'a -- A cold wind, -- kaneua bahakuôiui -- but refreshing.--

D' adali nodsintôkuak alômi pisouakamigw? -- Are there singers in the wilderness? -- Msaltoak, msaltoak! -- Many, many! -- Agemôgik d' *sipsak* -- they are the **songbirds**.[75] -- There is kejegigilhasiz,[76] that tiny, ebullient, friendly songster who brings such cheer into winter woods. There is kui'kueskas, "the whistler," of orange breast, whom the Pastoniak call the "robin."

---

[75] Sips, singular (animate plural sipsak) the word for "songbird," is highly onomatopoetic. You can hear the *seep!* of a songbird's note in the word. This is how the word must have been originally understood when it was coined thousands of years ago... possibly millions of years ago, if we take into account the views of such archeo-linguists as (the late) Zecharia Sitchin, &c., etc., who suggest that the first truly *polished* language evolved into existence on the planet Nibiru (a world of our solar system, but with an orbit of 3,600 years) where the inhabitants achieved technological proficiency eons ago, bringing the first truly literate language to the Earth. They are called, in the Semitic speech of ancient Mesopotamia, the **Anunnaki**; "Those Who from Heaven to Earth Came." That *sip* derives from the Anunnaki is indicated by the Sumerian-derived Akkadian (etc.), word for one of their antediluvian cities (in what is now Iraq), **Sippar,** interpreted (by students of extant clay tablets written in cuneiform script) as meaning **Bird City**. Extrapolating from Abenaki, we see bird in the prefix; **sip,** with the suffix 'ar' related to the European "urban." For other examples, now common in both Alnôbaiui and modern English, see Sitchin's *Earth Chronicles* series, the *Anunnaki Chronicles* by niece Janet Sitchin, Tellinger's *Slave Species of the Gods,* &c. The Abenaki sip**s**, rather than simply **sip**, as in Sumerian, indicates songbirds (*small* birds). The word-final s is a diminutive of the diminutive *siz*. In recent times, under the debilitating impact of European colonialism, "sips" has been broadened to indicate *any* kind of bird, as an investigator will discover upon perusing 19th and 20th century language textbooks. For the purposes of this narration the author is restoring the word to (what he thinks would have been) its original intention... especially in view of the fact that in the early 18th century the above-mentioned linguistic degradation was only just beginning. Such traditionalists as the author's Cloud Eagle and Wise Woman would have been -- presumably, -- particularly anxious to preserve the Peoples' language in its purity as part of their resistance to the cultural genocide being inflicted by the colonists. Including by the ***best-intentioned*** colonists, who, in that era, glibly assumed that their own culture was absolutely superior, especially in terms of religion. Lidooak, "Those that fly," is likely to have been used, frequently, to indicate birds *in general*, and would have included bats, who are also fliers.

[76] The chickadee: "Literally little kejegigi bird." *Western Abenaki Dictionary*, Volume II, p. 70. Chief Joseph Laurent's *Abenakis & English Dialogues,* pp. 37 - 38.

There is kejegigilhasiz, the songster who brings such cheer into winter woods. Also the joyously melodious nebesi-cogeleskok,[77] pond blackbirds, ta kassi msali kedagik! --and so many others!-- He was hard put to think of all of them at the moment.

"...kejegigilhasiz, the songster who brings such cheer into winter woods."   Author's photo.

Kui'kueskasak are among the first to return from nibenaki, summer-land, in the spring. And at the moment he was giving the drumhead one more vigorous slam, and stepped back with the other drummers, making room for assistants arriving with the large drum's blanket-material covering. The air felt damper now, while above, Padôgiak -- the Thunderers[78]-- spread their roiling, billowing dark wings, turning the western sky black, spearing the earth below with lightning bolts from their eyes. As with the pakessoak, the world is their drum. And their mighty beaks? Were they, like Seguanihla -- the Arrowhead Bird,[79]-- and the other nôbasasak, "knockers" (woodpeckers)[80] pounding on trees, the most gigantic trees of the mountains, to make the crashing thunder… in addition to the beating of their vast pinions..? Gusting dust accompanied last year's autumn leaves as they rattled dancing through the arbor.

Stuffing his drumstick into his waist sash, the shaman knelt down to help loosen the drum's bindings to the stands that had kept it suspended above the ground. The covering thrown over their treasured pagholigan, two Alnôbak lifted it and joined everyone else in the race to shelter inside the town's palisade, a howling wind inflicting "dekskôdelômsogon -- wind tangles the hair,"-- whipping peoples' long hair around. That is, of those who had long hair. Younger men had, in some cases, plucked their scalps to coxcomb "roaches" or topknots, and now put a hand to the feathers tied therein to keep the wind from ripping them out.

A convergence of people streamed through the stockade gate and made their way,

---

[77] *Dolichonyx oryzivorus*, the bobolink, *Western Abenaki Dictionary*, Volume II, p. 43. P. 38 in *Dialogues*.
[78] P. 409, *Ibid*.
[79] The pileated woodpecker, also spelled oziguaônihla, arrowhead bird, p. 415, *Ibid*, Volume I.
[80] P. 454, *Western Abenaki Dictionary*, Volume II, indicates woodpeckers in general, such as the hairy and downy woodpeckers. See also "nôba - rap, knock," p. LIII, **List of Selected Roots**, *Western Abenaki Dictionary*, Volume II.

as fast as they could, to the town's central structure, it's podauazeuigamigw, council - house. A few fat, random raindrops began to pelt them as they hastened inside. The last few barely made it within when suddenly a torrent of water gushed down, the rain falling in sheets.

The squared-logs community building was essentially kuena'tagigamigw, a longhouse, its gabled roof made of wide sheets of bark over stout poles, as of old. The longhouse's floor was of earth, with a central smoke-hole in the roof for the traditional council fire. Other modern improvements, along with the adze-squared logs, were six windows, three on each side. Originally the dauzôganal, "cut openings" -- windows, -- had been glazed with squares of thin hides. These allowed light to come in, but no one could see without. Recently these had been replaced by actual *dauzôganiya,*[81] window *glass,* shipped up the river by way of one of *le Roi Louis'* La Marine (i.e., Naval) sailing vessels. Wharves and a shipyard had been built alongside Fort St. Jean on the Richelieu River, at the head of the Rapids of Chambly. There the King's military, as well as mercantile *seigneurs,* were building Lake Champlain-bound patrol vessels and cargo batteaux. The French were intent upon dominating the Champlain valley and keeping its' riches, -- such as timber, naval stores,[82] furs, its' fishery, ginseng, potential farmlands, and likely mineral wealth -- out of the hands of the long-armed *Anglais.*

A decade or so previous it would have been much more problematical to transport such a fragile, breakable commodity as panes of glass all the way from the St. Lawrence to the delta of the Missisquoi River… and then up that river somewhat. If the panes were packed in cushioning, such as layers of straw, the large sailboats could bring them smoothly - in calm weather, - up the lake from St. Jean. An old problem had been the portage road from the river port (and fort) of Chambly, at the foot of the Rapids. The portage 'road,' formerly not much more than a foot - path, had lately been much improved. The improvements now enabled oxen or draft-horse drawn cargo wagons, even four-wheeled, covered wagons (rather than just the usual two-wheeled carts), to traverse the portage. Therefore, destined for St. Jean, more breakable commodities could be included with larger cargoes. Providing the weather was dry, of course. Otherwise the dirt track turned into a quagmire of gluey azesko -- mud. -- In the winter the wagons were replaced by sleighs and cargo sledges, the vehicles' runners turning pkuami ta uazôli -- the ice and snow -- to advantage. As thunder roared and the rain lashed down, the atmosphere inside the council house was one of merriment and profound relief. A'lôn and other matrons were there, around the cook fire, having just finished with the kettles of succotash they had been planning to bring out to the arbor. They had also brought bowls and platters for the community refreshment. Those that had them produced their amkuônak -- wooden spoons. -- Many kept personal spoons

---

[81] The suffix iya indicates material, substance, literally "cut - opening material," p. 450, *Ibid.*
[82] Meaning, for the most part, *térébenthine:* turpentine.

on them during their active hours, as you might a sheathed knife, the amkuôn suspended from one's waistband, secured by a slim buckskin thong (or hemp cord) by a hole drilled through the handle. This was the same custom as carrying a kinaôiui pipinaudsakuôgan -- personal mirror[83]-- suspended from your waistband. A small, wood - framed hand mirror, of course. They were carried, ali sanôbak ta p'hanemak kôdakiui -- by men and women alike -- often encased in a buckskin covering to protect them. Dômô'ua p'hanemak -- Some of the women -- auakan agemôuô pipinaudsakuôganal askua nikuôbi -- [were] using their looking-glasses right now -- ôbkuigôdahaluôn debkuan[84]-- [to] disentangle their hair -- yanegi aob dekskôdelômsogon -- after [it] had become wind-tangled. -- A few of the men were also, especially those with long hair. They were using artistically carved combs that had been made from bone or caribou antler… the almost flat, palmated ends of such antlers are often just right for fashioning into combs and other useful objects. Those warriors who had plucked their heads to achieve the coxcomb, scalp-roach effect, having applied auaas fat to make their debkuan zazibouad -- head-hair stand up straight,-- were not as concerned, having less hair to worry about. A few double-checked their ôgakw kôabial, scalp locks -- to make sure their gazalmômuk miguenok -- precious feathers -- aobanik askua aimek -- were still there. --

Another item routinely carried on one's person, though in a "bandolier bag," a couidebal pitôgan -- necessaries pouch,-- was another, smaller pouch. This one contained an array of small bags of paint. The paint containers were made out of auaasak segodabeskuak -- animal bladders, -- particularly of mikoak, squirrels.[85] There were those, possessed of very fine stitching skills, who managed to make the containers out of the bladders of such small mammals as anikusesak -- chipmunks -- ta pkui mikoak -- and red squirrels -- Others preferred the segodabeskuak of msaniguak, the bushy-tailed larger squirrels …called by the Pastoniak "gray squirrels." Their bladders being somewhat larger, they were a bit easier to convert into paint bags, and could hold

---

[83] *Abenakis & English Dialogues,* p. 27. Noted as "A Looking Glass," this listing is also extant documentation of the Abenaki custom of carrying a small hand-mirror suspended *on one's person* because it is listed under… 'Wearing Apparel.'

[84] The term debkuan specifically refers to the hair of the head, not hair in general. *Western Abenaki Dictionary,* Volume II. p. 178.

[85] Mikoak, plural, singular mikoa, is another Ô'banaki word that does "double duty." It specifically indicates the **red** squirrel, *Tamiasciurus hudsonicus,* but can be used to refer to squirrels in general, mikoa being the most common tree squirrel of northern conifer forests. When in doubt as to a squirrel's identity (such as when seen in silhouette) 'mikoa' is used until the exact species can be determined. Another such word is kuiguigemok (also another onomatopoetic term)… **ducks.** *More specifically*, what English speakers refer to as the "black duck," *Anas rubripes.* For squirrels reference p. 374, *Western Abenaki Dictionary,* Volume II. To reference ducks p. 120, *Ibid.*

more paint. The biggest were from agaskuok, woodchucks. Though a agaskw menoda -- groundhog bag -- took up more space (when full). You might prefer an assortment of smaller bags, for a greater variety of colors without the array becoming too bulky.

Those traditionalists who had, earlier, applied ceremonial paint to their faces, in anticipation of the rain-requesting ceremony, were now holding up their mirrors and inspecting the designs they had applied. If they found any smearing they brought out one or another of their zoguauan menodaal -- face-paint bags -- to repair the pattern. Cloud Eagle and Ôeoandamsko were also concerned about their face paint, but not very much. For one thing, they had not applied much. When they were younger they had been enthusiastic about painting on rather elaborate patterns, but now that they were older it seemed more important to concern themselves with other details when preparing for ceremony. For another, there was less to worry about because they had not applied any paint at all above their eyes. In such hot weather as at present, people tend to sweat… Even if you aren't doing very much, are supine, attempting to "chill out" in the shade, there is a tendency ôadsi ôpsazimek -- to sweat. -- If you have to be active in such heat, sweat runs down your brow, carrying elements of paint into your eyes, olitomek kia sizegol pogedzauaig -- making your eyes sting. -- No one needs that, especially when you're concentrating on doing the ceremony respectfully, with requisite devotion.

The glass panes of the windows of the council house were a special pleasure for the children. Not only could you see outside, but during a storm such as this the viewing was especially spectacular, with thunder crashing and flashes of lightning illuminating everything. Auôsizak --The children -- took delight in feeling protected from the stabbing lightning and lashing rain by the stout roof and walls of the podauazeuigamigw while at the same time they could look out and see it all.

Another dimension was that the view through the panes was somewhat distorted. The glass was imperfect, featuring locked-in bubbles and wavy undulations. This made the viewing even more interesting, adding a bit of other-worldliness to the experience. Often when the lightning flashed glaringly the radiance was caught by the bubbles inside the glass, the double refraction sparking so suddenly and brilliantly that some of the children jumped back, shrieking in fright. These were usually the smallest auôsizak, those only a few steps --and we say "steps" advisedly,-- from having recently been zôkhiguezidsik -- "crawlers,"… meaning "the crawlers who will replace us."--

At first the older children, and some nearby adults, had been startled as well, jerking back from what seemed like an explosion (or explosions, when the lightning "quivered") so close to them. Realizing that no one had been harmed, they quickly recovered, understanding that the glass panes were the cause, somehow… another "capability" of the curious substance. The panes looked like squares of ôuassa pkuami, clear ice, yet refused to melt, no matter how hot the weather. Older children embraced the terrified pabiusesidzik auôsizak -- smallest children -- to calm them down, reassuring them and seizing the opportunity to demonstrate that they themselves were *kagini* [86]...a word encompassing both "very strong," and "brave," because to be courageous is to be strong.

As they were served heaping ladlefuls of succotash[87] and gratefully retired out of the way, to the sides of the longhouse, Cloud Eagle, Wise Woman, their children, and other traditionalists, -- any who had taken part in the day's ceremonies,-- continued to ponder the question of the Pisouakamigw Medualui-Sôgemôk -- the Wilderness Medicine-Chiefs.-- At bottom, the impression Olôbao had gotten when he happened upon the three auaasak in the stream bed, that they were thirsty and wanted nebis dali -- the little water [that was] there,-- may have been the prosaic truth of the matter. Though Aligedaid is an extremely tough creature, impervious to so much -- an apt representative of eternal Mother Earth herself, -- he or she may have been midway on a long journey between bodies of water. Kuena -- Long -- for one of the "hesitant, delaying" nation, at any rate. Having quit one tributary of the Missisquoi (due to the drought, the tributary was lower and afforded both less cover and not as much prey), she was on her way to a deeper body of water, to the Missisquoi itself, perhaps. He or she was taking a shortcut overland, across terrain that eliminated a large bend that would enable her to reach the (hopefully) deeper downstream section sooner. Where she could not only drink, but would, sinking her entire self into the water, absorb nepi directly through her skin. That nebis -- little water -- in the dry brook bed, on her long, tedious *portage*... might have indeed looked (and smelled) tempting.

Regarding Mandaôasw, he may have been in the midst of climbing a nearby tree, intent upon reaching some especially juicy-looking leaves, and happened to look down. He had seen the sky reflecting from that piui baiala'ua nepi, small bit of water. Gulping, his throat felt dry. He decided he should lap up some actual water. Why not? The leaves could wait, but that cupful of water was doubtless evaporating, in such hot weather, even as he climbed back down the tree. Reaching the ground, for a change the Slow One may have hurried a bit ...getting there just as Aligedaid and Segôgw arrived.

Worried that the women's gardens would wither, that they would be short of vegetative provisions when winter came, in looking for signs of approaching rain, Asokw Mgezo and Ôeoandamsko pondered the possibility that they may have presumed overmuch from what their son had reported.

---

[86] *Western Abenaki Dictionary,* Volume II, p. 47. For simply "strong, stout," reference Chief Joseph Laurent's *Dialogues,* malkigit, malkigek, under *Vocabulary of Adjectives, Contracted and Variable* (also sôglizit, sôglak, "solid, strong, durable") p. 68.

[87] Frontier-era succotash -- and doubtless in previous centuries, -- consisted of more than the 20th and 21st century's modern version: lima beans and corn. Historic succotash was a mixture of corn and beans, yes (most likely red beans), but also of bits of meat and/or fish. The current word is a contraction of the Narragansett msickquatash. *Dictionary of Native American Terminology,* Carl Waldman, Castle Books, New York, p. 226.

Cloud Eagle finished the succotash, washing it down with a draught of mint-flavored water, and, rising to resume beating on the drum -- remembered another incident involving Aligedaid... seven aligedaidzik, in fact. An incident, one among a few others recalled from a number of summers ago. Olôbao's and Ôliuôgasku'sizo's "faces were yet beneath the ground..." -- they hadn't been born yet. The venerable head medaulinno at the Place of Flint, having recruited the likely couple (knowing they had been walking the Oligo Mkui O'udi so well among the Koasak), had urgently requested that the couple resettle at Mazipskoik. Kisikauo -- the One Who Makes, or 'He Produces,'-- the shaman, had known that his time was growing short, that he would soon be journeying to Akinna'ua Msaltoal Ô'igiuômal -- the Land of Many Lodges.-- The same was true of other aging medicine people at Mazipskoik.

Though they had mentored younger folk to carry on after them, too many of their hoped-for successors were influenced by the missionaries. Or else imbibed too frequently of blandi, traded surreptitiously "in the bush" by secretive *coureurs de bois*. Fortunately, thanks to watchful donnèak, there were not many of the latter. The friars had built a bark-roofed chapel at Mazipskoik. Kisikauo saw that, when they visited, holding services in the rude chapel with its minuscule belfry, they were undermining the People's traditional spiritual-medicine ways... as much as they could.

Cloud Eagle and his bride had responded to Kisikauo's appeal, knowing that there were competent medualinnoak, their own relatives among them, at Koasok, who would strive to keep up the Old Ways among the Little Pine Trees People. Something in their favor was that the Koasok-assigned missionary could not attend much of the time... the trail between Kanada and the upper Connecticut River valley was difficult. Yet the Mazipskiak needed the French as allies to enable the Ô'banakiak to resist the growing threat of the rapidly multiplying Pastoniak.

At times the friar and his donnèak were unable to return from Québec as soon as they would like. At Mazipskoik there exist no heights to the immediate north similar to the broken country to the eastward (and the Boundary Mountains, also called "the Height of Land," the waters of their southern slopes providing the sources of the Long River). Unlike that eastward region, daligen aob kaskak nepi ô'udi'a -- there was a broad water road -- to Mazipskoik all the way from Fort St. Jean on the Richelieu, enabling the Black Gowns to visit more frequently from their "civilized" parishes further north, in *Nouvelle France.*

Asokw Mgezo recalled that Kisikauo had been persuasive in urging himself and Ôeoandamsko (now formally honored with the name of Wise Woman) ...to attend, to participate, in a 'medicine' gathering on the north side of the delta of the Missisquoi. Alnôbak had collected not far from the river at a location on the southern shore of Missisquoi Bay, that rotund, northeastern arm of Pitaubagw.

Present day Medicine Man Mkazauiases, Black Horse, (Richard Philips), as the Mazipskoi shaman Kisikauo.

Photo by Laura Carbone, Plattsburg, New York.

The French called the bay *le Cul de Sac*. There was a rather permanent hunting/fishing camp there, as a central fireplace and a few conical wigwams attested.

Aob lômkipodiga -- Had the time[88]-- yagik kôgassigaden na Auanock --been [in] those years that the Strangers, -- both the French and British Strangers, called the 1690s…? Was it when that international, intercolonial conflict termed "King William's War" was being fought? The British Isles had been under King James II, who had been, like all *Anglais* monarchs, the head of the Church of England. But Kinjames Sakso was actually a Catholic… one of those the heretical Iglismôniak call a "Papist." The Dutchman "I'lliam'ua Olange, William of Orange," had invaded England, overthrowing Kinjames Sakso (Sakso from *Jacques*; in English "James"). Kinjames Loui of France had taken the side of his co-religionist and ally, Kinjames Sakso, and gruesome war flamed along the frontiers between the English colonies and Nouvelle France, drenching Ô'ban Aki, the Dawn Land, in blood.

Ônda --No,-- aob ni kôniui -- it had been after that time.-- When Williams' War ended there was an interlude of peace, until, in the early 1700s, another violent conflict

---

[88] A "modern" word (as of the introduction of the hourglass) meaning literally "sand wearing out," i.e., sand running out, p. 411, *Western Abenaki Dictionary*, Volume II. Older, very likely pre-contact, words for time are to be found in Aubery/Laurent's *French Abenaki Dictionary*, under *Temps*, p. 496, such as kôniui (or kôniôi), and *A temps* - in time: *8ri-tebi* (ôli-tebi), *tétebeska8i8i;* (tatebeskaôiui), *mañ8i* (manônui). *De temps en temps* - from time to time, on and off, now and then: *añkkañbékki* (aôkônbaki), &c., etc. Notice the affinity between "kôniui" and the common word for **long**: kuena. Kôniui: Something (or everything) ***long passing***.

between the English *infidèles* and Christian France broke out. This became widely known as "Queen Anne's War." Asokw Mgezo ta Ôeoandamsko zahagidebihlabanik itodsi -- Cloud Eagle and Wise Woman had a hard time then. --

It was a turbulent period, with both French and Alnôbak war parties passing south, through or near Mazipskoik, and Mohican (and Maguak) warriors, Pastoniak militia and Anglais makusauadak -- red-wearing soldiers -- pushing north to conquer Canada and Alnôbaiki --the (Ordinary) People's Land. -- English warships blockaded le Fleuve St. Laurent, causing acute shortages of food and supplies. The coming and going of warriors, the arrival of weary Pastoniak captives, the convening of frequent councils, plunged Mazipskoik (during the King William war not yet dubbed "Grey Lock's Castle") into turmoil. Worst of all were the stress-induced epidemics that swept through. Olôbao and Beautiful Girl were not the initial children of the medicine couple. Agemôuô ntami piusesid -- Their first "little one," baby, -- had died during an early epidemic, when the infant's parents had both been weakened by akuamalsouôgan. Though Cloud Eagle, summoning all his strength, putting down odamô, praying fervently, had feebly staggered about collecting medicinal roots and herbs …it was not enough. The infant had not survived. Perhaps his efforts had saved Ôeoandamsko..? And himself, of course, as well as others to whom he had administered herbal nebizon.

The little one who had died had been a boy baby. When it seemed that peace had come, the couple having recovered their health, they had tried again. Wise Woman's pregnancy resulted in ôskinôksku'siz'a -- a little girl, -- this time. Ta ac'hi, O'galiguômuk! --And also, O woe! -- Askua alômi kôniui -- Just in time -- ôadsi kedaga kôniui'ua aodin zokena! -- for another round of fighting to break out!-- Still the war went on. Would those grasping Iglismôniak never leave them in peace?

Again the Ô'banakiak of the villages along Pitaubagw became unusually busy, there were alarums and hurrying… many Strangers coming and going through Mazipskoik. The white-coated *soldats* and homespun-clad *miliciens* from Québec again came, heading south. Warriors were gone for weeks at a time, some never to return. Northward staggered the influx of starveling captives. Again *l' bloquer à les Anglais!* The shortages of provisions came once more, with so many extra mouths to feed. Ta mina! -- And again! -- Pedegibaiyô akuamalsouôganal! -- Again the sicknesses!--

Cloud Eagle was away this time. He had been recruited to a war party heading south to oppose an army of makusauadak and their Indian allies, said to be making its way into the Lake Champlain region. Asokw Mgezo had gone not so much as a fighter, but as a healer, as, *truly*, a medicine man in the both the physical and spiritual senses. The "papistical" Québecois who accompanied the warriors may not have thought much of him as medauinno'a -- a spiritually powerful man, -- but definitely appreciated his knowledge and skill in the *nbizon* sense[89]...the word for *physical* medicine. The Abenaki term is derived from nbisonbi -- mineral water. -- The initial part of the word is **nebi**, from *nepi* --fresh water.--

The *fusiliers* and warriors he had joined had a part in driving the enemy back, --or so it seemed, for *les Anglais* retreated. Later he found out that, despite all the black-clad ministers they had with them, daily offering up prayers, the makusauadak soldiers and Pastoniak militiamen had been stricken by an epidemic. Their army was unable to advance.

Had it been what the French called *l' vérole..?* What his own people dreaded as maskihlôgan... -- the **pox**? -- He hoped not. It was something you didn't wish on even your worst enemy. Especially when you realized that what was afflicting your enemies, no matter how malevolent they were... could easily spread to your own people. An epidemic of maskihlôgan could be even deadlier than the human enemy was. The detachment the medauinno belonged to followed the retreating Anglais quite a distance southward, seeking to snatch a prisoner, flank them on one side or the other. They forged down into the Taughkaughnick[90] mountains region... somewhere between the colonies of New-England and the Province of New-York. Into what was unquestionably the territory of the Ô'banakiaks' Muheconnuck cousins.

Though the young, aspiring 'medicine man,' had joined the expedition as a healer, as nodsi-nbizonhouad --a physician, a doctor[91]-- he had taken care to look the part of migakauinno'a -- a fighting person, -- the warrior. For one thing, he might have to fight, if only to defend himself. For another, the "war paint" applied to one's face was done not merely to appear ferocious, but served an identifying purpose. The band he was with used the same three primary colors in vogue at the St. Francis River mission of Odanak, to the northeast -- in fact there were a few Odanak warriors with the group. In the confusion of battle it was quicker to tell who was who by the colors on faces and hands... on arms, torsos and legs, if the weather was hot and ayhimal, clothing, should be dispensed with (except for breech clout, moccasins, and leggings). The sezouiganal --paints, -- were uôbi -- white, -- mkui, ta mkazaui -- red, and black.-- The streaks and other configurations of the design patterns also helped break up the lines of your face (or arms, etc.), serving to a degree as camouflage. While the Auanock soldiers were

---

[89] *Western Abenaki Dictionary*, Volume II, p. 247. Dr. Day's reference includes different definitions of medicine, such as gauôgan "a sleeping medicine"...which might mean, simply enough, getting *enough sleep* if one is sick from exhaustion.

[90] An early colonial rendering from the Mohican for 'Taconic,' referring to the Taconic Mountains Range on the eastern border of New York State down along the state lines of southwestern Vermont, western Massachusetts, and western Connecticut. See footnote 2, page 59, *The Western Boundary of Massachusetts: A Study of Indian and Colonial History*, 1886, Franklin Leonard Pope, Pittsfield, MA. Taughkaughnick is basically interpreted as "Forested Mountains Place (Region)."

[91] "Mechanical Arts, Etc.," *Abenakis & English Dialogues*, p. 34. Chief Joseph Laurent, 1884.

garbed in uniforms as a means of identification, this was not an option for the individualistic migakauinnoak, who weren't supplied by a quartermaster corps. At times a degree of clothing uniformity might be attempted, such as similarly hued blanket-material leggings, but if there was a shortage of blankets (and cloth in general), which British naval blockades certainly inflicted, such an endeavor went a-glimmering. You had to use your own locally harvested and processed buckskin if that was all that was available.

Asokw Mgezo usually wore his hair long, but for this war path he had plucked and shaved his debkuan --head-hair, -- to a debkuanimadagen[92] kôabi -- scalp lock -- or "topknot." In the event of working through thick woods to surprise (and then dash upon) the enemy, or the necessity for running through tangled brush to escape an outnumbering foe… something the combatant doesn't need --is long hair that might catch on branches and twigs when fleetness of foot is essential. Eliminating head-hair to a *soupçon* minimized this hazard. In a word, it was hirsute streamlining. Plus, the plucking or shaving of the hair of the scalp down to the roots affords additional scope for the application of war paint or ceremonial paint. The fighter's "wider palette," if you will. At the same time the warrior needs at least a strip of hair, a coxcomb, or a circle of hair at the very top, for the tying in of significant feathers, of amulets, a silver brooch perhaps, as an expression of *élan*, of *forêt élégance*.

Cloud Eagle had embarked on that particular war trail without the warrior's usual paskhigan -- explosion instrument (*fusil*). -- He didn't mind this in the least, as he had joined the war party more as a literal *medicine* man than as a combatant. There were other fighters without firelocks, who carried bows and arrows instead. Along with their atôbiak ta tiskuôdial one or two carried an astahigan -- stabbing instrument, -- a spear, as well. These weapons were not to be taken lightly, as they were highly useful when the fighters *didn't* want gunpowder to explode… when they wanted to strike noiselessly, such as when eliminating sentries (or anyone who might alert the enemy's main force). Even those lighter side arms, hatchets, knives, and migakaigualômal -- fighting bats (war clubs)[93]-- are useful in that regard, if that is all you have.

Cloud Eagle might have carried a slim-barreled, light-weight hunting fusil if he had harvested a sufficient number of furs and hides with which to trade for one (and

---

[92] *Western Abenaki Dictionary,* Volume II, p. 334. Debkuan: hair of head. The 'i' of debkuanimadagen shows that **debkuan** possesses madagen: hair skin, i.e., the scalp.

[93] Called a baskhôdebahigan, 'head breaker' club, as well. French: *casse-tete, Western Abenaki Dictionary,* Volume II, p. 77. Notice the onomatopoetic similarity between syllables in the words for a head-breaker club, a firelock, a drum, and the beating of a drum. The bask (!) for the club hitting someone's head (English speakers might say *bonk*(ed) or *bang*, as in "banged on the head"), the ***pask(!)*** of the gun discharging (English speakers might say *boom* or *bam!*), and, regarding a drum, the pag(!) of pagholigan, from the sound of a drumhead being struck. Holigan denotes the act of drumming -- holi -- combined with the instrument, igan. "To beat a drum" is expressed as ***pagholi.*** 'Pag (!)' from the sound, and holi related to hla -- go. --

"Asokw Mgezo had not been tempted by the employment of bribery to gain converts. He would make do with his bow and arrows and other traditional weapons. Spirit *would present a firelock to him when the time was right."*

The author as the young medauinno in a hand-made woolen green blanket coat and red leggings against the autumn chill. He is armed with his hand-crafted hickory long bow and hand-made arrows. His head having been plucked back to a scalp roach, with the face paint… doesn't necessarily mean that he is "on the war path." *Ceremonial* paint and hirsute streamlining are as important to the nadialouinno--hunter,-- as to the migakauinno -- warrior.-- Also, it should be taken into consideration that in the turbulent 18th century world of the Ô'banakiak an emergency transition from hunter to fighter could take place in a matter of seconds.

also the requisite ammunition, spare flints, and maintenance tools). At that time he had not yet done so, and was reluctant to hunt and trap more fur-bearers than was truly needed for his and Wise Woman's comfort to accumulate the necessary wherewithal. The French would most likely have gifted him with a paskhigan if he had undertaken to memorize their *prières* by heart, embracing their faith. Asokw Mgezo had not been tempted, not in the slightest, by this employment of bribery. How the Alnôbak had been treated by the oh-so-pious Puritans of Massachusetts, *traumatizing* survivors… yet rankled. He well remembered (or recalled from his parents' remembrances, having been only an infant at the time) how harshly the self-righteous English had treated his family during 'Williams' War,' even though his family, his relatives, had attempted to be neutral, trying to pose, even, as 'friendlies.'

Another incentive used by the friars was to grant an acolyte a bright red bead every time he or she thoroughly memorized one of the church's prayers. These were not merely wooden beads, or common glass beads, but were of bright *porcelaine*… made brilliant by the infusion of *gold dust*. This didn't persuade him or Wise Woman either.

There had been the occasion when they did accept something from the Black Robes... a certain confection. Why not? It was immediately edible. He and Ôeoandamsko had been in the vicinity of Père Antoine and his chapel on the Sanḓa when the Mkazaui Pitkôzon had been celebrating the Church's greatest holy day, *Pâques* -- Easter. -- It was after a High Mass had been said, the good father having led a procession through the town and back to the chapel. In high good spirits he had given out pieces of tsôkoulaṭ-covered aḅôn made in the shape of crucifixes.

The aspiring 'medicine' couple had accepted the treats along with everyone else. Indeed, they valued their tasty crosses so much that they had taken only tentative nibbles and put away the rest for later...taking care to store them in a container hanging from a high place in their lodge, where the always sniffing, ever-hungry dogs couldn't get at them. They had been able to trade for coffee beans recently, and on successive mornings following that Kisokw'ua Spemkik Alihlôḓ -- Day of the Ascension -- flaked the chocolate into the ḳapi, enjoying cups of mocha. While they leisurely sipped their mocha, the world slowly awakening from night's slumber, they discussed the puzzle of the Church's sacred symbol. *Le Crucifix*. It seemed a grim, a profoundly dismal, a downright macabre symbol with which to represent the "One True Faith." They knew of no native people, despite the Strangers' labeling of them as *les sauvages,* not even the inveterately fierce Iroquois... who chose the torture post as the emblem of their spiritual belief system. Supposing that the English had chosen to execute Sazos by... hanging? Would the Christians have then adopted the scaffold, with its dangling martyr, as their holy symbol? "Yes," Ôeoandamsko said, speaking in Alnôbaiui, "they probably would have." They considered that the missionaries' spoke Alnôbaiui so poorly, and their own grasp of French was so bad, that they couldn't understand half of what the friars preached. There were so many things about their ...*presumed*... doctrines that just didn't add up. While the friars preached honesty, mercy, and other moral virtues, they were not unique in that respect. Meḓaulinnoak'ua N'ḓ'akinna --The Spiritually-Powerful Medicine People of Our Land -- had been urging such values long before the Auanock had come ashore in Ô'baṇ Aki, the Dawn Land. Previously, honesty was *routine*. Money was... *non-existent!* It was virtually *impossible* to cheat people, materially, in a culture in which money doesn't exist. You could test goods on the spot.

Cloud Eagle thought about these things as he rhythmically slammed his drumstick down, chanting praises of Padôgiak, the Thunderers, hearing the grateful singing and rhythmic *shush! shush!* of the pebbles swirling in the si'zi'uanak being shaken by the other lintouôganak -- singers. -- While he outwardly praised the Padôgiak, sincerely appreciating their belated arrival in watering the fields and the surrounding forest, "olalokamek Sanôba ṭa Auaas nôbi -- benefiting Man and Beast alike,"-- the previous pondering concerning the putative wilderness "spirit-medicine chiefs" led him, on another level, to recall various events in his and Ôeoandamsko's past. Events such as that unexpected Pônbatami Podauazin -- Sacred Council -- nspi medaulak mikinakuak -- with the spiritually powerful turtles -- tali pmômanosek -- at the fishing place -- on the south shore of Missisquoi Bay..!

Ta ac'hi --And also-- that time, -- was it almost twenty summers ago? -- when destiny had brought him his first firelock -- rather unexpectedly,-- when the war party he had joined as a nbizonhouad was following the withdrawing *Anglais* who had advanced to Lake Champlain's southern "Wood Creek." He remembered that day quite well. It had been a brisk day in the spring, a good time for camping out, for campaigning, because the no-neck ones and mosquitoes were not yet biting. The maple trees were just beginning to bud… there were a few hovering peguesak -- mosquitoes -- when the day had warmed up. But they were not yet annoying.

The trail of the retreating enemy was not hard to follow. As they withdrew ever further south their footprints were easy to see, especially since the red-wearing soldiers wore hard-soled shoes. These imprinted splendidly in the soft spring soil. Some of their officers also, it would seem, wore boots, probably made of fine calf skin, but equally hard soled. Most of the Pastoniak militia also wore shoes, though some wore moccasins, as did, of course, their "running dog" (collaborating) Mohican and Maguak auxiliaries.

Authors' drawing of a calling mdauilha, described as a *spirit - goer* (spirit flier), the Abenaki name for the common loon… because the bird is believed to travel mystically back and forth between the material and spirit realms. The native name more reverently contrasts with the European translation of 'magic bird,' or 'shaman bird.'

7. Tôhné Asokw Mgezo Gauhouab Mkuigen Paskhigan'a ta kisi Aiyôba'i-Apenak[94]-Itaôalakw Kebahigan-Metsetsakw

-- How Cloud Eagle Acquired a Red-Colored Fusil and its Ballocks Dagger Plug-Bayonet --

At any moment the shadowing French and Indian force expected to see wagon-wheel ruts and the hoof prints of draft animals in the ever-widening trail as the English fell back on their baggage train. It would have been easy to race ahead and catch up with the enemy and attack them, as *les Anglais,* apparently plagued by illness, were moving slowly. But the commanders of Asokw Mgezo's detachment were not so reckless.

The war party moved cautiously, the presence of those native collaborators keeping them in mind that if they followed too quickly, too closely, they could blunder into an ambush. Even a sickness-debilitated enemy, if numerous enough, could be dangerous. All the French and Alnôbak commanders wanted now was to pick up a straggler or two, hopefully healthy ones, who could be interrogated for information and taken back to Canada as prisoners. They also wanted the enemy to fear their presence, so that they would keep pressing for home, abandoning any intention whatsoever of conquering New France and northern N'd'akinna.

Presently they discovered signs that some had indeed paused in their retreat. An ambuscade? Or merely a few back-trail lookouts assigned to determine how close the French were? While the main army had continued south along the trail bisecting the floor of the valley they were traversing, the forward Alnôbak and *coureurs de bois* nopaosauinnoak,[95] scouts, (who could also be called nadauahak[96] -- spies),-- had

---

[94] P. 53, *Western Abenaki Dictionary*, Volume II: "Aiyôba, bull, adult male of cleft-hoofed ruminants, *Cervidae* and *Bovidae*," and "stag, bull (bovine with full set of horns)," The reference here, "ballocks dagger," is to a particularly curious form of ***poignard,*** two-edged fighting knife, viz., "dagger," from the previous medieval epoch, a side-arm of knights in armor that was still extant in the colonial period. The wooden handle, at the hilt, was carved in the likeness of a certain portion of a bull's anatomy. Such surviving daggers were adapted for employment with early muskets as ***plug bayonets***. Their handles were whittled down to fit snugly into the muzzles of muskets, converting a firelock into a kind of spear. However, once the bayonet is inserted, the musketeer can't reload and fire again. This limitation eventually inspired the development of the ***elbow bayonet***, whereby a bayonet featuring a slotted metal sleeve is slipped over the muzzle, locking onto a stud. The blade extends from the sleeve by means of an "elbow," leaving the bore unobstructed. This enables the soldier to reload and fire while the bayonet remains fixed in place. *Baïonette:* "from F.:--bayonets were first made at Bayonne, France," *Webster's New Collegiate Dictionary*. **Apen**, plural **apenak**, can refer to the "ground nut or Indian potato, *Apios tuberosa*" **or** testicle, p. 269, *Western Abenaki Dictionary,* Volume II.

[95] Indicates "walk-far persons," from nopaosa, "go scouting, go on the warpath; literally walk-far," p. 335, *Western Abenaki Dictionary,* Volume II.

[96] The pluralization of nadauahôd, "The one who scouts, he spies on someone," *Ibid*, p. 335.

discovered moccasin tracks that quit the trail and angled up the side of the Taconics main range to their left. Were Maguak and Muheconnuck warriors, together with some of the more woods-wise Pastoniak -- they called themselves "rangers," -- climbing up the mountain in order to double back… and attack the French and Alnôbak column from the rear? The French commander, a Lieutenant Le Mercier of *La Marine,* ordered a halt. He hastily called together a council of his subordinates with the war chief and sub-chiefs of his allies. Should they fall back up the valley to thwart the presumed back-trail ambush, or remain in place, for the most part, sending a detachment of fighters uphill to follow the enemy moccasin tracks… and catch the would-be bushwhackers from behind?

Jonas T'sôngeba, one of their scouts who was Mohican himself, -- or *had* been of the Scatacôok Muheconnuck, -- who had migrated north with Grey Lock and now was considered Ô'banaki, -- stepped forward. He was quite familiar with their present location. Jonas pointed out that there was a dip ahead in the ridge rising on their left, leading gradually upward, northeasterly, to a sloping area where, he knew, some northward-venturing Dutchmen or Pastoniak had begun tentative logging some time ago. Apparently they were after certain hardwood trees such as hornbeam, rock maple, and ironwood. There ought to be a tote road leading from the valley to the place. It would have been carved out to enable them to haul out the heavy logs with oxen. He had not been there recently but suspected that, by now, there might be a water-powered saw mill up there so that the Dutsmôniak, as he called them, could more easily transport the valuable lumber down the mountain and eventually to market at *Fort Orange* (the French persisted in using the old Dutch term of "Fort Orange" even though the British had years ago renamed the town "Albany").

T'sôngeba, like Asokw Mgezo, the other warriors, and most of the woods-wise *coureurs de bois,* had been growing increasingly apprehensive the further they shadowed the retreating enemy. There was always the danger of walking into a well-concealed ambush, but it wasn't that. Kisi kagui agemôuô *melôdhigak* --It's something they *smelled.* -- At times the French marines and the habitant *fermiers* among the milice could smell it too. Of course, it was routine for an army, any large number of human beings, whether advancing or retreating, to somewhat "stink up" their route of march. People have to urinate and void their bowels no matter where they are. It was worse than that, however. And whatever was being defecated …wasn't easy to see. The French and Indian party was becoming increasingly worried that what they were smelling (and hopefully weren't stepping in!) was naaiahlauôgan… "down-flowing,"[97] that thin, watery, sometimes colorless form of obagidamen[98] that signifies that someone is sick

---

[97] *Western Abenaki Dictionary,* Volume II, p. 108. Also sabagezouôgan, "half boiled, lukewarm."
[98] Bagidam, "leave, abandon, renounce, give up, defecate," from obagidamen, "he leaves it, he abandons it," *Ibid,* p. 106.

with what the French call *diarrée*... and the Anglais-- diarrhea! Though microscopes had existed since about 1600,[99] and through them bacteria noted since the 1660s, only Lieutenant Mercier and his subalterns were likely to have even heard of such things. If they knew about bacteria, they still didn't know what the tiny *punaises* signified. Despite the lack of knowledge about bacilli and viruses by the average member of the strike force, there was some idea of contagion. If you come too close to those who are ill there is a good chance that whatever is ailing them can affect you as well.

The Lieutenant knew that he had to come to a sensible decision. If his *"sauvage"* auxiliaries became too alarmed... they would simply leave. They didn't consider themselves to be *soldats du France;* they owed no obeisance to le Roi Louis, or to whatever monarch happened to be on the throne of France at the moment. Yet he had his orders to persist in following *l'ennemi*, snatching a prisoner or two and maintaining the pressure that was motivating the Anglais homeward.

At this juncture Mercier knew that it was time to compromise. They would follow the withdrawing enemy no further south... by the looks of it, by the *smell* of it, *les Anglais* were in no condition to bounce back and renew their offensive. Not any time soon. The moccasin tracks up the nearby mountainside had to be investigated, however. They couldn't allow a detachment of rangers, Muheconnuck, and *Aniez* -- the French called the Mohawks "Aniez,"[100] -- to circle back and attack them from the rear.

Jonas ventured the opinion that a detail had been sent up the mountain to a highland sawmill that he suspected was there. There was a lively brook that began at the summit of the height, which flowed south-west, carving that dip in the range that he knew was ahead. Cutting logs with their saws and axes, the Dutsmôniak may have dammed up the stream at some point along its twisting course, constructing a rude sawmill there. Fort Orange burghers who had underwritten the operation would want their investment preserved. Since a few of them, the well known Schuylers, were officers with the English, they would have influence sufficient to divert a detachment. Les Anglais and their allies would 'fort up.' If the French and Indians missed the place in their shadowing of the main army, the mill's impromptu "garrison" could rest there, as doubtless they were weary and some of them might be feeling sickly.

The decision was made for half of the war party to remain where they were. These would retire to a likely spot nearby where they could defend themselves from behind trees, fallen trunks and boulders. The rest would follow the moccasin prints uphill and find out what that detachment was up to. The climbers would leave their

---

[99] P. 387, Volume 13, **M**, *Academic American Encyclopedia*, "...the first compound microscope is thought to have been constructed about 1600 by the Dutch lens makers Hans and Zacharias Janssen. * * * ...by the 1660s microscopists had discovered cells, capillaries, blood corpuscles, and bacteria."

[100] P. xiii, "A Short Vocabulary of some Words and Names used by the French Authors, which are not generally understood by the English that understand the French language (&c.)," *The History of the Five Indian Nations Depending on the Province of New-York,* by Cadwallader Colden, 1727 (Part I), and 1747 (Part II). Facsimile reprint, 1980, Cornell University Press, Ithaca, NY.

blanket rolls, knapsacks, thicker raiment and heavier haversacks with the stationary party to move faster and more easily. If they ran into trouble up on the mountain, the others would hasten to reinforce them.

Jonas led the way, Cloud Eagle, much younger then and in excellent physical shape, close behind him. The upward forging enemy had made an attempt to conceal their tracks, scouring their back trail with broken-off, twiggy branches. This didn't fool the sharp-eyed T'songeba, as the obscuring effort left the normally (at this damp time of year) flat carpet of last autumn's leaves somewhat disturbed. And here and there the back trail scourers had missed a footprint. These enemies were either clumsy -- the Pastoniak rangers? -- or …feeble? Infected with the first stages of their army's sickness..?

Asokw Mgezo was armed with a hunting knife, the pipe-tomahawk that he kept wedged behind his waist sash at the small of his back, and, in one hand, aǥma aodouôgan astahigan -- his war spear. -- Climbing uphill under the branches of stout trees, the spear comforted him with something of a sense of security in that, its blade pointing skyward, it was a very quick means of defense… should a hungry pittôlo, that tawny cat "of very much tail," leap on him as he passed beneath overhanging limbs. Not that such was likely with so many others around. But the spear was very handy in that he was now using it as a kind of hiking staff to help him up the steep slope. Not far behind was Lieutenant Mercier, huffing and puffing with effort but determined to be one of the first to sight *l'ennemi* on the mountain. The higher they climbed the steeper the slope became. They found themselves falling into column along a beaten trail. The dim path, most likely, had not been made by human beings (not originally) but was an ancient game trail.

Then, just as they climbed to some old, prostrate trees that had obviously been cut down with a cross-cut saw, indicating that they had indeed reached the Dutchmen's lumbering area,-- the slope leveled off. They could hear foot-falls somewhere ahead..! They were getting close!

Then they saw him! One of them, who had been wearing a wide-brimmed hat of bast,[101] was almost helpless before them. He had thrown down his fusil and unbuckled his leather waist belt, throwing that down also. As the French and Alnôbak emerged over the lip of the hillside onto the more level area, he saw them as well. Saw exactly what he was afraid of seeing. Just a moment before, afflicted with the onset of acute naaiahlauôgan, he had dropped his firelock, frantically hopping from one foot to the other, and torn off his bayonet-hung waistbelt to pull down his breeches. He had grabbed a slim tree that was fortuitously convenient, leaning out at just the right angle.

At first, because he was wearing woolen hose and knee breeches (and had been

---

[101] In appearance just like a farmer's straw hat but, rather than straw, woven of strips of the inner bark of the linden or **bass**wood tree. "Bast" from *bass*wood, *Tilia americana*.

wearing the hat of bast), the warriors and Plac'môniak who surged onto the level area assumed that he was a Dutch or Pastoni ranger. He had been wearing a kerchief under the hat (though those hats of straw or bast are light, they can still make you sweat, especially if you have been toiling up a steep hillside), both of which had been snatched off by an overhanging branch as he lunged for the angled tree. However, his bared head revealed a scalp roach, which together with his bronze coloring indicated that he was either Mohican or Magua (a "Mohawk"). Seeing that he was unarmed and helpless as he squirted out watery obagidamen, Jonas spoke to him in Muheconnui -- the Mohican Way, -- as he approached, his fusil pointed skyward. He held his other hand palm out as he assured the afflicted that he had nothing to fear. He was their prisoner, but would be among Alnôbak brethren, among friends. One of the party's warriors, of the Kaanauagihnono,[102] or French Iroquois, -- who had also been among the first to arrive, called out "Yongya'dén'lon! -- My friend!" --[103] addressing their presumed captive in Iroquoian, anticipating that he might be a Magua rather than a Muheconw. Assurances identical to those offered by T'songeba had started from his lips when a shot rang out and the Kaanauagi scout flinched and dodged aside. His name was "Sken'nenhahson'a dsi'ile -- He Who Walks Softly,"[104]-- but now he wasn't walking, was lying down, aiming his fusil as more musket blasts rang out. Plac'môn and warrior scattered, seeking cover behind whatever was nearby (some behind the old saw-cut logs). They tried to train their front sight blades on the enemy fighters, but there were many trees and saplings in the way. They could see the gunsmoke as it quickly rose and dissipated, but to merely fire in the direction of the smoke wasn't good enough for them… that might only waste valuable ammunition. The Canadiens and *les naturels* were highly experienced hunters who were used to firing a single, snugly seated ball at a clearly sighted-on target. L' ennemi, however, apparently had fired "buck and ball," -- several smaller buckshot (sometimes goose-shot, &c.) and *one* large ball that took up most of the bore. Buck and ball isn't as accurate as one tightly seated full-gauge ball, but your fusil can be loaded much faster. The wider impact of buckshot also compensates for the lack of single-ball accuracy. Luckily for the French and their allies there were so many protruding old stumps, so many trees and saplings with low-hanging branches (and what have you) between the opposing parties that the English shot struck intervening tree trunks and branches for the most part. Some pellets rattled through the boughs of the evergreen trees -- there was a copse of hemlocks near the old logs -- that various French and Alnôbak took shelter behind. With the first burst of gunfire Cloud Eagle and

---

[102] Kaanauagihnono is more popularly spelled "Caughnawaga" today. *Abenakis & English Dialogues,* by Chief Joseph Laurent, p. 52.
[103] P. 108, *One Thousand Useful Mohawk Words,* by David Kanatawakhon Maracle, 1992, Audio-Forum, Guilford, CT. [103] P. 85, *Ibid.*

Lieutenant Mercier had dodged behind the stout trunk of the same hemlock, bumping into each other, making them laugh. Asokw Mgezo, being armed with only edged weapons, couldn't shoot back, but Mercier, having slipped down behind the lip of the mountain shelf, extracted a rather expensive-looking *pistolet* and prepared to retaliate. Crouching, he used a largely horizontal root of the hemlock for a parapet.

Their would-be prisoner took advantage of the distraction: he yanked his breeches part way up and ran to join his compatriots. French and Alnôbak alike tried to aim at him, bringing the hammers of their fusils back to full cock, but, despite the weakness he must have felt, and the frantic hitching up of his breeches, he moved with surprising speed and adroitness, zig-zagging between trees, stumps, and protruding ledges. He was such a comical sight as he fled, trying to hitch up his breeches as his "necessaries pouch" and haversack flapped loosely at his sides[105] that the French and Alnôbak fighters couldn't help but laugh, which *definitely* threw off their aim. He quickly disappeared among the tree trunks and low-hanging evergreen boughs. *Le Lieutenant,* like everyone else, couldn't make out a clear target when he attempted to aim his pistol. There were too many trees, stumps, leaning or fallen trunks, and outcrops in the way. He felt around in his canvas haversack and produced that gleaming object that Cloud Eagle had seen him look through a few times before... an interesting instrument that he would like to know more about.

The company's nbizonhouad was also taking something from his form of a necessaries pouch, a beads-patterned cloth pitôgan. It contained his medical kit. Keeping his head down, he slid over to where the wounded Kaanauagi warrior was lying on the lip of the hillside, aiming his fusil, trying to pick out a clear target. Asokw Mgezo could see where Sken'nenhahson'a dsi'ile had been hit. He was bleeding from his right thigh. Not badly, though... apparently the ball had nicked him without penetrating. Telling Walks Softly what he was going to do, the medical man pulled down the top of the brave's torn legging. He cleaned the gash with a bit of cloth, applying a ready-made herbal poltice, and then wrapped it securely with a strip of cotton "uôbaksiziya -- white little material."[106]-- Walks Softly grimaced slightly as this was done, continuing to concentrate on Dyol'henhshā'geh, Kaanauagiui for "the English."[107] When Cloud Eagle was finished he patted Sken'nenhahson'a dsi'ile's leg reassuringly, to indicate that he was going to be all right. Walks Softly murmured his thanks, remembering that Oliôni is the Abenaki expression for "Thank you." There was a considerable degree of intermingling among the Kaanauagihnono and the Ô'banakiak, including (these days) even intermarriage. Both nationalities were closely allied as constituent parts of the French-aligned 'Seven Indian Nations of Canada.' It was

---

[105] The Magua (Iroquois) or Mohican had originally placed the converging straps of his necessaries pouch behind (under) his waistbelt so that it wouldn't flop about if he had to run.
[106] *Western Abenaki Dictionary,* Volume II, p. 76.
[107] *One Thousand Useful Mohawk Words,* D. K. Maracle, p. 116.

inevitable that many of the Kaanaugihnono would pick up elements of Alnôbaiui and that their Ô'banakiak allies would learn snatches of Iroquoian. Walks Softly said 'oliôni' correctly, but then lapsed into the Kaanauagiui "Yon'kyadén'lonh[108] --My friend,"-- before remembering to say 'Nidômba,' the same thing in Abenaki.

In the meanwhile Le Mercier had taken up a brass-bound telescope and was peering through it in the direction of the enemy. Occasionally *les Anglais* fired another volley, apparently just to keep the French and Alnôbak at a distance.

"Sang du chien! --**Dog's blood!**--" *le officier* swore. Then he noticed that Walks Quietly[109] was looking in his direction with a curious expression on his face. Of course the warrior knew some French too. *"Non vous! Pardon!* -- Not you! Sorry!"-- the Lieutenant apologized, realizing that since the Kaanauagi had been bleeding, he thought that the Frenchman may have meant him. Le Mercier grinned ruefully and tapped his spyglass, to indicate that something about the telescope was the problem.

The problem was not the spyglass. It was as it should be. The problem was the officer's position on the lip of the hill, behind the large root of the hemlock. He was too close to the ground. In order to achieve an adequate view he would have to get higher up. What he needed to do, *oui,* was to climb the tree. He should be able to see where the enemy is from among its branches. And whether there *is* a purported sawmill. However, that entailed a larger degree of risk. Should he chance it?

Judging by their gunfire l' ennemi was somewhere to their direct front. That was plain enough. But… *exactly* where? For the nounce, however, he should get his men into a more effective position. They needed to spread out more, to the left and right, to cover their flanks. *Les Anglais* and their *sauvage* auxiliaries might outnumber them, for all he knew, and conceivably might launch a counterattack. The resistance they were putting up *was* something of a counterattack. The French and their allies were clinging to the edge of the shelf area, their backs to the steep slope. *C'est mauvais!* Not good!

The Lieutenant passed word to both sides to direct the marines and *la milice* to spread out; and then press the enemy on both flanks. They should seek to compress the foe into a smaller area where they would be more vulnerable. He relayed the same -- as a suggestion, -- to Pmauikho, the Mazipskoik war captain. The sagacious Pmauikho, living up to the meaning of his name -- He Who Goes Ahead [110]-- (from Pmauikhoud, which can also mean "He [or She] Who *Walks* Ahead"), returned that he had already launched, with his fighters, what Le Mercier was advocating.

---

[108] P. 117, *Ibid.*

[109] Sken'nenhahson'a dsi'ile means both "He Walks Softly" and "He Walks Quietly," interchangeably.

[110] P. 435, *Western Abenaki Dictionary,* Volume II: "He walks ahead (of his followers, of the herd)." The author has modified Dr. Day's animate intransitive verb pmawikhowa to pmauikh**oud**, a *personality* going ahead, and further to Pmauikh**o**, deleting the suffix *ud*, the word-final **o** indicating that it is the chief's formal name.

Seeing that their medical aide was finished with Walks Softly, Mercier pondered Cloud Eagle's further usefulness. The warrior lacked a missile - throwing weapon. What could he do from here? The Lieutenant had heard that their "medicine man" was something of *un Jongleur:* a Sorcerer. Indeed, he wasn't wearing a crucifix-hung rosary-necklace like some of the other Mazipskiak. Le Lieutenant had, every now and then, briefly noticed him engaged in what might have been heathen practices. Had he seen him off to the side, solemnly putting down a handful of tobacco… to propitiate one of les sauvage jongleurs' *génies?* -- And that time he had noticed him staring -- seemingly -- into a rather commonplace, small puddle of water. Had he been engaged in some manner of *diablerie clairvoyance…?* In addition to his *physique médecine compétences,* he was, you could tell just by looking at him, *un conjuror;* what les Abnaquies' called mandokôzid: "one who sits and thinks or reflects, a conjuror, he thinks."[111] And of his war paint, typically red, white and black like the other Mazipskiak and Odanak warriors, -- but all that white paint across his brow, just above the eyes..? To help him see better, not so much into the geographical distance, perhaps, as into *le monde du esprit…?* However, if he was in league with *le Diable,* he was certainly on the wrong side! Le Diable was, no question about it, on the side of *les hérétiques* who were shooting at them.

And another thing… he thought he had heard the other Mazipskiak refer to him as 'Missal.' Something -- Missal. Wasn't Missal the Abenaki or Algonquian way of saying *Michael?* After Saint Michael… then perhaps their medicine man was a Christian after all, or had been duly baptized at some time in his life. Le Mercier had heard 'Mgezo,' which, pronounced in non-labial frecktle, indistinct to his Canadien ears, reminded him of the Ô'banaki Missal for *Michael.* And isn't St. Michael the patron saint of soldiers, and therefore of warriors--? Had he heard them say San Missal --? Not paying much attention, the Lieutenant, having other things on his mind, had picked up on the consonant s of Asokw, and now thought that he heard *San* (French for "Saint").

However, be that as it may, whatever his spiritual proclivities, if their warrior "San Missal" did have extraordinary talents, perhaps he could make use of them in helping the French defeat the *hérétiques* at hand. Especially if the nbizonhouad's "clairvoyance" -- clear seeing -- was enhanced by the instrument the Lieutenant possessed, a triumph of the latest in ultra-modern "state of the art" optical technology, *l' télescope.* Le Mercier requested that Pmauikho sidle over to his impromptu "command post" position. He knew that the chief was quite familiar with French. He wanted the war captain to act as an interpreter between himself and their "San Missal." Le Mercier had decided that it was too much of a risk to climb the hemlock himself to 'scope out' the enemy. If les Anglais saw him and he was shot out of the tree, the French detachment would be rendered leaderless. Of course, ranking subordinates would then,

---

[111] *Western Abenaki Dictionary,* Volume II, p. 83.

presumably, provide a degree of substitute leadership… However, they might not render as effective service as he was capable of. He wasn't the commanding *officier* here for no good reason. Even if he was "only" wounded, his leadership capability would be seriously impaired.

Le Lieutenant made his request known by way of a mélange of his own pidgin-Algonquian, the limited Plac'môniui -- Frenchmen's Way, -- that Asokw Mgezo knew, hand gestures, and the interpreting of Pmauikho. At first the medauinno had inwardly bristled at the Lieutenant's proposal, suspecting that he was being asked to take the risk of climbing up the tree because, like any commonplace *"sauvage,"* the French considered him to be expendable. However, in mulling it over, he thought that this chance to demonstrate how kagini he could be might be well worth it. When he had joined the scouting party, as the fighters made their way south against *les Anglais,* he thought that he detected an attitude among his fellow warriors that… he might be using his nbizonhouad role so as to hang back and keep out of harm's way, for the most part, when the detachment did come to grips with the enemy in mortal combat. Not that anyone had chided him outright with such an opinion. But had he seen indications of such disparagement in nuances of expression on their faces… in subtle tones of voice..? Or was he being paranoid?

There had been a time when he could have determined the truth by reading their minds. Ôhôô, when he was a mere boy, he had been able to read people's minds, and very accurately, at that.[112] He had not been able to read their ôndamal, minds, from any distance. His method had been to place his head against the back of the head of the other person (they would be, preferably, sitting down). Would place his forehead/eyes area against their head, and, eyes closed, would psychically "look" into their minds. He would literally *see* what they were thinking. When he told them what he had seen, the subjects were always astonished. They had fondly assumed that it was a childish game… they were humoring him. He recalled an indulgent okem -- paternal aunt, -- who silently thought: "O, agma kisi'ônda kisito -- Oh, he can't do it."-- When he had withdrawn his head and told her what she had been thinking, she had jumped up and whirled around in complete astonishment, telling him that he was absolutely correct.

However, as he had grown older he had neglected this ability, distracted by the "more serious" pursuits of hunting, fishing, wild edibles and herb-gathering, canoe-building, tools and weapons-making, playing such fiercely competitive games as pabaskuhamauôgan,[113] caught up in suchlike more mature endeavors. Among his adult peers he declined to propose that he attempt to read their innermost thoughts, concerned

---

[112] Conjecturally applied to Asokw Mgezo from the author's own ability to read minds as a youngster. As described above, this was not done with any distance between himself and a subject, but required head to head physical contact.

[113] The French term is lacrosse. *Abenakis & English Dialogues,* Chief Joseph Laurent, p. 50.

that this could imply that he didn't trust them …that their spoken words might not be absolutely honest. His traditionalist elders, however, seeking to maintain and revive old spiritual practices, had taken his boyish psychic ability into consideration. It had been one of the factors that, early on, had motivated them to encourage the youth (him especially) to begin walking Ôligo Mkui Ô'udi -- the Good Red Road, -- the path of spiritual power and enlightenment. If there were any doubts among his brother migakauinnoak about how much courage he had in the face of the enemy, here was a golden opportunity to definitely allay such uncertainty!

Now he was quite eager to climb the tree, hazardous though it might be. He was intrigued, profoundly, by the prospect of using the Lieutenant's shiny lôbodi -- seeing instrument.[114] -- Le Mercier was careful to instruct him on the proper employment of the telescope, the use of which was unfamiliar to him. To, for example, very firmly stabilize the instrument when looking through it. Otherwise, if held too loosely, the sensitive device would be more of a hindrance than a help to far-viewing. When looked through, the sections fully extended, any shakiness, or trembling, made it hard to see anything. If casually holding up a stick and pointing with it revealed no shakiness (of the stick), the same light pressure applied to a telescope, as seen through its lens, would allow what in the case of a stick was unnoticeable… to be multiplied to the point of difficulty by the magnification of the sensitive lens. Therefore Cloud Eagle should very forcefully press the instrument against the trunk of the tree, or press down on a branch extending in front of his face (better yet if the two could be combined) to adequately stabilize it. This closeness to the tree trunk (or trunk and branch) would also help conceal him from the enemy, who had eagle-eyed Mohican and Maguak warriors among them.

Not having his spear, which he had loaned to the wounded Walks Softly, Asokw Mgezo placed the telescope in his necessaries pitôgan to leave both hands free for climbing. Pmauikho and Le Mercier spread the word that, on their signal, half their force should fire at the enemy. It didn't matter if they were zeroed in on a target. All of those close to the hemlock their man was to climb were to shoot. The Lieutenant told his men to put a little extra powder in their fusils. He would also fire with his pistol. The object was to emit a screen of gunsmoke to conceal their medauinno / spy as he started up the tree. There were a few branches extending from the trunk where it grew closest to the ground; as the smoke wafted upward and dissipated he should be higher up among more numerous, concealing boughs. The abrupt striking of musket balls in the area where the enemy was hunkered down should make them pull their heads behind whatever stumps or other cover they were hiding behind.

---

[114] *Western Abenaki Dictionary*, Volume II, p. 399.

8. Asokw Mgezo Lôdaua Alnizedi -- Cloud Eagle Climbs the Hemlock Tree --

This would give the climber another, albeit brief, margin of safety. A highly practical rule of the French and their *naturel* allies, in such circumstances as the present, was that when a soldier or warrior fired, the shooter's (previously agreed-upon) teammate would refrain from firing. He wouldn't discharge his own fusil until his partner had reloaded. That way, the recharging *fusilier* would remain covered until ready to fire again.

Cloud Eagle lunged for the branches that were closest overhead as flints sparked against striking steels. The fusils of the French and Alnôbak roared as he climbed with alacrity. He was scrambling upward with the speed of an apanakes[115] or of an olanigw,[116] he thought, even as he climbed frantically, trying to keep himself behind the trunk as much as possible. However, having done, on the way to the present juncture, all the requisite spiritual-medicine propitiations, as far as he was able, he felt little fear. The Grandfather and Grandmother Spirits should be with him! If the Christians thought they are protected by nanaôalghed ôzaliak -- guardian angels, -- ...so did he!

As he climbed the thought crossed his mind that this would be a good time -- an excellent time! -- to engage in the practice of lôgihla - azuaôzimek, shape-shifting. He had previously discussed the subject in council with Kisikauo, Wise Woman, and others who were striving to follow the old spiritual ways. He had not, to date, seriously attempted to lôgihla azuaôzi, shape-shift, for the simple reason that he had not felt any pressing reason to. And there was the nagging thought that, supposing he succeeded in changing into something else... would he be able to *resume* his human form..? There might be certain advantages in becoming a high-soaring mgezo'a, an eagle, or, for example, ali moôuin'a -- as a bear, -- being able to sleep the winter through, -- but..! Would Ôeoandamsko, for one, accept such a drastic transformation? Would she want to change into a moôuinaskw -- female bear --? And, if she did... would she be **able** to...?

It was obvious that shape shifting is not to be taken lightly. You had to have a powerful reason for making the attempt. Was there a strong reason for trying it now? Certainly... to fool the enemy! If the foe glimpsed hands and feet as he reached for branches to haul himself up, if they saw, instead, the form and fluffy tail of a mere msanigw -- gray squirrel,-- they wouldn't give it a thought. Of course tree-dwellers such as squirrels would be frightened by the shooting and all the commotion, and would flee for safety to the treetops. They would expect that. O'hôô, Yes, even the less woods-wise Pastoniak and Dutsmôniak from the streets of Fort Orange would expect that. To change into msanigw, or, better yet, a smaller mikoa (red squirrel) would certainly fit

---

[115] *Western Abenaki Dictionary,* Volume II, p. 244. Pine marten, *Martes americana.*
[116] The so-called fisher, also called 'fisher cat,' *Martes pennanti,* p. 148 Ibid.

the need of the moment. Could he, should he…?

This line of thinking ended suddenly when he abruptly glimpsed what he was after. With a final heave up onto branches stout enough to hold him, he looked around the trunk, revealing only part of his face, and saw… the building. Aha, o'hôô, there *is* a sawmill! And there was apcikozidzik -- *l'ennemi*,-- their fusil barrels protruding from windows, a doorway, from outbuildings, from behind stacked logs and piles of debris, from behind stumps and trees still standing… though the boughs of the hemlock spreading in that direction, and intervening growth somewhat obscured the view, his eyes were sharp enough to see exactly where the enemy is. He really didn't need the telescope. However, since he had it with him, he might as well use it. There might be details he could pick out that weren't apparent to the naked eye, which, if noticed, might provide crucially valuable information to Pmauikho and the Lieutenant.

Cloud Eagle extracted the spyglass, and, with his left arm encircling a westward-protruding branch to steady him, having pulled out the scope full length, rested it between the trunk and the southward-extending bough that was in front of his face. He held it in place firmly with his right hand, contorting somewhat to also steady it with his left hand, looking eastward toward the mill.

He squinted as he gazed through the glass, first looking through it with his right eye, and then his left, testing to see which was better. 'Iahi!' He could see so far with the amazing instrument! And he understood Le Mercier's warning about the trembling if the glass was not 'grounded' enough. He pressed down harder with his right hand to stop the slight shakiness the lens reflected. As he gazed at the enemy in the mill and around it, turning the glass slightly to increase the magnification, the scope's view projected his gaze well beyond the extending, intervening boughs of the hemlock. Talk about shape-shifting..! He is a mikoa, looking down on l'ennemi from the branches of a tree much closer to the mill! Had a view like that of a tiny ahalôdauasid, tree toad.[117] He definitely *felt* like one, clinging to the trunk of the hemlock and attempting to spy out as much as he could. How many of the enemy, exactly where they were… who are their war captains? He saw that the mill was on the far side of the brook, across the impounded water of the mill dam. There was a rough log bridge across the upper brook, just before the point where the water fell into the mill pond. That was good… it would take fire arrows to pry them out, and the intervening water should prevent the consequent blaze from spreading to their side of the stream. Hopefully. Or delay it from spreading toward the French and their allies, while at the same time driving away the foe, sending them fleeing down the mountain on the old tote road leading back toward the main body of their army. Satisfied that he had seen enough, Asokw Mgezo began to

---

[117] Ahalôdauasid, "the Tree Toad: He who climbs customarily, the climber" (technically a frog). *Western Abenaki Dictionary*, Volume II, p. 74. Related to ahaligid, '*one that is like*,' referring to, in this case, the arboreal frog's bark-like camouflage. *Western Abenaki Dictionary*, Volume I, p. 17.

desend. The Lieutenant and Pmauikho had been keeping an eye on him, and when they saw that he was coming down, called out that their men, particularly the ones closest to the hemlock, should fire another volley. This was to make the enemy duck and to generate a rising cloud of smoke to conceal their spy as he desended. Before his moccasins even touched the ground Asokw Mgezo was telling Pmauikho where the mill was, how far away, and that his warriors should alight fire arrows and dodge forward to launch them at the sawmill, and at the associated outbuildings and piles of debris as well. What the enemy was using as sheltering "bastions" should be used against them, forcing them to withdraw.

Pmauikho had already anticipated the need for fire arrows…Certain warriors, equipped with pouches containing fireproof clamshells or scallop-shells harboring almost-glowing coals couched in punk,[118] had elbowed their way forward, crawling behind concealing stumps or hillocks. They were now ready to apply the coals (gently blowing on them to increase their heat) to the small "collars" of jute wrapping tinder and various flammable materials around their shafts just behind their arrowheads. Now their war chief relayed word to them to set the arrow combustibles aflame and take aim at specific targets. Their signal to let fly was when Lieutenant Mercier shouted for his *troupes* to open fire. The fire arrows streaking out in the direction of the mill seemed to emanate from the abruptly billowing clouds of gun smoke that erupted. Flaming arrows, thunking into the mill and nearby outbuilding and debris pile "ramparts," their fires spreading quickly thanks to the volatility of the solutions of potassium nitrate that the jute "collars" had been treated with …might have been extinguished by defenders (anticipating fire arrows) who rose to beat them out with wet blankets or containers of water. However, only about half of the Canadiens and their *naturel* allies had fired. As these fusiliers quickly reloaded, the other half rose to their feet and opened fire, taking direct aim at the wielders of the blankets and containers of water. The waving, slapping blankets made excellent targets even through intervening saplings and boughs. As they fired and reloaded, taking advantage of the distraction of the fire arrows, the French and Alnôbak dodged forward to handy tree trunks, boulders, and outcroppings, shortening the distance between themselves and the sawmill. This increased the accuracy of their marksmanship, their musket blasts further driving the *Anglais* and their allies away from extinguishing the spreading flames. In addition, more combustibles-wrapped skueḍa tiskuôḍial -- fire arrows-- were launched, and at closer range, the archers also dodging swiftly from tree to tree, taking advantage of the rising smoke and flames that plagued an enemy forced to duck the rain of balls from the fusiliers. The musketmen

---

[118] *Webster's New Collegiate Dictionary:* "[Of Algonquian origin.] 1. Wood so decayed as to be useful for tinder; touchwood." In the case of preserving faintly (or *almost*) glowing coals with which to ignite tinder at some indefinite future time, the rotten wood, "punky wood," is selected so as to be damp enough not to ignite the coal… yet *dry* enough to keep the coal alive. It should also surround the coal closely to keep oxygen from igniting the coal to flame while **also** admitting *just enough* air to prevent the coal from suffocating.

had also formed the outline of a pincers, working their way closer to the stronghold of the Dutsmôniak and *les Anglais* from the right and left, harassing the defenders with a storm of fire that increased in lethality as the element of *crossfire* was added to it.

Looking on, Cloud Eagle was intent not only on observing the progress of the fight, but watched to see if any of the French and his fellow Alnôbak had become casualties. If he saw any wounded, he was poised to immediately make his way to them (taking advantage of cover to avoid being hit himself) and render first aid. In anticipation of this, when he saw how much the billowing smoke must be obscuring the defenders view, he abandoned his position at the foot of the hemlock. He risked moving forward, joining a *milicen* behind a quite decayed, but massive birch that had fallen a long time ago. He remembered that he still had the Lieutenant's spyglass, having returned it to his pitôgan as he climbed down the tree. Mercier had been too busy absorbing his spy's intelligence (relayed more quickly by Pmauikho's translating) and directing his men to think to ask for it back. It was too risky to seek out the Lieutenant to return it now, so Asokw Mgezo decided to make use of it himself. He focused on the area immediately downstream from the milldam, where the logging road started downhill, to see if any of the enemy was breaking. Intervening trees, a trash pile, and ledges blocking his view from behind the old birch, he moved to the bulwark of a nearby koa -- pine -- with a sufficiently thick trunk, and spied again from there. And sure enough! He was rewarded by the sight of one of them hastening down the trace, one who was fleeing. Moreover, he was a familiar sight. The fugitive carried no fusil and the medauinno knew why… he was the scout they had nearly captured when their detachment had debouched onto the mountain shelf of the lumbering area. He was the sufferer from naaiahlauôgan, "down flowing." Having abandoned his fusil, and the musketry from the French and their allies making it too hazardous to extinguish the spreading flames, he was prudently 'abandoning ship.' In his weakened state he was not much good to the defense; he knew that he had better get away while he could. Understanding that the fugitive was a fellow Alnôba, Cloud Eagle felt a pang of sympathy for him… it was too bad that they could not have captured him. He, Pmauikho, T'songeba, and Walks Softly would have seen to it that he was treated well. Returning north, there would have been a chance that they could have won him over, making an ally out of him. *Ôzoka!* -- *On the other hand!* -- seeing that he was ill …it was just as well that he was getting away! His sickness was likely contagious, and they didn't want to become infected also.

As the unarmed, rather pathetic figure lurched feebly downhill, Asokw Mgezo turned his attention back to the fight for the mill. Clouds of smoke swirled copiously from it and its nearby "outworks," bright sparks streaking upward as fires crackled and snapped with increasing vehemence. He could hear coughing, punctuated by shouts, from the mill, and could discern no gunsmoke blossoming from *Anglais* fusils. They were too busy attempting to quench and beat out the flames to continue to shoot back.

They had to worry about sparks igniting cartridges in their hands as they extracted them from their pilaskuigani'nodaal -- paper's bags, -- i.e., cartridge pouches.[119] Edging closer like the Canadiens and his brother migakauinnoak, Cloud Eagle looked again at the downhill road leading away from the embattled mill. He was so close now he really didn't need the spyglass, and put it away. Here he saw what he rather expected to see -- more of the enemy abandoning the place, four of them carrying another on a stretcher hastily rigged from two poles with a blanket or something between them. They were immediately followed by more stretcher-bearers with other wounded supported between two of their fellows. The entire force was abandoning the now fiercely burning mill. The victory halloo rang out from the French and Indian fighters, Mercier and Pmauikho shouting for their men to cease fire. The Lieutenant and the war chief didn't want them to waste their limited supply of ammunition on an enemy that was plainly defeated and was fleeing. Let them go! *Anglais* reinforcements might be marching uphill, "to the rescue," for all they knew, and whatever powder and ball, and arrows, they still possessed might be needed to enable them to make an orderly withdrawal from a more powerful force.

    The band's nbizonhouad now advanced to the edge of the mill pond. Remembering that he still had the Lieutenant's telescope, he took it out and started looking through it at the withdrawing enemy. For those emerging from the mill, just across the water, he didn't really need it. He wanted to more closely examine the majority, who were now further down the trace. He wanted to know exactly how bad off were they, how much damage the French and Indian detachment had done. For all he knew, some of those being carried on stretchers might be fatally wounded... could be dead already. Their compatriots might be taking them away so that their bodies wouldn't be consumed by flames in the mill or the burning areas around it. To honor them with military interments further down the valley. An officer's corpse might be carried all the way back to Hudson's River and Fort Orange. Even with the far seeing lôbodi it was hard to tell if the stretcher-borne wounded were dead or not. He could see that even those prostrate ones retained their firelocks. The Pastoniak didn't want to leave any of their weapons behind for the French and their "savages" to find. As it was they had already lost the firelock and its bayonet that had been thrown down by the diarrhea-plagued scout.

    Seeing the last Pastoni ranger and Alnôba auxiliary leave the mill, running quickly, none of them attempting to fire a parting shot as they left, Cloud Eagle advanced right out onto the mill dam. He was limited only by the fast-flowing spillway. His audacity was rewarded when, using the lôbodi, he glimpsed one of them, well down the trail, suddenly stop, and bending over, erupt in segaguôgan -- vomiting. -- "Segago! -- He vomits!"-- the young *naturel docteur* whispered to himself, thinking that the up-

---

[119] *Western Abenaki Dictionary,* Volume II, p. 300. *New leaf,* paper, i.e., 'bila' or *pila* from pilaskw.

chucker was probably suffering from smoke inhalation. Scrutinizing more intensely with the spyglass, he spotted yet another give in to the throes of sickness. This one had stopped by a young leaning tree, grabbing it with one hand while he pulled down his breeches with the other. Like the one they had thought to capture, this one was afflicted with "naaiahlauôgan -- down flowing."-- "Kdemôginôgw!"[120] Asokw Mgezo muttered to himself. They certainly were a sickly bunch! Not to be laughed at, however..! What they were suffering from could just as easily afflict his own people.

Then he heard a voice from behind, seeming to be directed at him. It was Le Mercier, calling out something that sounded like 'San Missal!' From his beckoning gestures he apparently wanted his labôdi returned. For a while the Lieutenant had not known where their *homme de médecine* was, but now had found him. Cloud Eagle hastened over, holding out the spyglass, and at the same time called out to Pmauikho. He needed to warn the chief that he should call back fighters who had crossed the upstream bridge -- it had not caught fire yet, not quite, -- that they should absolutely stay away from the apcikozidzik -- enemies. -- Though the fugitives were demoralized and nearly defenseless, and it shouldn't require much exertion to run down and capture five or six, the medical man knew that the easiest to capture would be *akkuadsala!* (*alas!*)… the sickest ones. Those are precisely the ones you don't want! Whatever was afflicting them would, *very likely,* be passed on to their captors.

"He Who Goes Ahead" certainly lived up to his name in this instance, more so than usual, instantly understanding the wisdom of their nbizonhouad's warning. Telling the Lieutenant that he should keep his men away from the enemy also, he dashed over the bridge, pursuing the warriors who were now on the other side of the mill. Môdzahazimek pitta nanabi -- Moving very swiftly, -- calling out, he caught the most advanced fighter. The warrior wanted to pursue, but Pmauikho caught him in time. The war captain, thinking quickly, then put those of his men who were on the east side of the millpond to work dousing fires. Not that he was interested in saving the mill… it was burning much too fiercely, with vesuvian intensity. He of course was glad to see it destroyed -- as a northward outpost of *les Anglais* it needed to be eliminated -- but they didn't want to have a forest fire on their hands. Not only would it be annoying to have to fly ahead of a roaring conflagration… but they should be mindful that they were in Mohican territory. This thickly wooded Taconic Mountains region provided an abundance of resources to the Muheconnuck …various wild animals for meat and hides, the flesh and feathers of birds such as turkeys and grouse (appreciated, too, should be the mere commonplace familiarity with so many fascinating auaasak ta lidooak) …vegetative bounty for food and medicines, bark for wigwams and containers, spiritually significant pine groves, rocky summits for vision quests… Cloud

---

[120] Chief Joseph Laurent, *Abenakis and English Dialogues, Interjections:* "Articulations expressing commisseration or pity," p. 90.

Eagle, and also Kisikauo, if he was present, would be quick to point out that Olakuika, the Good Forest, needed to be valued and protected no matter whose territory it was part of. It was all part of the Creation of Ktsi Manenioiw -- the Great Mystery, -- and therefore is sacred, deserving of veneration and of every consideration.

The warriors found, scattered here and there, wooden buckets, two or three yet damp blankets, and some *bego* - sealed Mohican-made bark containers that the enemy had used in attempting to quench the fire arrows, and then had abandoned in their flight. Some were snatched from the spreading flames just in time, and were quickly refilled from the stream flowing into the millpond, or, in the case of the blankets, dipped and soaked again. Those equipped with gourd water containers, "canteens," filled them with more water. Le Mercier's *troupes* crossed the bridge also and joined in, those with leather-covered bottle canteens using them to douse spreading flames. In the meanwhile Asokw Mgezo was busy administering first aid to a few slightly wounded warriors and fusiliers, applying poultices and bandages as he had done in the case of Walks Quietly. The eyes of a large Canadien marine sergeant twinkled with merriment as the *naturel docteur* applied a poultice to his left arm, which had been grazed by a ball. From a small ball, most likely, probably from one of the Anglais' scattershot loads, as the wound was not severe. What made him laugh was that he had been struck by an *arrow* to his other arm, at the *same time*. At least one of the Magua or Mohican auxiliaries had been armed with a bow and arrows. The iron-bladed arrow had not actually penetrated, or even scratched, his arm. Leaving his heavier wool regimental coat at the foot of the mountain, for a less sweaty ascent he had climbed in his *veste* (sleeveless waistcoat) and of course his white shirt under that. Typical of 18th century shirts, the sleeves were generous, one might even say "billowy," the arrow catching in the copious underarm sleeve gusset, and hanging there. Le Sergent, intent on keeping *l'sauvage's fléche* as a memento of the successful combat, felt quite proud of his inadvertent acquisition.

Cloud Eagle diligently searched the forested, uneven ground between the edge of the mountainside and the millpond's feeder brook. He looked for anyone who was so badly wounded that he was now completely prostrate and out of sight behind a moss-grown, granite slab or fallen trunk. He wanted to find such casualties, presumably rendered unconscious (he couldn't hear any outcries or moaning), before they slowly bled to death. He was beginning to be slightly concerned that he might not have sufficient bandages and poultices on him to administer adequate first aid to everyone. He needn't have worried, however, because various of Le Mercier's men were also carrying bandage rolls in small haversacks, his *cadet-aiguillettes* and *sergents* especially. As he rounded a dense copse of ôski alnizediak -- young hemlocks,[121] -- he

---

[121] Alnizediak: "common evergreen boughs; Eastern Hemlock, *Tsuga canadensis*," (singular Alnizedi), p. 187, *Western Abenaki Dictionary,* Volume II. Not to be confused with 'ground hemlock,' sagaskôdakw, *Taxus canadensis,* and especially not with 'water hemlock,' cannaps madzinebizonoo, "turnip [that is] bad medicine," *Cicuta maculata* L. P. 187, *Ibid.*

found one of the Lieutenant's subalterns, exactly one of those carrying bandage rolls, putting the finishing touches on the wounds of the staunch warrior Nikola… what was his surname? Ah, yes, it was M'Sadokues (pronounced 'M'Sado*q*ues' by the French), a well-known family name. His brother Llobal was with him, though at present on the other side of the millpond, helping in the effort to keep the fire from the mill from spreading. Speaking of that edifice, just then they harkened to the sudden sound of flaming timbers crashing down as the structure partially disintegrated, sending an eruption of fiery embers streaking skyward.

The subaltern was somewhat expensively uniformed, being a "gentleman cadet," a *Garde de la Marine* of the "Dos Blancs"-- so called because the marine uniform coats were *blanc* [though, in his case, borderline gray]. The cadet, assigned to Le Mercier's detachment to acquire actual experience in the art of war, had prudently left his well-tailored, but heavier, uniform coat at the bottom of the slope, his blue waist-coat leaving him appearing sufficiently military. Luckily he had thought to bring along his lightweight haversack containing a bandage roll, small vials of medicines, and even a new probe and forceps for extracting balls or splinters from any wounded.

M'Sadokues had been struck in two places, obviously by "buckshot" balls of the scattershot loads. Another missile, a full-sized ball, had whacked into the shoulder stock of agma paskhigan -- his fusil. -- The firelock was still useful, however, missing only a shard of wood. He had hoisted his upper garment, his overshirt, to allow the cadet to attend to the wound in his torso. The ball may have been kept from a fatal penetration by striking a rib. "N' olinkauadsinô ônda zokuab n'pigasen -- I hope it hasn't broken my rib,"-- Nikola had thought, wincing from the pain, as the young soldier tightly wound a long bandage around his body, not only to stop the bleeding but to "set" the rib if it was broken.

Le Garde was now bandaging M'Sadokues' "winged" shoulder, having placed absorbent cotton padding under the strip of uôbaksiziya -- white small material -- that he was securing in place. The warrior's arm should also be put in a sling, to better allow the shoulder wound to heal.

Nikola now stood up (both had been sitting on convenient moss-grown protrusions: a low boulder for one and an old stump for the other). Mes'ôghaid -- The gunshot - wounded one -- greeted Asokw Mgezo, who had been scrutinizing the first aid that the downy-cheeked youngster had been administering. He wanted to make sure it was done right. The location of M'Sadokues and the cadet was not too far forward from the area where akuamalsiui -- the sickly -- Alnôba had taken to the angled tree for urgent relief. Nikola, advancing against the enemy, attempting to keep behind whatever cover the terrain afforded, had been hit a little in advance of the present spot. Knocked down, he had then crawled behind a fairly decayed, but sufficiently large fallen trunk to hide. He needed to examine where he had been hit and to assess the damage to his fusil.

Nikuôbi -- Now -- he called their nbizonhouad's attention to akuamalsid'i -- the indisposed one's -- abandoned fusil, waistbelt, *baïonnette,* and other articles. "Odena dôniyo k'sidaldamô -- Take what you wish,"-- Nikola said. The items were prizes of war. The medical man / fight-person realized that, since he had loaned his spear to Walks Softly (as a staff, to favor his wounded leg) he no longer had much in the way of weaponry. None of the other fighters would, most likely, want the booty, already having their own firelocks and edged weapons. M'Sadokues and the cadet -- whose name was Clément de Sabrevois, -- accompanied Cloud Eagle over to the discarded items. Picking up the musketoon (he was surprised at how heavy it was, the barrel being so short), he smiled to himself… though he had difficulty imagining himself hunting with it, the fusil feeling rather clumsy in his unpracticed hands. But it was plunder, an unasked for *gift..!*

He had always believed that the Great Spirits would guide him to his own firelock, without having to trap or otherwise kill numerous fur-bearers to obtain it. And **here it is,** on a mission where his role had been more to heal than to fight..! Another indicator that it was meant for him was that the wooden stock had been stained red (the stocks of most military muskets were painted black). Les Anglais know that "ye Indians" favor mkuigen -- the color red. -- The barrel's gauge was probably .75 caliber, in common with most British-made muskets. It had, most likely, been gifted to the Magua or Mohican scout by Queen Anne's government. Carved into the wide shoulder stock, near the large brass butt-plate, was the emblem of the 'King's Broad Arrow,' a design incised, carved or stamped onto government property. Though the English may have been generous in gifting the weapon to one of their trusted "salvages," simultaneously… they couldn't help but wax parsimonious. Counting pence, there was no tendency to "waste" brass on a trigger guard or on ramrod-channel "thimbles" (brass or iron guides ordinarily installed to secure the ramrod in the forestock's channel).

The ramrod itself was a thick but simple wooden rod, lacking the usual (somewhat trumpeted) brass tip. The ignition system was powerful-looking but featured a safety-catch that was, in these modern times, obsolete, called a *dog-lock*. The catch was a steel hook secured to the outside of the lock-plate. The 'dog' hooked into a notch in the base of the cock (the lock-hammer), to provide the "half-cock" safety catch. It was an exceedingly clumsy arrangement. Especially when, at the onset of a fight, or the hunter, upon spotting game well within range …needed to disengage the catch and thumb the hammer back to full cock. At a moment when haste was of the essence, the firelock had to be held between one's arm and body while the shooter used *both hands* to release the 'dog.' Its only utility was that it was better than no half-cock safety catch at all. The up-to-date, modern era's "state of the art" internal sear safety catch released (at least!) twenty times faster, and with no difficulty whatsoever. And you can't even see it; the mechanism is entirely inside the breech (lockplate-ignition area) of the fusil.

"Cloud Eagle's" putative battle-ground plunder. Among sprouting mozilalo --moose's tongue -- (trout lily) leaves are: Royal largess 'doglock' musketoon and medieval vintage dagger, "updated" as a plug bayonet, with leather scabbard above "hat of bast."

Author's replica items.

The internal sear was (naturally) a French innovation. The unwieldy external dog-lock sometimes was referred to as *"la Platine Anglais* -- the English Lock." Though M'Sadokues and Asokw Mgezo may not have been informed about the French origin of the silky-smooth internal sear catch, young de Sabrevois could well have known about it. He would have accepted the information with suave aplomb; *of course* such a salubrious invention would be French! The people of *La Belle France* are *supérieur* in every way...

La médecine homme examined the curious firearm, holding it this way and that. He admired in particular the brass 'side plate' (opposite the lock-plate). This had been cast in the serpentine likeness of what was referred to, in Alnôbaiui, as 'auahônedo.' This can be roughly translated as a "dragon." The brass imagery, commonplace on hunting fusils, was considered to contribute a deadly serpent's striking power. Disdaining the clumsy *Anglais* half-cock "dog," -- which M'Sadokues and Cloud Eagle referred to as an alemos[122]-- they and the confident cadet were in for a surprise, however. De Sabrevois and Nikola, being more familiar with firelocks than Cloud Eagle, were the first to notice it. Though the fusil's "alemos" hook was hanging loose, was *not* set into the notch in the base of the cock…yet the hammer seemed to be set on half-cock anyway! The flashpan-cover combination frizzen (striking steel) was closed… the fusil, undoubtedly primed and loaded, had been ready to fire when akuamalsid -- the sickly one -- had dropped it. Was it really set on half-cock, or was the ignition spring-

---

[122]*Western Abenaki Dictionary,* Volume II, p. 114. A more recent word for dog, alemos, "ordinary canine."

mechanism so strong that the flint-hammering cock needed only half the arc that other muskets require? Clément proposed to experiment, asking for the musketoon. First he tried to pull the trigger, aiming at a decayed stump nearby. Try as he might, his face almost red, the trigger refused to budge. *Oui!* It *must* be set at half-cock! Then he attempted to bring the hammer back to full cock. *Click!!* He thumbed it back easily. Obviously the firearm *did* have an internal sear half-cock mechanism! It featured *both* the outside dog-catch **and** the internal sear half cock!

Voila! *"Succés!"* le cadet exclaimed as their eyebrows lifted with surprise. Cloud Eagle was in luck! The seemingly obsolete firelock was quite modern after all. But why had *les Anglais* gone to the trouble and expense of providing the internal sear safety catch and then *added* the external dog-catch..? With the internal catch the external dog was unnecessary. They looked at each other in puzzlement. The mentality of les Anglais was difficult to understand.

"Gizila -- Perhaps,"-- M'Sadokues ventured, the locksmiths (i.e., gunsmiths) of *les* Iglismôniak didn't have full confidence in the internal sear half-cocks they built. The mechanism, after all, was a *French* invention. It had been devised circa 1605 by the brilliant Norman locksmith Marin le Bourgeoys --if de Sabrevois remembered the name correctly, -- who was, naturally enough (being French), also a brilliant *artiste,* clockmaker, sculptor, and all-around incomparable genius.[123] The English locksmiths, being new to the mechanism, likely lacked full confidence in their fabrication of the device. So they added on the dog hook as "backup" in the event their internal sear failed. Or perhaps it was a matter of simply leaving the alemos on an old lockplate and (already notched) cock they were using in building a musketoon* with an entirely new internal ignition mechanism.

Asokw Mgezo indulged himself in the pleasure of easing the hammer forward to half cock. An additional quite positive feature, M'Sadokues and Clément pointed out, was another safety measure. It was the accidental discharges - preventing hide "hammer stall" (or 'frizzen boot') sheathed onto the striking steel. By the look of it, *le* akuamalsid had provided it himself. The leather appeared to have been home-cured, stitched together from two small pieces of the hide of some game animal. Such sheaths were usually attached to a thong that was tied to a fusil's trigger guard. As this firearm lacked a trigger guard, the thong was wrapped around the "wrist" of the shoulder stock.

As their *naturel docteur* retrieved the scout's waistbelt, an unquestionably obsolete feature, they noted, was the weapon sheathed within the belt's leather scabbard. Dagger-bladed, it was a "plug bayonet." An antique, it was the original form of *baïonnette*. Its haft had been whittled to fit directly into the muzzle of the musketoon.

*A musketoon is a firelock that has a *shorter barrel* than the standard full length musket.

---

[123] "An Invention of Genius — The Flintlock," Chapter 5, pp. 22 - 26, *Pageant of the Gun,* by Harold L. Peterson, Doubleday & Company, Garden City, NY, 1967.

Informed by the cadet and M'Sadokues that the formidable dagger might be kebahigan-metsetsaka -- a plug bayonet, -- from the look of the brass – tipped wooden handle, Asokw Mgezo experimentally inserted the *poniard* into the muzzle. *Oui,* it fit snugly. O'hôô, kisi! --Yes, it is! -- The firelock's muzzle was somewhat "belled," or flared, and this helped you seat *la baïonnette* quickly and easily. By the same token the "trumpet" flaring enabled the fighter to recharge powder and ball more swiftly. A handy blade to have on you in a desperate, close-quarters fight when, suddenly, there was absolutely no time to reload the barrel, prime the flashpan, close it, and then thumb the hammer back to full cock. But you could instead very quickly insert the bayonet.

Rather than featuring an iron or brass guard where the blade emerged from the handle, there were instead, in that area, two rotund protuberances of wood that bulged spherically. All three looked curiously at this feature, not having seen such on the plug bayonets being carried, hither and yon, by habitant *milicens* who carried old-fashioned muskets. Fusils probably inherited from their *grand péres*. This bayonet seemed to display another rather incomprehensible *Anglais* oddity.

Yet, to young de Sabrevois, to whom many things were new, it was vaguely familiar. The feature was not exclusively English, he began to realize… He had seen one or two like it in Québec City, perhaps, even in his own relations' ivy-grown chateau back in la Belle France. That was it! Now he remembered! He had seen such a poniard sheathed at the waist of one of those suits of armor left over from the age of chivalry, standing along the walls of the grand hallway of the château. And it signified..?

Suddenly he burst out laughing. Now he knew what it is! He explained to his *naturel* companions that it's called a *bouvillon poignard*. Originally such blades had been an auxiliary sidearm supplemental to the arms of knights such as swords, battle-axes and jousting lances. *Bouvillon* in Iglismôniui is "bullock," he guessed, for a bovine male, a bull. As a "*ball*ock dagger" it is intended to invoke the powerful beast, and at the same time signify something more directly associated with the knight himself. With his manliness, Clément explained, chuckling. He elaborated, mentioning *testicules,* which M'Sadokues adroitly translated into apenak,[*] indicating the same thing. Grasping the cadet's meaning, the two Alnôbak could not help but laugh as well.

The peculiar knife would somehow help enhance the potency of his zanôbauôganui --manliness,--?? Cloud Eagle smirked. "Aligek oligo! That's good!" he laughed. Not that he thought he needed such enhancement. But the more the merrier!! This curious plunder from the poor fleeing ozigôuzo -- sufferer, -- is getting better by the minute. Something else good about the red stained firelock, Nikola observed, was the lack of a trigger guard, *even if* it had been left off for a parsimonious reason. Pmi tka'ua pebon -- During the cold of winter, -- when you don't want to touch metal without gloves or mittens on, and when any mechanism tends to be stiff, you could pull

***Or** can be understood to describe what are called "ground nuts" or Indian potatoes, *Apios*

the trigger wearing quite thick mittens, there being no trigger guard to make it clumsy, difficult. And the lack of a ramrod-securing "pipe" didn't matter... the barrel was so short, and therefore the fullest part of the forestock so comparatively long, that the hole in the forestock to return the rammer to was quite sufficient to protect the stubby ramrod. The lack of an iron or brass "thimble" was just one less detail to worry about.

The hybrid internal sear half-cock safety catch / "doglock" musketoon was strictly a fighting weapon, a close-quarters paskhigan at that... there were no sights on it, neither a front sight blade nor any kind of rear sight. This might seem a problem if you wished to hunt with it, but then you could do as did the Iglismôniak and Tesasemôniak[124] -- Dutchmen.-- Load it with "buck and ball," one large full-sized ball and several smaller balls, whereby the scattering of multiple missiles will compensate for an errant single ball. Ac'hi -- Also, -- M'Sadokues emphasized, in time the medical man could trade for a longer barrel, replacing the present one, a barrel furnished with front and rear sights, or a front sight blade at least.

Cloud Eagle buckled on the bayonet-scabbard - hung leather belt, concealing it under his waist sash. He didn't want sunlight reflecting off the metallic belt buckle, alerting enemies to his presence. Other warriors and fusiliers were flowing around them now, the flames around the mill having been brought under control. The Lieutenant's / Pmauikho's mountain detachment was withdrawing back down into the valley. Le Mercier had no intention of garrisoning a charred, smoking ruin. A few paused to look at Asokw Mgezo's plunder, drawn by laughter and the bemused expressions on the faces of the three. The medauinno aspirant looked at the hat of bast and the kerchief that had served as a sweatband, which still lay where they had fallen. He decided not to take them. Somehow they didn't appeal to him, especially the kerchief. It looked like it might still be damp from the sweat of the sufferer... a sixth sense nagged at him not to touch it... the same for the hat. They had been in too much contact with the skin of the ozigôuzo. And the broad-brimmed hat would interfere with the warrior's feathers tied into his scalp roach. If he needed something over his head in inclement weather, he had the wool flannel hood that was tucked away in the blanket roll he had left at the foot of the slope. If anyone else wanted the abandoned items, they could have them. As the detachment gathered at the copse of hemlocks and rotting saw-cut logs preparatory to filing downhill, they met two *fusiliers de la Marine* who had finally attained the edge of the recently embattled area. Le Mercier's valley contingent, hearing all the shooting from above, had become concerned that the mountain detachment might be in trouble. *Le pair* had been detailed to climb the slope and find out what was going on.

They were relieved to find that all was well, that the enemy had been soundly defeated. L' Mercier's / Pmauikho's war party was about to come together again.

---

tuberosa. Reference *Western Abenaki Dictionary,* Volume II, p. 269. [124] Flemish or Dutch: "The word is taken from the English: Dutchman." *French Abenaki Dictionary,* p. 262, the Rev. Joseph Aubery, circa 1690s - 1700, English translation by Chief Stephen Laurent, 1995.

Curious as to what his new acquisition could do (it was still loaded), and to again demonstrate that he was as kagini -- strong, brave, -- as any who had fought that day, Cloud Eagle volunteered to cover the withdrawal. Might an especially bold enemy shadow the retiring strike force and attempt a parting shot? As the allies descended past him, their nbizonhouad was focused so intently on covering their backs that he nearly tripped over one of the old saw-cut logs! Ôigôdamiui, Happily, that constituted the most untoward event that was experienced as they filed unmolested downslope. When the mountain detachment rejoined the rest of the war party in the valley, accepting the congratulations of those who had remained below, a few scouts were sent forward. Their mission was to advance within sight of the cut in the range ahead that Jonas T'songeba had alluded to. They would observe the exit of the apcikozidsik -- opponents; enemies -- from the mountain tote road and ascertain whether they were resuming their withdrawal toward Fort Orange.

In the meanwhile the majority of the reunited war party fell back somewhat. They settled down for the night in a good defensive position among the trees on a rock-ribbed hill affording a good view southward. The clamor of battle had brought forward the main French and Alnôbak *armée*. They were needed. Having engaged in a knock-down, drag-out fight with the enemy and having wounded among them, it was time that Lieutenant Mercier's / *Guerre Capitaine* Pmauikho's men were relieved. Though not all would retire northward… Le Lieutenant himself, proud of the day's accomplishment and seeking yet more *honneur,* would continue on, the Marine *troupes* under his

The author as Asokw Mgezo keeping a sharp lookout as he "covers the back trail" with his newly acquired doglock musketoon, following column of French and Indians withdrawing down mountainside, Monkton, VT.

command having no choice but to accompany him. Chief Pmauikho and his fighters, however, planned to fight no more. "Apcikozidsik aaok poleuadak... -- The enemy is on the run....-- "cigitaua agemôgik alosak -- let them go." --

And it wasn't just that the foe was withdrawing, seemed toothless, but that a continued southward course presented another hazard. The enemy threatened danger in another way. Not even intentionally, but with what could be dangerous in any case. Kizi agemôuô zôgelamalsouôgan -- It's their health-condition, -- agemôuô akuamalsouôgan -- their sickness. -- By coming into close contact with the sufferers the warriors could become infected themselves -- and could bring the disease home to their families! Cloud Eagle, Pmauikho, Jonas, Walks Quietly, and others had seen the fusil-abandoning one up close; and their nbizonhouad had observed gagasoui akuamalsidzik -- more and more sick ones -- through the Lieutenant's far-seeing lôbodi. Pmauikho, "He Who Goes Ahead," was not volunteering to continue ahead in this instance. Asokw Mgezo was emphatic about returning home. Sôgemô ta agma migakauinnoak idziak olestôuadinak... --The chief and his fighting-men brethren agreed...-- agemôuô acouiba -- they should -- "poniadoak kuôgueniui agemôuô d' nikôni -- quit while they are ahead."-- The dawn brought great relief to Cloud Eagle as he stepped northward.

Soon he would be seeing Ôeoandamsko, he thought joyfully, and their little one. Agma linkauadsi na agemôuô maôuito -- He hoped that they were all right. -- He had joined the southward expedition with reluctance in the first place, loathe to leave Wise Woman while their little girl was still so small. However, he *had* to go. They had to throw back Neskamegueziak -- the Destroyers -- before they reached Mazipskoik!

9. Nebizon Ôadzapkol, Piseuakamigw-Môdsagimek Apenak, ta Ôskahla Minigha -- Medicine Roots, Wild-Growing Tubers, and Fresh Greens --

The weather remained fair as they took the trail northward, making for the marshy headwaters of Lake Champlain liuitam 'Abazi Sibo' -- named "Wood Creek"-- (at that time the waterway was, in places, blocked by fallen trees). The members of Pmauikho's war party had originally gone south from Mazipskoik by different routes. Some had been detailed to go as pemosauinnoak -- walkers, -- trekking inland on the east side of Pitoubagw -- the Water Between -- (Lake Champlain) while others went in their bark canoes. Yôgik medzessalak lipabadegibiak,[125] These latter paddled in a zigzag pattern, so as to search for enemy spies, visiting various islands, and didn't want to draw too far ahead of the inland nopaosauinnoak -- scouts, -- (literally "far walking persons"). The

---

[125] "Paddle zigzag," Lipabadegibia. *Western Abenaki Dictionary*, Volume II, p. 278.

entire group had started out in canoes, but, after paddling a certain distance south to a point where *les Anglais'* Mohican and/or Maguak vanguard might have penetrated to, half of the band had gone ashore to scout inland. They had agreed to rendezvous on the peninsula where a Dutch / English expedition had built a small fort in 1690 (and subsequently abandoned; the present-day Chimney Point, Vermont). They had continued the same pattern as they went further south; exchanging the canoes, scouting inland, former far-walkers paddling. Tạ nolemibiạk -- And paddling softly, very slowly (silently)[126]-- the lake below the point narrowing and therefore increasingly pregnant with the danger of being fired on from shore. At times the paddlers coursed among concealing reeds of paludal margins. Some extensive 'looks' south of (what is now called) the Crown Point Narrows, the canoes were finally beached along Wood Creek. There the lake was considered, at that time, to be riverine. The Iroquois-derived "Ticonderoga" -- meaning 'Noisy,' refers to the falls of the Rivière La Chute, from Lake George. -- Also reputedly "Where the Two Waters [Rivers] Meet," the other 'river' being Lake Champlain. French swivel gun-armed *batteaux* were also drawn up there, though military *pionniers*-bearing batteaux pressed yet ahead, their axe-wielding crews cutting away fallen trees restricting onward navigation. Still further they found fresh-cut trees pushed out of the way… the work of British pioneers hewing their way north. South of that was found evidence of boat construction and encampments. All recently abandoned. Rejoined by the landward scouts, Pmauikho's band had merged with Lieutenant Le Mercier's vanguard troop, continuing forward under joint command.

It turned out that it wasn't necessary to trek as far as anticipated to recover their canoes. Rear guard members of the Canadian array, the creek now more navigable thanks to the hard-chopping *pionniers,* had borrowed the canoes and paddled them further south. This was good news for the wounded, who could now relax restfully in the bark boats while others wielded the paddles homeward.

Recovering their mạskuạiuiguạolạl[127]-- birch bark canoes, -- the detachment didn't embark immediately. By now they were running low on provisions. The injured would remain by the canoes, looked after by Cloud Eagle, while the able-bodied deployed in the forest to hunt. Their medical man also searched around their temporary camp, looking for early-flowering herbs, the nebizon of which would be helpful to his patients. This was a great relief to M'Sadokues, the most grievously wounded among them, who needed to rest, to be still for a while, so that his injuries could begin to heal. Asokw Mgezo, always on the lookout, had noticed certain early spring flowers blossoming in the area of the camp when they had passed this way south, the roots of which should be good for medicine. There hadn't been enough time to collect any then,

---

[126] *Ibid,* p. 278.

[127] Literally **birch bark** canoes, rather than simply "canoes" or 'bark canoes.' The term can be broken down into at least six components: 1. Mạskuạmozi: Birch tree, 2. Mạskuạ: the **bark** of the birch, 3. uigi: piece, 4. uạ: *of,* 5. ol: boat, and, 6. ạl: inanimate plural suffix: Boat**s**. *Western Abenaki Dictionary,* Volume II, p. 37 and p. 60.

but now he would find them.

The first herb he looked for, somewhat hurriedly, was a species that was among the earliest to blossom. He remembered some nearby... they featured rather austere maroon flowers. They came in brighter colors as well, occasionally, such as white, pink, and greenish-yellow.[128] Among brighter, cheerier flowers she might be called "austere" but certainly lending a note of (what the French would surely call) *"gaieté de cur"* -- against the rather bleak early spring background. Their roots were highly medicinal. He soon found them, and was relieved to find that they had not yet gone to seed. Not that he needed the petals. The blossoms only made them easier to find. The Canadiens, he recalled, also dubbed the flower *lis* -- lily -- though he thought it was quite different from those large, creamy white blossoms he had seen painted on walls and icons in their prayer-houses at St. Jean and Chambly. He called the purplish-flowering plant minôbouigen sippen,[129] and, when digging up a portion was careful to leave most of the root system intact. In a less hasty situation he would have set himself down next to the flower, calmly put some odamô in the bowl of his pipe-tomahawk, lit it, and had a casual smoke while mentally explaining to the plant why he needed its nebizon. At the same time he studied the herb's characteristics, engraving its features in his mind for future reference. He then would have raised the pipe, gratefully releasing smoke to the Four Winds. But for now he dug up some of the roots, putting down an offering of tobacco or killinick when finished. Would clean the roots and pulverize them, mixing the fibers and crumbs into a brew for M'Sadokues and the other casualties. While the bandages that de Sabrevois had applied kept Nikola's wounds from bleeding externally, the nbizonhouad's trillium concoction would help keep him from bleeding from the inside. He also mixed the shreds of a few other medicinal herbs into the potion to ntôuiha ali kagininôgw ali peguatôsw -- make [it] as powerful as possible. -- As he did so he remembered that, about a year ago, he and Wise Woman had gathered elements of trillium ôadzapkôl -- roots -- as her time drew near, well knowing such root material is excellent medicine for stopping bleeding after parturition.[130] They had ranged from flower to flower over a wide area. The object was to take only a small amount of ôadzapkuiia, roots material, from each plant, leaving each one largely intact. The Alnôbak custom was to allow them to continue to perpetuate, as they are not abundant flowers (the same rule applies, or *should* apply, to herbalists today, whether or not there are local laws for the protection of trillium).

---

[128] Pp. 20 - 21, *Trillium,* in **Roots** *An Underground Botany and Forager's Guide*, Douglas B. Elliot, 1976, The Chatham Press, Old Greenwich, CT.

[129] Minôbouigen: 'It is violet,' p. 45, *Abenakis & English Dialogues*, Chief Joseph Laurent, 1884. For sippen, lily, p. 341, Rev. J. Aubery's *French Abenaki Dictionary*, c. 1700, English by Chief Stephen Laurent, 1995.

[130] Genus *Liliaecea, Trillium erectum,* **(red) trillium,** cited in Elliot's *Roots* as having "astringent properties useful for all kinds of bleeding, from simple nosebleed to more serious internal hemorrhaging," p. 20. It is also a "tonic to the female reproductive system, and to treat related "squaw" disorders," Elliot, *Ibid,* p. 20.

Akisitôn'i
maasa
siguan
kadauik -
hôgan'ua
mkuô -
bamegua
sippen'a
môdzagi -
mek ônda
nôui odagw
agma
uigiuômo

-- Author's early spring photo of a reddish trillium growing not far from his home. --

Having warmed the brew over the band's campfire and given it to Nikola, others among the more lightly wounded being urged to drink some, Asokw Mgezo returned to the flowers he had taken material from, lowered himself, taking out agma odamôgan -- his pipe -- to perform the ritual of explaining his need, and his gratitude, that he had put off. In the healing arts time is often of the essence, and he was now rather contrite for having been so hasty, having dug up root material with only rushed apologies. He carefully explained that M'Sadokues was kassôuadik -- a very valuable person, -- even more valuable, in fact, than tebaï minaôngan[131] taba pabasiui -- a bushel and a half -- of *ginseng*. Ônda, nisal tebaï minaônganal! -- No, two bushels! -- By citing that other highly valued medicinal root he hoped the trillium spirit would be duly impressed. Even Auanock, 'the Strangers,' who were not as familiar with various herbs in Ô'banakik -- Abenaki Land... -- held such a high regard for ginseng that it is, to them, as precious as "uizôuimôni -- yellow money," -- i.e., **gold**.[132]

That done, exhaling a sigh of relief -- he hoped Spirit would be satisfied ...he set out to explore the terrain around their campsite more thoroughly. Other early herbs, such as those green-leafed from tubers, he knew were coming up now, about the same time that trillium flowered. One such was mozilalo -- moose's tongue.[133] -- What, if he

---

[131] *French Abenaki Dictionary*, Aubery / Laurent, p. 362. Aubery's Tebaï minaôngan equals eight gallons; a bushel. The umlaut over i of **tebaï** is from Father Aubery's French spelling of Abenaki words.

[132] *Western Abenaki Dictionary,* Volume II, p. 170. The equivalent for silver is simply môni, p. 351, *Ibid.*

[133] P. 413, *Erythronium americanum,* popularly called, in English, 'dog-tooth violet,' 'adder's tongue,' and 'trout lily,' *Ibid.* Also Petersen's *Edible Wild Plants*, 1977, Houghton-Mifflin, New York, pp. 74 - 75.

remembered aright from when he had been small, his family making their way northward from Massa'tzosek -- Massachusetts[134]-- the Pastoniak called "adder's tongue." Adder's tongue? Wasn't an adder (he pronounced it *addaɬ*) some kind of snake? The leaf didn't look much like skog'i ilalo'a -- a snake's tongue -- to him. Much more like a moose's tongue, quite. -- And also "trout lily"..? Is he right? Agma ao maôuigek, agma namito na -- He is right, he could see that.-- The mottled leaf indeed resembles the dark green and black sides of zibos skotam'a -- a brook trout,-- and the peskuasauôn -- flower,[135]-- that is, *uizôua*taua, the *yellow* flower, might be, he supposed, the same as what the French call *lis*. He knew they were up, as he had seen them growing on the late mountain battleground, especially where the akuamalsid, sickly one, had dropped the musketoon and the ballock - hafted bayonet.

He didn't have to go very far before he found an abundance of mozilaloal, moose ('s) tongues, sprouting. Mingled among them were, indicated by their small but cheerful pink and light blue blossoms, another tuber that the Pastoniak, if he remembered correctly, called "fairy spuds."[136] "Spuds" wasn't hard to pronounce, but he had trouble with "fairy," thinking of it as p'halie. And just what is *'p'halie?'* "Spuds"… that 's' at the end -- did that indicate more than one, in Iglismôniui? -- In Alnôbaiui the word would be pluralized as spudsak. They are small, round tubers that in his own tongue are called apenak.[137] They are much like what the French term *patate,* (sometimes put as "pomme de terre.") The apenak of the "p'halie spudsak" can be termed apen*iz*ak because they are so small. In fact the tubers of the mozilalo and the spring beauties (fairy spuds, so-called) are both so tiny that they are hardly worth all the trouble to dig up …even though you don't want to uproot all of them, wishing to leave sufficient for self-propagation. Msalid alokauôgan…-- So much work… -- ôadsi dagasiatta! -- for so little! --

Though it was a tedious employment, Cloud Eagle was quite glad to be availing himself of the tiny "patates." They came under the category of fresh greens, which was exactly what his company needed right now, especially the wounded. Though they

---

[134] P. 91, *Abenaki Indian Legends, Grammar and Place Names,* Chief Henry Lorne Masta, 1932, Odanak Reserve, P.Q., the chapter *The Meaning of Indian Names of Rivers, Lakes, Etc.*

[135] Literally "opening one," i.e., a blossom, p. 151, *Western Abenaki Dictionary,* Volume II. The prefix pesk has in common the sense of *opening out* as with a gunshot, *bask*ha, p. 346, and gun, *bask*higan or paskhigan, "exploding implement," p. 177, *Ibid.* A flower opens with infinite slowness, an explosion instantly. Both "pesk" or baskaka, open. Baska*b*a: "It is open water," p. 274, *Ibid.*

[136] Peterson Field Guides, pp. 32 - 33, under "spring beauty," *Claytonia* spp. *Edible Wild Plants,* 1977. Also pp. 108 - 109 in *Wilderness Harvest, A Guide to Edible Wild Plants in North America,* Alyson H. Knap, 1979. Pagurian Press Ltd., Toronto, Canada.

[137] "Ground nut or Indian potato," *apios tuberosa*, apen, singular, apenak, plural. *Western Abenaki Dictionary,* Volume II, p. 300.

wouldn't be eating the green *leaves* of the plants above ground; the underground tubers contained vitamins and minerals that would stave off scurvy and other illnesses.

When he had set out, others had stepped into the forest as well, such as Pmauikho, T'sôngeba, and that new acquaintance, 'Pepôkuan.' As they were carrying their firelocks, he assumed that they were after fresh meat. Pepôkuan was not only carrying his usual kuena paskhigan -- long gun,-- but, the nbizônhouad assumed, also his short-barreled, much smaller alômsauaiyas... -- a word that is also a sentence, as it means an *inside the clothes thing.*[138] Otherwise called a pistel, the latter drawn from French and English. This firelock is so stubby (carried as "backup" in the event that your long-barreled fusil misfires) that you can indeed carry one inside your clothes. As he presumed Pepôkuan was doing. He had ventured forth wearing, over his shirt of fustian, a woolen pebonibitkôzon -- winter's coat -- (the morning temperature having been quite cool), this one a short-skirted garment that *les Anglais* term a "coatee." The pebonibitkôzon opens down the front, as any pitkôzon would, but for extra warmth there is additional cloth there, at the opening, the two sides overlapping one over the other. The coatee didn't really need buttons or ties to close it (though you might want to add a toggle at the throat) since the average hunter cinched his waist with a leather belt or woolen sash. Often both, leather giving more support to your hunting knife (if carried on your hip), small belt pouch, and tomahawk. On your upper torso the garment is kept closed by the shoulder straps of your necessaries pitôgan and powder horn. If you aren't carrying a fusil the shoulder strap or straps for your arrows quiver can serve. The material in front is so generous that, once overlapped and waist-cinched, you can easily make an extra 'bag' out of it, carrying all manner of things. In battle, in the event that you suffer a "flash in the pan," an onrushing enemy, bayonet-fixed musket leveled (or war club upraised) -- giving you no time to re-prime your flash pan,-- can be in for a devastating surprise when the "defenseless one" whips out his loaded and primed alômsauaiyas..!

Now that he possessed his own firelock, he was interested in learning everything he could about using it efficiently and accurately. He planned to ply Pepôkuan with a number of questions. If anyone was a firearms expert he should be, as his very name indicated "Firelock." The Pepô of the name is related to baskha or 'pask,' shot, that is, explosion, in Alnôbaiui. This is thanks to Algonquian linguistic affinity, Pepôkuan being a member of an Algonquian nation to the south -- quite far to the south and west,-- whose very name, Suônniak, means (in their dialect) Southern People, suôanni being related to the Alnôbaiui souanaki -- southern *land.*[139] --

---

[138] P. 291, *Ibid,* "Inside the clothes thing, a gun hidden inside the shirt, a pistol."

[139] *Western Abenaki Dictionary*, Volume II, p. 367.

[140] The so-called "onions" should not be confused with Europe-derived domestic onions. The "onions" of the Winooski Valley and the northern U.S. (and southern Canada) in general are more accurately termed *leeks,* wild

Camping overnight on their way south, following the enemy, Cloud Eagle had noticed that Pepôkuan was closely associated with Jonas, two fighting men he had been, until then, unfamiliar with. He Who Goes Ahead had introduced them, their nbizonhouad learning that T'sôngeba was Mohican, one of those from the southward whom the Pastoniak call a "River Indian." The English appellation stems from the Mohican heartland along what they, *les Anglais,* termed "Hudson's River." It is that stream the Muheconnuck themselves are named after, indicating that they are the people "of the Rising and Falling Water," i.e., the tidal nature of that great river. As he talked with Jonas Cloud Eagle assumed that Pepôkuan was also Muheconw, as the latter and T'sôngeba conversed easily in the Mohican dialect. He could understand some of what they were saying, as Muheconui is an Algonquian language, a variant of Alnôbaiui. Their speech was comprehensible since they, avoiding the Albany rum purveyors, were integrating themselves into the Ô'banakiak, having established themselves among the Ôinuzkiak near the mouth of the Ôinoztekw -- Onion Land River.[140] --Tiring of digging up the tubers of such peskuasauônizal -- small flowers, -- Cloud Eagle moved on, determined to find less tedious pickings. He had made a quick circuit of the area on the way south, remembering seeing what *might* be, seen from a distance, -- clusters of edible greens. He called them megoakw kizoskôganal -- swamp sunflowers. -- The Pastoniak called (if he remembered correctly after all this time), such early greens "cowslips," or "marsh marigolds."[141] "Marigolds" indicate their bright yellow peskuasauônal, he surmised. Because the soil was well - watered in that area, was rich, he would also look for the vine-like stalks trailing from those much preferable apenak --tubers -- the Ô'banakiak know as skibô.[142] These would be *true* apenak, larger in size,

---

leeks, *Allium tricoccum,* also called "ramp." *Edible Wild Plants,* Peterson, pp. 52 - 53. Notice, though, how ôinoz (leek), if spelled with a circumflex 'o' -- ô -- rather than with a w, *does* resemble the European word 'onion.' And leeks *do have* an oniony *taste*. An ancient Asian word, 'onion,' having migrated west to Europe, and a similar word, ôinoz (*small* onion) having migrated east, long, long ago, across the Pacific... coming back together (in a manner of speaking)... in North America? [141]*Caltha palustris*; reference Knap's *Wilderness Harvest,* 1979, Pagurian Press Ltd., Toronto, Canada. pp. 56 - 57.

[142] *Abenakis and English Dialogues,* Chief Joseph Laurent, p. 32. "Skibô" because they're good even when uncooked... "a group name, ôskipoôg, what is eaten fresh," p. 455, *Western Abenaki Dictionary,* Volume I.

Author's photo of megoakw kizoskôganal, swamp sunflowers (cowslips), showing bright yellow blossoms and fresh green leaves.

Had *agemôuô* -- **they** -- done it here too? He wondered, --had assumed the present location of Goes Ahead's band was a bit too far north for enemy Auanock to have wreaked their vegetative depredations… as they had done in their colonies to the east and southward. *Ônda! Ônda yo ac'hi!* --No! Not here too! -- Then he remembered that they were camped not all that far from the ruined sawmill.

he was confident, the "potato" tubers much worthier of his harvesting efforts. The latter were not, he understood, leafing out or flowering yet, not for another moon. He felt that he could spot them anyway. *Pmi pebona* -- When winter came -- the plants had shed their leaves and clusters of seed pods (resembling pea pods), the stalks drying out to somewhat of a light hue, their delicate branches (now) showing tentative buds. The stalks ought to be still of a whitish color. Occasionally seed pods stubbornly hold on all winter, instead of falling off. If you notice even one such pod (soon to be pushed off by new growth), you know you are looking at *skibô*. The next step is to dig down for the tubers, which should have survived winter's frost. *Tali yo lômpkipodiga'ua pamigadek* -- At this time of year, -- *siguak* -- in the spring, -- some of the tubers might be rotten from winter's frost, but others will be good. Usually they are strung along their root similar to beads on a necklace. Like the leaves of the cowslips, you *may* want to cook them in boiling water. Then fry the *skibôiia* some more *alômi moôuin bemi* -- in bear fat -- (*ala dômô kalaa bemi* -- or some such grease) -- *ôadsi uigatôzo* -- for the best taste. *Skibô* indicates that which can be eaten raw. You can cook them if you wish.

He found the slough, and saw with satisfaction that there were no *uizôuataual* -- yellow flowers -- blossoming as yet, though the bright green leaves were *ôlibaguezo* -- well developed. -- It's the leaves you want. They contain the healthy nutrients. Now they would have fresh, very fresh greens. "*Oguaskô kagui nodzi nbizonhouad* kassauighôzab -- Just what the doctor ordered." -- He had to step on mossy hummocks and so forth to keep from sinking ankle-deep in the cold water of the slough, but the effort was worth it. As he cut clusters of leaves and deposited them in the hemp sack that he was carrying his tubers in, he kept looking around for skibô. Attempting to concentrate on thoughts of appreciation for the abundant "cowslips" …as he glanced around, expecting to discern at least one skibô growth, an emotion of bitterness crept in, inspired by his (so far futile) search for the latter.

Axe-wielding Iglismôn/Dutsmôniak pioneers had, probably, cut away obstructions in the creek this far north… not all the evidence of chopping had been executed by Canadien *pionniers*. Enemy scouts, their pioneers, and the vanguard of soldiers guarding them …all would have had to camp along the waterway. And, most likely, would have looked around for skibô to supplement their rations.

The more he thought, the angrier he became, double-thinking as he apologized to Spirit for allowing himself to be distracted from gratitude toward the greens he was harvesting. Agma aob ibi ôskinnos'a zibiui -- He had been a mere boy then, -- he recalled, but remembered his elders commenting on how their ancestral Alnôbak of the coast had, when the Iglismôniak first came, only a few and famishing, prevented them from starving by, among other things, showing them where to dig up and how to process skibô (the olden Alnôbak called the tuber *ô'pniss*).[143] When the newcomers had increased in number, buying and claiming more and more land, they built grim - looking "gebahoduigamigol -- shut-up houses."--[144] They called them "gaols" (i.e., jails). The ancestors had never seen such structures before. *Les Anglais* then forbid their former benefactors, along with other hard rules, from harvesting skibô in the woods near Iglismôniak dwellings. You could be, and some **were,** thrown into those kacibainôguezo[145] uiguômal -- terrible - looking houses -- as punishment. Caught harvesting skibô there again, and the "offender" could be whipped![146] The Iglismôniak are strong believers in what they call "private Property," which doesn't merely indicate clothing, a hunter's bow and arrows, personal articles, but, to them, especially applies to ki -- land, the earth.-- Just like pots and pans, it, in their system, is something that can be bought and sold, and, once purchased, becomes sacrosanct to the new owner. Unless it is *N'd'ákinna* -- *Our* land, *our* ground, -- "Alnôbai aki -- Indian's land."-- That they regard as pizeuakamigw, *uninhabited* land, "wilderness," where they feel free to come

---

[143] Knap's *Wilderness Harvest,* p.106.

[144] *Western Abenaki Dictionary,* Volume II, p. 207.

[145] *Ibid,* p. 401.

[146] P. 106, *Wilderness Harvest*, Knap: "Upon the arrival of the Pilgrims at Plymouth Rock, the natives shared their knowledge of the plant with the newcomers, helping the settlers through their first, hard winter in the new world. Alas, ***, less than twenty years later laws were passed forbidding the Indians to harvest groundnut tubers on English lands, on penalty of jailing, and whipping for a second offense."

and go, some hunting animals, taking out deer, to name one auaas that the People depend upon for meat and hides. As if the forest is wholly and totally theirs, but at the same time waxing wroth if Alnôbak nadialuinnoak -- Native hunters -- kill and carry home the nidazoak, domestic animals, they call *cattle*. Even if the cows or pigs are roaming freely about just like wild nolkak, deer. It is acceptable for them to kill the People's 'cattle,' the nolkak, but an awful offense if Alnôbak harvest any of the blithely wandering kaozak. Was it any wonder that the warriors of the Chief Metacom -- "King Philip" to those Anglais who called themselves "Pilgrims"-- finally gathered into a war council and struck out? They fought to push the expanding Iglismôniak back to their coastal enclaves. It had been a good thing to trade with the Strangers, exchanging commonplace furs and hides to acquire goods of metal and cloth that the People are unable to manufacture themselves. But their early new - found "brethren" had multiplied into tebaldônsuak -- dominators. -- Acting as if they were conquerors rather than nidômbak -- our friends.--

Asokw Mgezo was sure that his ancestors had advised the Pilgrims that, when harvesting skibô, they should dig up only a few of the "Indian potatoes" of a given plant, leaving some of the roots intact… allowing the plants to perpetuate themselves. Agemôuô 'aoakdsi dali --They will be there -- pmi kia coualdô baami -- when you need more. -- However, the Strangers had haughtily ignored this, the advice coming from "meer Salvages," tearing up the entire plant and consuming all of its tubers. They arrogantly assumed there would always be more, a perpetual supply, "out there" in the "endless wilderness." When they carved out farms further and further inland, claiming wide areas around them as exclusively theirs, they found that the tubers were no longer as abundant as formerly. They became jealous of anyone gleaning skibô from the earth that the Alnôbak had harvested from, and conserved, for millennia.

Beached maskua-iolagol -- birch bark canoes -- such as *Guerre Capitaine* Pmauikho's scouts had on Lake Champlain's Wood Creek, following firefight at the sawmill and used to carry wounded fighters home.
Photo is of birch bark canoes owned by author.

10. 'Kullos'kahp' Ôpcito Pemôuzouinnoak --"Man from Nothing"[147] Creates [Living] Human Beings --

As Cloud Eagle contemplated the injustices that had been wreaked on his forebears, who had done so much to enable the Pilgrims and Puritans to survive …simultaneously striving to harvest the swamp-sunflower leaves with a grateful attitude, his hitherto clouded brow brightened quite unexpectedly. His face split into a grin …remembrance of an atookuakun -- wonder tale, -- a creation story, insinuated itself into his mind. A favor bequeathed by all - knowing Spirit..? Debidahôdamenmek pabômiui tsibaginôguezoui'ua 'T'saukuakuak' --Thinking about the ugliness of the "Sword Men,"-- even though of their ungrateful *moral* ugliness, not so much physical, may have triggered his access to the story.

When the Great Mystery had sent the creative force known today as Kullos'kahp[148] to the world, the first beings he had given life to were namasak, fish, auaasak -- animals, -- ta lidooak -- and those that fly.-- Ônda Pemôuzouinnoak ali askua[149]-- No People as yet.-- Even Kullos'kahp himself had the appearance of an olanigw[150] (and still does, presumably, wherever he is). Being mighty himself, and as yet rather inexperienced, Kullos'kahp naturally made those beings quite large. Gigantic, compared to the auaasak of today. And rather aggressive, as the earth they were born to was itself rather new… saki gôuigen -- quite rough, -- rather crude, kassi auaasak uadzônabanik gôuigen ac'hi -- so the animals had [to be] rough as well. -- Later, as we know, he squeezed those fish and animals down to size. Minaguiba, auani ualdam? -- Though, who knows? -- He may not be quite finished yet. Those ocean-dwelling auaasak, podabak -- whales[151]-- are still, even today, quite enormous.

Kullos'kahp lived an interesting life, in those dawn-time seasons of the world, his spirit of creativity given absolutely free rein. Even the weather was fascinating, constantly changing, ranging from fiercely raw to sweetly mild and everything in between. Especially here, in Ô'ban Aki -- the Dawn Land, -- his favorite region of the world. But the day came when he felt dissatisfied. Something was missing, something that he felt a need for. He realized what it was. He needed beings like himself! And yet not *exactly* like himself, not as olaniguak. Beings not the same, but who could *think* as

---

[147] *How Glooskap Outwits the Ice Giants*, Introduction, retold by Howard Norman, 1989, Little, Brown Co., Toronto, Boston & London.
[148] Called Nanabozho by the Anishinaabeg, Moshup by the Wampanoag, the Niantic, Nipmuck, &c.
[149] *Western Abenaki Dictionary,* Volume II, "person," p. 286. Adding the animate plural *ak* makes pemôuzouinno, person, into the equivalent of "people." Pemôuzouinno literally means **living** person, a more specific designation than the more abstract English 'person.'
[150] P.148, *Ibid, Martes pennanti*: "Fisher, black cat."
[151] "Blowing out water" creatures, *Ibid,* p. 444.

he did. Who he could talk to, could engage in interesting conversations with. He decided to create... Nitami Pemôuzouinnoak -- ...the First People.--

What made the greens-gatherer smile was the reaction of all those auaasak when Kullos'kahp's new-borns appeared. Of course, well before he attempted to create the first human beings, the Hero had wandered widely, searching out his animal, fish, reptile, and bird creations mezi ôdauiui akinna -- all over the world. -- They were so huge, for the most part, and aggressive, that if he made his People modestly sized (compared to himself) as he planned, the enormous, and habitually hostile auaasak would easily wipe them out. Cloud Eagle surmised that Kullos'kahp, looking ahead very wisely... didn't want a potentially ambitious one among the humans to conceive that he or she could rival him. *He* would remain their guide, their Elder Brother, their Chief. If they were diminutive no one among them could entertain such an ambition. So he polled all the creatures he could find. And indeed, when questioned, almost every one haughtily declared how badly he or she would treat such small, feeble creatures. How forcefully they would trample, tear up, devour, kick apart, throw trees down on, and otherwise destroy the contemptible new comers.

Spontaneous Man, therefore, acted to protect his People even before they were brought into being. Grappling with the giants, by various means he diminished them in size. Some he *squeezed* smaller. Kicimahom Moz ta Kicinigô Moz -- Great-Grandfather Moose and Great-Grandmother Moose,-- who charged him, he stopped with his powerful hands against their faces, *pushing* them down to the size you see today. Have you ever wondered why the faces of mozak have the configuration that they do? ...he recalled questioning his young nephew Tsadzigôuasko. He had then proceeded to give "Persistent One" the answer. Descendants of the original mozak continue to bear the impression made by Kullos'kahp's kaskak, meliki eldsial -- broad, strong hands, -- yo nitta kizogw -- [to] this very day.--

Mikoa, Squirrel, was originally as big as a full-grown moôuin is now. After listening to the boastful chatter of what Kicimahom Mikoa and Kicinigô Mikoa would do to human beings, the Hero picked them up bodily, one by one, and *smoothed* them down. Mikoak are still testy about being reduced to their quite manageable size of today, despite Kullos'kahp's gentle way of reducing them. They sometimes angrily scold people when they see us, and that is why.

The day came when Kullos'kahp finally thought enough auaasak had been reduced and the First People could be created. It was a gala affair -- he let all of the creatures know that it was an occasion of great importance, and they gathered from far and wide. Where this happened seems to have been tali na guina menahan alemakiuik at that large island far away to -- pebonkik-ô'banaki -- the north-east. -- Mi'kmak and

Atmanuk[152] cousins call the place Uktamkw.[153] That island is off the coast of n' guina Ktsiatta Menahan -- our much Greater Island -- that all Alnôbak live on now. Msaltoak lidooak ta auaasak abitahabanik -- Many fliers and animals were invited, -- except for a few exceptionally aggressive ones, who, despite having been down-sized, remain too belligerent. Kalaa ali yanmôgik ktsi uôbi moôuinak -- Such as those great white bears, "ponki moôuinak -- northland bears,"-- i.e., polar bears, whose forebears Kullos'kahp exiled to the frosty winterland regions where they are today. Where only a few Alnôbak live now. None at all back then.

Dodziui d'yanmôgik auani idak --There are those who say,-- pôbabahami gottliui Mikmôzak -- especially among the Mi'kmak,-- that Elder Brother created the First People in a dazzle of blinding light and burst of thunder. This shocked and surprised the on-looking creatures, bowling many of them over. Ta dodziui d'yanmôgik -- And there are those, -- gottliui Odanak ta Mazipskoiak -- among the Odanak and Missisquoi, -- auani ida na Ntami Pemôuzouinnoak -- who say that the First People -- Kullos'kahp olitoab -- Man from Nothing made, -- agma olitoab ali alakôsaônsmek alômiui nenizoak pemôuzimek ôgemakok -- he made by chisling into two living ash trees. -- He animated the two carvings, a man and a woman, by shooting arrows just above them. Which is the true version is anybody's guess. Cloud Eagle refused to choose between them… one story is as good as another, as far as he was concerned. Quite unlike the teachings of the Plac'môniak Black Robes or the Pastoniak manistelak -- ministers.-- They insist that the stories from their Up Biblum are the only true ones, and, on pain of being condemned as "zahagauakôzouinno -- a sinner,"[154]-- …you *HAVE* to totally accept them. But that is not the way of Alnôbak traditionalists. Anyone's creation story should be taken into consideration. Ôadsi kinauitigamek kusihoduôgan -- To show due respect. -- The People's stories were of *possibilities*.

In fact, when you think about it, he mused, -- standing up and cautiously making his way back to firm ground (having harvested a sufficiency of cowslip greens) …you can take what seem to be different versions of the same basic event, and, by using your

---

[152] *Abenaki Indian Legends, Grammar and Place names,* p. 84, Chief Henry L. Masta, Odanak, 1932. The chapter *Meaning of Indian names:* "Etchemin from **atman** meaning gut string." Also p. 241, *Western Abenaki Dictionary,* Volume II: "Malecite: **Muskrat,** Moskwas a Malecite." Etchemins (or Atmanuk) and Malecite are alternative names for the same people. Combining the two definitions, we perceive that the Malecite/Etchemin were known for their expertise in fashioning snowshoes webbing ("gut string") from muskrat innards, moskuasak -- muskrats -- (p. 260, *Ibid.*) -- being abundant in their well-watered territories.

[153] *Glooscap and His Magic, Legends of the Wabanaki Indians,* Kay Hill, 1979, McClelland & Stewart Ltd., Canada, p. 19. Kullos'kahp anchored his *stone* canoe, "…which he turned into a granite island covered with spruce and pine. He called this island Uktamkoo, the land we know today as Newfoundland. This, in the beginning, was Glooscap's lodge."

[154] P. 351, *Western Abenaki Dictionary,* Vol. II: Zahagawakôzowinnowiak, "miserable ones, hence sinners."

imagination, "fill in the details" that others have omitted (have forgotten..?) In the instance of the atookuakuṇ that he was cheerfully recalling, he thought of a way to reconcile the two, *seemingly* two, versions. As he contemplated the creation story, he synthesized the disparities, making them one. He smiled with wry irony when he realized that it was the recalling of the arid dogmatism of the Strangers, their grim insistence that their *La Bible,* or Up Biblum, whatever they call it, is absolutely true, every tiny ink-mark in it, and his contrasting that rigidity to the friendly regard shown toward Alnôbak stories. To the traditionalists' attitude of tolerant acceptance of all stories, no matter who is doing the telling. Atskiato -- In fact, -- Alnôbak tsôi kôgezaldamak ôadsi debestauamek pildoui ôtlokôganal! --The People absolutely love to listen to different stories! -- To hear about what might be, or had been ... possible.

Ôtlokôganal ôtlokak alômi pabilouinôgw liui'a? --Tales told in a much different way? -- *Mezi maui! -- All the better!* -- as far as *we* are concerned, he thought. To be regaled with cleverly different stories is grand entertainment! Children and elders alike look forward, eagerly, to hearing new stories when around the cook-fire in the family wigwam, especially of a winter evening.

What had clued him in to his synthesis was when he realized that there were some points of similarity between Alnôbak'i atookuakunal -- the Peoples' wonder stories,-- and some of the Plac'môniak'i atookuakunal -- Whitemen's wonder tales -- preached from their La Bible. He had been reminded of the story concerning a powerful shaman of theirs, one "Moses," who had climbed up one of the mountains in far-off France ...Ôadso Sinai -- *Mont Sinai,* -- is that what they call it? Intending on a vision quest, apparently, he had encountered the Whitemen's Ktsi Kagôssal'Misiui -- Great Creator, -- their deity, their version of Ktsi Manitou. They call him *Dieu.* Much like our Great Mystery and Kullos'kahp, but both at once. Their Dieu gave Moses a book of stone into which the deity had engraved the rules that those early Christians were commanded to live by. Ôdziôzomek mdala mezi -- Adding [up to] ten, in all.-- And here is the crux of the similarity between that event and Spontaneous Man's creation of the First People. Dieu had carved those commandments into the stone *nspi gassakuad'ua skueda -- with fingers of fire!* -- Which must have been something to see! Ôadsi cegasamek alômiui **asen!** -- To burn into **stone!** -- Pakalmeguad kagininôgw'ua padôghi! -- Certainly the power of lightning! -- Another spectacle that the medauinno was treated to was that Dieu spoke to him through ...pmakadamek abazis'a! --...a burning bush! -- Saki kuaguahlimamek! -- Quite astonishing! -- In that form Moses was told everything that the French need to know. When story - tellers speak of Kullos'kahp carving the first two Alnôbak out of the ô'gemakw trees, -- that we make snowshoes and baskets out of, -- it can be expected that listeners envision the Hero doing the carving with a knife. ...Nsakuagw'ua mazipskw --...A knife of chert, -- we may imagine, on that day in the Dawn Time. *Some* may even imagine that Spontaneous Man used *nhenol* nsakuagok -- *three* knives -- (considering the importance of his intention)... Uiguashigan'a -- a bark-peeling knife -- (to begin with), a common-place flint-bladed knife, and, -- especially if it was just after his battle with nigikeda nizuak kagici 'abagôloak' -- those two gigantic "flat-tails,"-- (they had dammed up *much* too much water) "belaghagenigan'a -- a crooked knife."-- Using an incisor tooth for the blade of the first belaghagenigan.

"Kaneua -- But,"-- thought Cloud Eagle, continuing to contemplate as he made his way back to the camp site, "...has anyone ever actually said that Kullos'kahp used Dômô auakôganal *tali mezi?* --Any tools *at all?* -- "Ônda -- No, -- ônda pegua -- not really."-- His method is left to the imagination of the listener. In that way menagezoiak -- those seeking stories, -- participate in the shaping of the story *also*. In our own minds we fill in various "missing" details, easing the load that Nodôtlokad, the Story Teller has to carry, enabling him, or her, to get to the point more quickly. Get to the moral of the story, or to the amusing "punch line" of the tale sooner than later.

Gizidahôdamek ni negoni atookuakun, Considering that the old wonder-tale, pabômiui medaulinnoid 'Mozes' 'ua Plac'môniak -- about the spiritually-powerful person "Moses" of the Whitemen -- involved their Nônguic'hi-Ntatôgw -- Almighty Being -- appearing to him as a *burning bush,* auani peskuelab auighigauôgan *alômiui ôhagaôio asen!* -- who burned writing **into solid stone!** -- ...it stands to reason that Spontaneous Man might have -- might *well* have -- ac'hi -- also -- used lightning to make the first people! Why should such a powerful being as the Man from Nothing, such an obvious agent of the Great Mystery, bother with mere cutting tools ...when he could command the lightning? Bringing down lightning to sculpt the first man and woman would have been much faster... not tedious at all. And what does lightning engender? O'hôô! --Yes! -- Padôgi! -- Thunder! -- Kassi kisi ônda guahlialeuamek --So it's not surprising -- ni mezi nagik sipsak ta auaasak gibtahabanik odauiui! -- that all those birds and animals were bowled over!-- In addition, they were treated to the amazing sight of Kullos'kahp shooting arrows into the two trees to animate his sculptures. The creatures wouldn't have even seen a bow and arrows before that time. Na tôbi, That bow, ta yagik niznol tiskuôdial... -- and those two arrows...-- aobanikba agemôgik dadebad n'auakôbena pamegizegak? -- would they have been the same [as] we use today?-- Ônda! Kaalatta ônda! -- No! Certainly not! -- Kullos'kahp ao mameliksani -- Man from Nothing is mighty, -- ôadtak agma tôbi ta tiskuôdial d' miliki ac'hi! -- hence his bow and arrows are powerful as well! --

Atskiato, na tôbi -- In fact, that bow,-- yagik tiskuôdial -- those arrows,-- ato ônda aobanik dadebad -- may not have been the same -- ali yagik n'kelozôbena'ua

pamegizegak -- as those we speak of today. -- Liuitamek agemôuô 'tiskuôdial'
--Calling them "arrows" -- ato *tebeskôsui'ketoangan*[155] ôadsi kagui agemôuô
gôgizi aobanik -- may be a **metaphor** for what they really were.-- What they may have
been... were strong bolts of *lightning!*-- The heartwood of the ash trees was already
alive. But his hurled lightning, striking just above them, made First Man and First
Woman step out of their trees. Now they were animate ...could walk about, could
talk... do many things. Ala, kuinôgui -- Or, at least, -- uadsônabanik *tônega'alagha*
kisito msalto ôakasenal! -- possessed the *potential* to do many things!--

After the birds and beasts had recovered from the shock of all the flashes of
lightning and blasts of thunder (pekeda -- smoke -- was probably still rising from the
cavities where the first two had been), they stared with great curiosity at these latest
creations of their master, the powerful Kullos'kahp. The new creatures were certainly...
mos'haginôguak -- strange-looking, -- they all agreed. Dôdaka d'agemôuô miguenok?
nadodemauabanik lidooak.-- Where are their feathers? asked those that fly. -- Dôdaka
d'agemôuô osuadagen? -- Where's their fur? -- Ala dôdaka d'agemôuô piasso? -- Or
where is their hair? -- nadodemauabanik auaasak -- asked the animals.-- Gahalaki,
agemôgik uadsônabanik *azi* piasso... -- True, they had *some* hair...-- Kaneua ônda
nôdami -- but not much.-- Nspi nadauziui dômô piasso -- With scarcely any hair, --
tôhné aobanik agemôgik ôadsi ozôlôuzimek tkegizegad? -- how were they to survive
the cold weather..? -- auaasak pabômidahôzibanik -- the animals wondered. --

Lidooak pabômidahôzibanik: -- Those that Fly wondered: -- Nspiônda
miguenak -- Without feathers, nspiônda ôeleguanak -- without wings, -- nspiônda
ozogenal -- without tails, -- agemôgik gizito'ônda tousaoak nopaiui -- they couldn't
fly away -- li nibenaki ôadsi boleuamek pebon -- to summerland to escape winter. --Ta
aobanik agemôuô kassi piuseso! -- And they're rather small! --

Everyone had expected bigger creatures, at least somewhat larger... beings as
great as Kullos'kahp himself, ala aleua -- or almost. -- Minaguiba agemôgik masegilek
ndaki madeguasak ala ôkusesak --Though they're bigger than hares or foxes, -- they are
much smaller than magôliboak -- caribou, -- moôuinak -- bears, -- ta, pôbabahami,
mozak --and, especially, moose.--

Agemôgik d' *ketemôghinông*w! -- They are *ridiculous!* --
Auaasak ônbdalmôtasinak mamesaniui --The animals smiled sardonically. -- The fliers
(their beaks make it hard for them to actually smile)... began to cackle. Dodzi môtsak
ôadsi mamilegokuazimek... --Then began different calls and cries...-- Sipsak ta

---

[155] For **metaphor** reference the Rev. Joseph Aubrey's *French Abenaki Dictionary*, p. 360. The credit for the English translation, completed in 1995, belongs to Chief Stephen Laurent, the son of Chief Joseph Laurent.

auaasak *nspôbedalembanik!* -- The birds and animals were **laughing!** -- Snorting, guffawing, shrieking (and what might be called giggling), -- broke out among them. The ayiôbak --bucks, bulls, -- of such ungulates as the nolkak, uabôzak, and mozak scooped up twigs with their antlers and tossed them in the air in their merriment. The alhlak, female ungulates of the magôliboak, also, since they too have antlers. The moôuinak ta alaskanak -- bears and wolverines -- laughed so hard they rocked back on their heels and had to hold their sides. Môlsemak, the howler-canines (wolves), emitted yips and high-pitched howls. 'Ôigudi' pezoak -- The "no-tail" wildcats -- ta pittôloak -- and the very much tails -- (cougars), being cats, of course ...caterwauled. The original two mandaôasak -- slow ones, -- mahom ta okemes mandaôasw -- grandfather and grandmother porcupine, -- *aomek guinaui cigabi ali ac'hi ali manni...* -- being largely silent as well as slow... -- expressed their hilarity by getting up on their hind legs to... pmega! -- dance!-- No one had ever seen *two* porcupines dance, and dance together, at that, gagiui ta gagiui -- round and round.-- They weren't slow that day. Ônda! No! On that day you could instead call them kôguak,[156] "prickly ones." As the laughter subsided, many deliberately attempting to calm down and desist because their sides hurt so much, auaasak, mamilegokuaziak -- the animals, speaking in their many different voices,-- sipsak lintômek -- the birds singing,-- were fulsome in their praise of Kullos'kahp. He had such a wonderful sense of **humor!** Kalaa Ktsi Dalbadak'a! --Such a Great Master! -- Kagui pabôladakauinno'a! -- What a showman! -- They had never enjoyed such a good time. It was an entertainment they would always remember. They would regale their grandchildren with details of the gloriously funny day in ages to come. All that astonishing thunder and lightning, all that splendorous razzle-dazzle! *Just* to emphasize the absurdity of the pathetically vulnerable, comically puny First People!

As the creatures departed, going their separate ways -- it was getting late, -- Kullos'kahp grinned broadly. Then he started chuckling out loud... he couldn't hold back. The last of the departing auaasak assumed their own hilarity was infectious... was "catching." That he couldn't help but laugh at himself.

But that wasn't it. It was because he knew the joke was on ***them***. His new people were "helpless" were they? Are naked ...are "vulnerable," eh? He would see about that. True enough, he had concentrated on making the new creatures like-minded -- that is, nspi ilôdebônak nôbi agma -- with minds like his [own], -- but too modest and feeble for one of them to ever conceive that he could challenge him (which *would*, probably, turn out to be a *he*). In so doing, he had not given much thought as to how they were to survive and prosper. For sustenance he had equipped them to sustain themselves on

---

[156] From kôuigen, "...rough, ***prickly***," author's emphasis, an allusion to the spines of the porcupine. *Western Abenaki Dictionary,* Volume II, p. 326. Dr. Day spells it "gôwigen."

nuts, berries, fruit, and tubers. Nada oligen dabi --That [is] good enough -- ôadsi nolkak ta mikoak -- for the deer and the squirrels, kisi'ônda? isn't it? He had not given much thought (ônda *dômô*, pegua! -- not *any*, really!) -- about how they were supposed to get through the freezing cold winters. Nor did he consider how they were to fend off the predatory animals. Who now had such scorn for them! Various carnivores, still imbued with traces of the belligerent natures they had when they had been gigantic, were sure to see such "weaklings" as fair game.

Nagik auaasak uadsônakdzi kuahlialeuauôgan'a --Those animals are going to have a surprise, -- ôlaui --however. -- Pemôuzouinnoak aaok *agma* saki kinaôighen Alnôbak --The humans are **his** quite special People, -- aaok agemôgik ônda? -- are they not? -- Agma ao *kaginiatta*, ônsaaghi'nôtatw Kullos'kahp -- He is the *mighty*, the miracle-working Man from Nothing, -- kisi'ônda agma? -- isn't he? -- He would make his people strong. And *without* increasing their size! He would enable them to survive winter's cold. *Without* the need to hibernate or fly away to summerland every autumn! The more he thought about it, the happier he became. Solving the quandary of his people's vulnerability was just about the most interesting task yet. It was clear… that the Great Mystery had dispatched him to the world precisely to solve such problems as this… why he possessed such great power. Pabakiui! -- Obviously! --

"…grandmother and grandfather porcupine expressed their hilarity by getting up on their hind legs ôadsi pmega! -- to dance! -- They weren't slow that day!"

Drawing by the author.

The means to accomplish all this were ready to hand. There were three good ways that his People could survive winter's cold. Nôbi tmakuak -- Like the tree-cutters (the beaver) -- like nest-building fliers, they would build shelters from materials of the forest. While such wigwams would keep out the wind, he would show them how to harness skueda -- fire, -- to heat them from within. They had, *themselves,* been carved into existence with fire.[157] They had no reason to be afraid of it, ali d'lidooak ta auaasak -- as the fliers and animals are. -- Agma kinauitigaba agemôuô -- He would show them-- tôhni ôadsi olitomek alsauômek... -- how to make clothing...-- warm, snug clothing for winter and lighter clothing for the warmer seasons. Where would that come from? From the animals themselves! Not only would his People utilize auaasak furs and skins to cover themselves, but they would harvest them for *food,* also. When vegetation withdrew into hibernation with the onset of tkegizegad -- cold weather, -- unable to produce any more fruit... his Alnôbak would instead harvest animals. Ta kinaui namasak ta lidooak, ac'hi --And certain fish and fliers, as well.-- Spontaneous Man would even show his People how to fashion various implements and tools from their very bones, and menodal --'bags,' containers -- from bladders, rendering bemi to cook meat and for greasing buckskin raiment... He would show them how every part of a creature could be put to good use. Everything would be utilized, wasting nothing.

How would his People overcome all the living, walking, running, some flying, others swimming ...creatures, so as to accomplish all this? Kullos'kahp would show them. He would instruct them in how to make nsaônkôsônal ta abapskadahiganal --weapons and snares, -- nspi enni ôadsi gadonkamek, with which to subdue, auaasak agemôuô coualemakba noskop'hak --the creatures they would need to catch.-- Auani aoakba ôbedalemimek *adotsi?*-- Who would be laughing *then?* -- Ônda auaasak! -- Not the animals! -- Agemôgik kuaguadadakakba ôadsi kôdakamek odsi "nolemi" pemôusouinnoak --They would be trying to hide from the "puny" humans! --

Ta kassi uadsônaba mezi zôghizaosaik -- And so it had all come to pass.-- Asokw Mgezo, recalling not only creation atookuakunal of his own people, but also satisfactorily synthesizing two *seemingly* disparate versions of his peoples' fundamental atookuakunal ...by employing insight gained by recalling a Plac'môniui Bible tale, was in a much better humor. He thanked the ever-watchful Grandmother and Grandfather Spirits for reminding him of "Mozes ôtlokôgan, the Moses story." As he made his way back to camp he still kept an eye out for skibô, or any other herbage that could be useful. Also for enemies ...not only for their lurking spies, but for stragglers, ôanosadak -- lost ones.-- Who could be now stumbling toward the creek, famished and

---

[157] Which explains - ? - Why the People are not as light-colored as the heartwood of ôgemakok -- *white* ash trees.

panic-stricken, not knowing that their army was long gone. Hardly had he reminded himself that he should be watching out for danger, or for ôanosad'a -- a lost one, -- when he heard a shot ring out. Not close by, but not very far away, either. He stood stock still, wondering if he should look for cover. Then he heard two more reports. Still… No cause for alarm. Most likely it was the hunters who had gone out. Of course, they might have encountered enemy scouts. Then a fourth shot. Cloud Eagle retreated to a shallow dip in the ground where he slipped behind a sizeable beech, adjacent to a massive tree that had fallen years ago. The prostrate elder's bark, now long gone, left the trunk a smooth, silvery gray. He still thought that the firelocks had been discharged by the hunters, but to be prudent was putting the beech and the fallen trunk between him and the direction the reports had come from. His caution was probably entirely unnecessary, but in a war zone you can't be too careful. If a fight had broken out, it was an unusually quiet one …he couldn't hear any war cries or shouts, any exchanges of derision.

    Then a fifth report. So many shots, and so close together… whatever was being fired at, agizouôganak'ua paskhamek -- the number of shots -- indicated that the hunters had come upon a herd, or perhaps a flock, of something. There might be a body of water in that direction, a small lake, perhaps. If it was shallow enough, they could be shooting at large fish, ones close to the surface. Dahôlaui nagik melikiui sôgli namasak -- Possibly those formidably armored fish -- kabasak -- sturgeon. -- Perhaps garfish.

    Cigabi mina -- Silence again, -- ibi ôadsi nouigen lôbaktakhiganmek'ua --except for the distant rapping of -- ato gezalmamek -- a presumably amorous -- nôbalha lôbatahigas'a -- male woodpecker.-- Ato nôbalha -- Presumably a male,-- considering that it's the mating season for birds.

    Asokw Mgezo waited, watchfully patient, first looking past the left side of the beech, then angling his head to gaze beyond its right side. His left arm and side rested comfortably against the silvery, almost satiny trunk of the fallen giant. Nôntmaôadoaunui, Comfortably, *sakiatta* nôntmaôadoaunui, **quite** comfortably, because the trunk had grown so warm. It had been steadily soaking up the rays of kizos, the sun, the cold and dampness of early morning now long gone. Olabeda kizosoho psakuelamek dabsiui -- Pleasantly warm sunshine beaming down,-- gauikhamek agma nolemekusouôgan -- making him feel drowsy.-- Ôski siguan odzauasak odenigamek ôdabuôgan alômi olôda kizos ac'hi -- New spring flies were taking comfort in the warm sun as well,-- ôakasoak cacakigenmek ôpetauakua'ua negônia odabazim, a few speckling the upper part of the old trunk. Oliôniui ôadsi olôda -- Grateful for the warmth, -- agemôgik ônda kaghigihamek -- they weren't annoying,-- kassi agma alidahôzia ônda laldamuôgan'ua odamihamek agemôuô -- so he entertained no thought of bothering them.-- Agma alidahôzia na agma 'aob alômi pazegw'ua pagatlôdadok -- He realized that he was in one of those warm, sunny places -- where it is difficult to stay awake. A determined effort to keep watch is required. His dilemma ceased upon hearing kinaôsadôsw alokôasw'ua nôbalha nahama -- the distinctive sound of a tom turkey.--

11. Oladialimek Gimskasoldin'a --A Good Several-Together Persons Hunt--

He sensed that the *gobble - gobble!* -- though sufficiently shrill,-- was not quite authentic. What was it that rang false? Ah, Kisi pôuidahôziatta! -- It's too cheerful! -- Humanly cheerful. Agma adagidahôzouôgan 'aob môuigek pmi agma namitab odouinno Pmauikho -- His suspicion was confirmed when he saw that distinguished personage He Who Goes Ahead...-- mosko odsi gottliui abaziak -- emerge from among the trees. -- The war chief carried his fusil in the crook of one arm. He carried the turkey that he had bagged slung over the other shoulder.

Cloud Eagle rose and gobble-gobbled in reply, letting the chief know where he was. Though their location was, most likely, secure enough to signal to each other in Alnôbaiui, to be on the safe side they imitated the calls of various forest creatures. Nahamak, Turkeys, in this instance. Appropriately ...there actually was a flock of them in the neighborhood. Somewhat reduced in number at this point. Nabi migakauinno 'Pepôkuan' mosko -- Soon the warrior "Firelock" emerged, -- pmenigamek kedag nahama -- carrying another turkey. -- Dodzi paiyôb Sôsas, pemenigamek agma --Then came Jonas, carrying his.-- He was closely followed by the Missisquoi warrior Ôiguahlo --Whistling Swan,-- ta Pkôgihla Sibo'i[158] 'Ôlebmôuzo' -- and Crooked River's "He Lives (viz., The Survivor)," -- auani ac'hi môdsadobanik lidooak -- who had also taken birds.-- Nônnoak nadialuinnoak; -- Five hunters; -- nônnenol nahamak -- five turkeys.--

As the hunters joined their nbizonhouad, quite pleased, and justly, with their success, -- the chief explained the method by which they had bagged the succulent birds. They had stealthily advanced up a hill, having formed what might be called a "skirmish line." Looking across an intervening ravine to another hill, they had seen a flock of turkeys moving, in a leisurely manner, parallel to them and downslope on the opposite height. They aimed at those the furthest in the rear of the flock. As they shot those rearward ones, each hunter in turn firing at the next forward, the gobblers had expressed muted alarm. Puzzled, but, not thinking to look behind them, the nahamak had not become upset enough to panic. The hunters could have shot more, but, out of

---

[158] Pkôgihla Sibo: "Crooked River" (it goes crooked), the original Abenaki appellation for what is now called Otter Creek, Vermont, which flows into Lake Champlain. So designated for the upper river's winding, twisting course.

consideration for T'songeba's Mohican relatives, restrained themselves. The five successful hunters lingered with Cloud Eagle by the soaring beech, two of them sunning themselves on the fallen ancient. Ah! Kisi kassi negemi! -- Ah! It's so comfortable! -- They were waiting for the sixth member of their party, the young one who lacked his own firelock. He had originally joined them with his hickory long bow and quiver of arrows. When the meandering flock had been seen, he had not attempted to let fly across the intervening gulf. The range was just right for those with paskhiganal, but it was just a bit too far for his bow. He didn't want to alarm his intended turkey by narrowly missing it, wasting an arrow in the bargain. He had waited patiently until each of the fusil-armed hunters had fired. When the flock had moved on sufficiently, they crossed the ravine to claim their kills. The archer accompanied them *into* the cut, but not up the far side. His name -- only a nickname at present, -- was "Nespokusino -- He Dreams of Someone,"-- because he was quite enamored of a particularly attractive young woman. He instead bent low, hastening down the defile, using it as cover to pursue the flock. Emerging where the gully dwindled, he had stealthily shadowed the birds, using whatever cover was available, flitting wraith-like from tree to tree. He attempted to avoid walking on last autumn's fallen leaves, now dry (and "crunchy") thanks to the warm sunshine. Stepping from lichen-thick old fallen trunks to moss-covered rocks (and such) instead, he was quite successful in his stalk, only occasionally

"Dreams Of *let fly, accurately pinioning his bird.*"
Taking aim with hickory long bow is the author, in an Abenaki hunter's trade cloth / buckskin regalia and accoutrements, as would have been typical in northern Muheconnukik --Mohican Land -- as well as in Ô'banakik -- Abenaki Country -- of the 18th century between the contending French and British colonies. Arrows quiver is of onegigua -- otter skin,-- made by the author.

Photo credit: Tomas Azarian.

forced to step on crackling leaves. Finally drawing within close bow - range of the tardiest turkey, he notched an arrow to his bow-string. Covering the last few yards at a rapid pace, he steadily pulled the cord back. His moccasins crunched rather loudly into the forest debris underfoot (loudly to *him*). He not only didn't mind... the "noise" was part of his plan. Harkening to the suspicious crunching, his intended prey, who had been gazing blithely ahead ...now turned to see if some kind of predator was coming on. Nespokusino didn't want to loose his arrow while the bird's back was turned. That made too narrow a target. Turning half-way to scrutinize the terrain behind it, the semi-alarmed turkey was now largely broadside to him. A *broader* target. That was when "Dreams Of" let fly, accurately pinioning his bird. He saw his arrow penetrate, and, quietly articulating "*lahi!*" (expressing satisfaction) Nespokusino leapt forward to claim his prize. The luckless turkey thrashed about briefly... and was still. Snatching it up, he hastened to join the others. Agma ni oladialiab! He too had made a successful hunt!

Hearing another merry *gobble-gobble!* ululate from the forest, Asokw Mgezo and the hunting party now looked back the way they had come. Hearing increasingly distinct footfalls crunching into the carpet of autumn leaves, it was the bright-eyed Nespokusino hastening to catch up with them, his nahama slung triumphantly over one shoulder. "N' leguasiôôb'ua kedag! -- I dreamed of another!"-- he quipped as he joined them, making a joke out of his own recently acquired nickname. A man in love, he didn't mind the moniker at all, -- gladly accepting the truth of it.

The hunting / gathering party, back together, now started toward their waterside camp. They weren't the only ones who had gone out to hunt. Others had also, but in different directions. Some had remained close to camp, fishing in the creek and acting as sentinels at the same time. Breakfast had already included a few fish caught at dawn, thanks to the exigency of having sunk a few fish traps in the water beforehand. The traps, roughly resembling baskets, were made from green withes woven together. The "adelahiganal, barring-of-the-way-instruments,"[159] namas pitamal -- fish traps, -- in this instance, wider at one end, narrowed toward the other end. Namasak swam into them and couldn't get out. On such far-paddling journeys as at present the handy fish traps were kept with the canoes as part of the *voyageurs* equipment, along with nodamaguôganak -- fish spears[160]-- and hooks and lines. The party's return was leisurely. To hurry could be wasteful. As they progressed it was prudent to keep watch for lurking enemies, for 'lost ones,' and for more game. They wouldn't be completely finished with hunting until in camp. As they went there were low-keyed commentaries on turkey hunting.

---

[159] *Western Abenaki Dictionary,* Volume II, p. 417.
[160] *Ibid,* p. 369.

12. Kaoz Zôkukuahiganal ta Nahama Kauakunigamek

-- Cow Ringer Instruments and Turkey Harvesting --

Cloud Eagle recalled a way of turkey-"hunting" that the crafty Pastoniak had developed to the southeast, in their Mass'atzosek colony. He inquired of Jonas and Pepôkuan, especially now that he knew that the latter was Shawnee, from a nation whose traditional homeland was a considerable distance to the south-west... if the Dutsmôniak and Pastoniak, who had settled in the original territories of the two, especially of the Muheconnuck ...engaged in the same practice. Particularly since Pepôkuan had, like T'sôngeba, been born and raised in the country of the Mohicans.

    This particular Auanock way of 'kauakunigamek'[161] pizeuakamigw nahamak --"harvesting" wild turkeys -- *harvesting* is a more appropriate term, as the method could hardly be called hunting-- was dependent upon the presence of the Strangers' domestic animals. Particularly the ungulates, kaozak -- cattle, -- asesak, ta azibak -- horses, and sheep.-- Even gotsal might serve. Pigsak, too, probably, on occasion. The key to it were fields, "pastures," where thousands of trees had been cleared away, the ground plowed up and sown with grass seeds for the sustenance of those foreign animals. Rather than hunt the wild-roaming auaasak, that were already here in abundance, for food and hides, this was another instance of the Auanock taking up enormous stretches of land... to replicate their system in far-off Agômenoki -- Europe Land. -- A system that had, ôauinôguadui! -- apparently! -- led to great overcrowding. It was pressuring innumerable Strangers to risk crossing the vast ocean to this Great Island.

    When the pastures were created, not all wildlife became alienated from them. There were creatures that prefer, exactly like the kaozak, to browse on the lushly growing grasses, not caring a wit where the seeds came from. Certain insects also. Côlsak -- Crickets and grasshoppers, -- thrived in such fields. Though when such large animals as kaozak grazed, chomping contentedly, the côlsak, whether they were of the smaller, black kind, or the larger, green-hued ones, had better get out of the way. They could be accidentally eaten or stepped on. The Iglismôniak didn't call the askaskui-latstak -- green-colored [ones] -- "grass-*hoppers*" for nothing. The threatened côlsak acted with alacrity, leaping out of the way. Away from danger... ala kassi agemôgik *lidahôzibanik* -- or so they *thought*. -- Sometimes, however, their splendid leaps brought them to the quickly-thrusting beaks of nearby nahamak. The birds, meandering

---

[161] Kauakuniga, "gathering in (especially *unplanted things*)," author's emphasis, in contrast to kikauôgan, p. 95, *Western Abenaki Dictionary*, Volume II, "cultivation, literally field working," plural kikauôganal. Kauakunigamek: "One harvests (by pulling), gathering in." *Ibid*, p. 181.

to the margins of the meadows, had been attracted by noticing all the côlsak leaping frantically away from the grazing cattle. At first they didn't know what to make of the huge herbivores, but soon perceived that they were harmless. The leaping insects were definitely edible, scrumptious, juicy *midzouôgan* -- *food,* -- and the birds seized their opportunity. A factor that made the situation crystal clear, distinguishing the inadvertently benevolent cattle from any other creatures, beyond doubt, were curious, idly clanking instruments hanging from the necks of the cows. "Kaoz zôkukuahiganal --Cow ringers" -- i.e., cow bells.

The cow bells were collared to the ungulates to enable the farmers to more conveniently find them when they needed to, even if the kaozak wandered off into the woods. The colonists also lifted thousands of rocks and cut down innumerable trees to build enclosing fences, but such labor required time. Fence-building was scantier the further into the frontier that cow pastures were developed. Initially, investigating turkeys were nonplussed by the bells, which clanked or tinkled erratically --and which at other times were completely silent, -- not knowing what to make of them. Soon they concluded that the metallic clinking was not only harmless, but, recognized as an integral feature of the cattle themselves, perceived that the bells were part and parcel of the large animals' côlsak-stirring beneficence.

While the colonists depended on their tame ungulates for most of their meat and leather requirements, coming, as they did, from a needful, grasping culture, they were not adverse to also shooting free ranging auaasak if the wild ones innocently came within musket range. It wasn't long before they took notice of the nahamak who, emerging from the surrounding forest mingled with their grazing stock as if… they were all members of the same pastoral family. However, it wouldn't do to fetch one's firelock and attempt to hunt the birds while they were among the cattle. You might get a turkey, but by ill luck could also wing one of your own milch cows. Even if you were quite accurate, the sudden, thunderous blast, right among the herd, was greatly alarming, provoking bovine panic.

How the Iglismôniak were finally able to devise a way to harvest such nahamak without resorting to explosion-instruments, with a minimum of fuss and bother, was most likely discovered by sheer chance. Probably a farmer had walked through his herd carrying a cow bell -- a collar had broken, and he was retrieving it -- when he noticed that the turkeys were not running or flying away from him, as they usually did. As he walked along, the casually-held bell clanking with almost every step, the birds remained in place. They seemed to regard him …as merely another cow! A very *strange*-looking cow, oddly enough upright on only two legs, but the peacefully moving creature *aiyagô* kaoz'a! --***must be*** a cow!-- Kisi aghoda nspi kaoz-zôkukuahigan'a..! -- It's hung with a cow-ringer instrument..! -- They focused on any côlsak jumping out of his way.

Pondering the unusually tame behavior of the côlsak - catching birds, slowly realizing that the turkeys had, thanks to the retrieved cow bell, taken him for one of "their" symbiotic bovines, the colonist was reminded that he greatly enjoyed roasted nahamaiya -- turkey flesh. -- It may have been his idea, or he may have idly mentioned the curious nahamak behavior to a neighbor, but the upshot was that the initial farmer, or said neighbor, ventured, one day soon after, out into a cow-pasture where the birds mingled among the cattle. He walked casually -- haste would have been counterproductive, -- cowbell idly clinking in one hand …and a stout club held in the other. Strolling close to one of the turkeys, the gobbler looking in anticipation at his "hooves," his feet, for a vaulting grasshopper, the club was quietly raised. To be brought down on a hopeful head with lethal swiftness.

Pepôkuon and Jonas replied in the affirmative to Cloud Eagle's query. O'hôô, Yes, the Pastoniak and Dutsmôniak to the south, from whence the hostile army had come, had learned the cow-ringer trick and had "hunted" nahamak in that manner for many summers. As per usual, the Auanock farmers couldn't restrain themselves from continuing to harvest the unsuspecting birds in that way when the flocks markedly dwindled. As a result they rarely saw them in their pastures any longer. If you wished to hunt turkeys it was necessary, in those parts, to libmosa môlôkipiui -- go deep in the woods -- to find them. Fortunately those Auanock peasants were, usually, much too busy on their farms to take their firelocks far into the forest and discover the roosting places of surviving nahamak.

Pepôkuon remarked that, where he was born and raised, in Muheconnuck territory, eastward of Fort Orange, across the river, up among the Taconic Mountains (the northern extension of that range rising to their east even as he spoke), it was well forested and still possible to encounter wandering flocks of nahamak. Those hills were too steep for farming, the colonists much preferring level land… though they sometimes arrived to cut timber or engage in mining. Even there, they preferred the lower, more gradual slopes. To the east of the Taconic Range there were still more forest-cloaked hills, some quite high, where the Muheconnuck and their handful of Suônniuk --Shawnee -- cousins roamed, only rarely seeing a Pastoni visitor. Both Jonas and Pepôkuon speculated that the lack of Iglismôniak there might be because there seemed to be an argument between the Pastoniak of Massa'tzosek colony, to the east, and those of what they call "New-York," along "ye North River," or 'Hudson's River.' Dutsmôniak had founded that colony, only to be later conquered by *les Anglais,* and now the Bostonians of Fort Orange were disputing the westward claims of the "New England" Pastoniak. There was, apparently, confusion as to where their separate jurisdictions began and ended.

Among the Muheconnuck, of course, there was no confusion. The land was under their stewardship. But the quarreling Pastoniak, in terms of jurisdiction, acted as if their "dusky allies," the Muheconnuck …didn't even exist.

13. Muheconnuck Migakauinnoak li Ôidzokaduôgen
-- Mohican Warriors to the Rescue --

Asokw Mgezo and his nahamak-harvesting companions finally arrived back in camp, where all was quiet. Some members of the homeward-bound party had begun to construct overnight shelters. The hunting, fishing, and gathering looked quite good in this area, the southward flow of Canadien supply batteaux not very disruptive. The wounded should be allowed more recuperating rest before the paddle north was resumed.

As Cloud Eagle put kettles of tubers and greens on the fires to cook (two fires had been built, to prevent overcrowding around just one) and otherwise tended to his charges, he continued, when opportunity offered, to converse with T'sôngeba and Pepôkuon. Having heard little about the Suônniuk previously, he was interested in learning more.

The cheerful Suônni warrior explained that his grand-parents or *great*-grandparents had lived further to the southwest, much further, in a region belonging to the Lenapéuk. The Iglismôniak were now calling Lenapéhocking, the ancient territory of the Lenapéuk, "Pennsylvania," a name meaning 'Penn's Woods.' "Firelock's" forebears, even further back, had lived in a yet more distant region to the west, where there are great bodies of water. Calamity had overtaken (a northern extension of) the Shawnee Nation in that land. The northerner's sovereignty had been questioned by an expanding confederacy, an Iroquoian alliance. They were unlike the Shawnees' time-honored neighbors, the friendly Erie and Huron Iroquoians. Old enemies, increasingly restless enemies, as time went on. Those western Suônniuk (the northern extension of the Shawnee as a whole, who live further south) had come under forceful pressure exerted by the Iroquois alliance of Five Nations. The aggressive Maguak demanded that the Suônniuk bow down in subordination, becoming tributary to them. The proud Shawnee rejected the haughty command. Attacked, they fought back with great courage! But soon found themselves surrounded... threatened with utter annihilation. Their Algonquian cousins to the east, the famous Lenapéuk, being notified of their plight, sent fighting men to assist them. They found that yet more Algonquian allies were needed to fend off the fierce Maguak, calling upon their Mohican relatives. The Suônniuk recognized the then-powerful Muheconnuck as "Grandfathers." To keep endangered Shawnee families out of the reach of revenge-seeking Maguak, numbers of rescued Suônniuk were relocated to Lenapéhocking, settling in a pleasant valley called, in Lenapéui, 'Ô'yoming.' It is not far west of the river the Iglismôniak are calling "ye Delaware." Others were conveyed to Mohican territory. A few families were brought to the eastern side of the great river (of the Muheconnuck)... in an area, quite rich in game, that is at the foot of, and up among, the Taconic Mountains, well east of the river.[162] It was quite a ways south of where Pmauikho's party was now, of course. That range is said to vaguely constitute the border between "Wilderness lands" (Mohican territory) claimed by the magistrates of Massa'tzosek, in Boston, and the Fort Orange - centered Pastoniak of "New-York."

Cloud Eagle listened, appreciating the northward evolution of such exiles as Pepôkuon and T'sôngeba. His own history was similar, as was that of He Who Fools Them. He wondered if the chief might soon ask him to accompany one of his war parties into those very Muheconnuck forests to the east of the Taconics, again as nbizonhouad for the band. Grey Lock knew those forested hills intimately, having roamed them himself when young …where his raiders could shelter while scouting the Pastoniak settlements that now dotted the valley of the Long River. No matter how much the native Massa'tzosek and Kueniteguak -- Long River people -- helped the Pastoniak, their assistance went unappreciated. *Les Anglais* kept chipping their sovereign territories smaller and smaller. Even those cousins of the Muheconnuck, "the Mohegans" of eastern Connecticut, who had served the English so well in the "Pequot War" and "King Philip's War" of the 1600s, couldn't keep their land base from being constantly whittled away. If they forcefully resisted, they would be declared *Rebels!* and attacked by militia bent on their annihilation.

The day steadily grew warmer, with two of the turkeys, gutted and pskuiboaalôbanik'ua miguenok -- plucked of feathers, -- now being cooked. Asokw Mgezo, hearing the screech of a jay in a nearby pine, some boughs of which extended over the creek, looked up. Just in time to see one of the bands' canoes, saki pili pazeguen'a, a quite new one, being paddled toward shore. The paddler's deb'kuan --head-hair-- was plucked back to a scalp roach. He wore a headdress that the French call *crête d'un coq,* -- a cock's comb. Cloud Eagle could translate that. Naskuaha is 'comb.' For *coq,* rooster, he used nôbalha, the common word for a male bird. It was made up of deer and porcupine hair, the white nolka hair, from a deer's tail, now dyed bright red. The prow's emblem was a sun edged with red serrations, the yellow and red ochre still bright. The warrior's name was Olitôguezo,[163] so named because of his pleasant voice, indicating it was a pleasure to hear him speak. When Cloud Eagle and those with Pmauikho had gone into the woods on the west side of the waterway, Olitôguezo had taken his own canoe (called a 'lake canoe' fully sixteen feet long, the lakes referred to being *quite* large, saki kaska -- *quite* wide) -- …and embarked toward the eastern shore. He would see what could be obtained on that side. The boat had been built as a joint project by himself with family members and various relatives.

---

[162] The Taconic Mountains township of New Ashford, Massachusetts, was originally designated as the "Shaweno Purchase" tract, indicating that it was part of Mohican territory granted to Shawnee people brought east.

[163] "He (his voice) sounds nice." *Western Abenaki Dictionary,* Volume II, p. 366.

Asokw Mgezo's focus on Olitôguezo -- had he hunted successfully? Perhaps he had found some useful herbs? -- was interrupted by the sound of knocking close by. He looked over to see that an uncle of Walks Softly was busy. The Kaanauagi warrior Kyâs'hūtâ was working on another canoe, also recently constructed. He had put it upright and was using a freshly-made pagamôgan, pounder, its handle and mallet-head

Kuena tôbi ta tiskuôdial pit'halôn nikôntag agma --Long bow and arrows quiver in front of him, -- bringing his new - made 'lake canoe' toward shore is the author as the early 1700s warrior Olitôguezo.

Photo: Tomas Azarian

carved from a single piece of wood, to knock auakôdsi giuhlauôgan ôginak -- slightly wandering ribs -- back into place. To tighten them against interior cedar - strip "planking" and the bark hull. The canoe was splendidly constructed, built by Tanial Salasin, the famous Algonkin canoe maker. Nspi agma lakamiguezo ôidzokadimek -- With his family pitching in -- acoui -- of course. --   It had occurred to "Fire on the Mountain" (Kyâs'hútâ) that, now that the former enemies (or a large faction of the 'Maguak' enemies of the 1600s) were not only no longer enemies, but were fast *friends* of the Algonkins (as well as of the French)… that he should travel deep into Canadian Algonkin territory, where he would find out if the inhabitants there were as friendly toward such 'reformed' Iroquois as himself as the various Algonquians close to the Rivière St. Laurent. Such northerners *had* viewed him with suspicion, but soon warmed to him when they were assured that he was a friend. There he had happened to meet, far north on the Ottawa River, the renowned canoe-making Salasins. Wanting only the best, Kyâs'hútâ had engaged the family to make a birch canoe for him. Appreciating its value, it's amazing stability in the water… it was almost impossible to tip over, even if you *tried,* to name one attribute, the veteran Kaanauagi warrior wanted to keep the excellent boat in as good condition as was humanly possible.

Earlier, as the returning turkey hunters approached the camp, Cloud Eagle had noticed guina mkazaui skog'a -- a large black snake -- slither out of the way. Though the reptile, -- sluggish from basking in a sunny spot -- was vulnerable to anyone who was of a mind to harm it, none of the warriors made such a move… quite the contrary. They knew that such a snake was harmless. Some of them smiled, two murmuring (words to the effect of) "Kuai, Mahom! -- Hello, Grandfather! -- N'ozigaldak ôadsi aueskôlauamek kia adalôdabid -- We're sorry to disturb your repose. -- O'hôô, Yes, kizos'ginakula ao olabeda -- the sunshine *is* pleasantly warm. -- Uadzôna olegizegad'a! -- Have a nice day!"--

The sight of the skog reminded Asokw Mgezo that, where they were now, in a more southern region, there were indeed poisonous snakes. Si'si'kuak, Rattlesnakes, to name them. Ônda na agma odamidahôzab -- Not that he was worried.-- If you wander near one, you will be given fair warning. He will shake si'zi'uan -- the rattle -- that Kullos' kahp, long ago, affixed to his tail. At the same time, it is wise, in this country, to be a bit cautious. If you blunder, quite inadvertently, close by, mahom Si'si'kua might shake his rattle all right… But then, because you have stepped *too* close, might strike. Vowing to keep a sharp lookout for those skogak, Cloud Eagle regarded Olitôguezo as the latter, having beached his canoe, approached. He had bagged something on the other side of the waterway. He carried a buckskin sack that sagged, containing… kagui?

-- something? --

Kyâs'hútâ was almost finished. When he was done knocking ribs into place the young medauinno would inquire.

Bow section of one of the author's bark canoes, 'Olitôguezo' putatively paddling, displaying (author's) artistically decorated paddle, his hickory long bow and part of otter - skin arrows quiver.

"The veteran Kaanaugi warrior Kyâs'hútâ was working on his own canoe. Using pagamôgan'a -- a pounder, -- head and handle carved from a single piece, to knock slightly loose ribs back into place." Drawing of Kyâs'hútâ is from information tendered to the author by the late Royce E. Coburn, of actual "Caugnawaga" Iroquois heritage.

Craft was made by the famous Algonquin bark canoe-maker Daniel Sarazin of Golden Lake Reserve, Ontario.

Kyâs'hútâ put his pagamôgan aside and, straightening up, looked closely to see what else could be done to assure that the canoe was absolutely ship shape. Noticing something else that (he thought) required tending, he began to turn the craft upside down.

    Asokw Mgezo and Olitôguezo, being close, hastened to assist, helping him turn it over. They were as anxious as he was to make sure no damage would afflict the fine boat, not even slightly. The woods-wise Kaanauagi unsheathed his trade knife and, kneeling, employed the blade, held horizontally, to applications of *bego,* conifer gum, that covered the balsam - roots stitching holding the hull together. Gum had also been smeared, here and there, where there was no stitching, had been added "just in case" the bark *might* leak in such places. The bego (on bark canoes mixed with bone marrow) appeared to be a *bit* rough, *somewhat* too thick, ridged, in a few spots. Should be smoothed down, excess material, *however* slight, scraped away. Streamlined, enabling the craft to slide with absolute smoothness and speed through the water.

    Na minauitôzo -- That done, -- môlhinôguak lessano -- curiosity inclined -- Cloud Eagle ôadsi limosamek atali -- to turn toward where -- Olitôguezo had put down the buckskin containing kagui -- something. -- Strolling casually, when he reached the spot a cloud drifted over, briefly darkening the hitherto sunny day. Olitôguezo had spread out the skin, revealing what he had brought. Immediately Asokw Mgezo's face broke into a smile. His eyes gleamed with delight, banishing the gloom cast by the shadow of the asokw overhead. The young man had harvested skibô! Those larger, much more preferable apenak -- tubers -- that the band's *naturel docteur* had despaired of finding earlier in the day! Olitôguezo was more successful than he knew... he had accomplished just the right thing in bringing joy to Cloud Eagle's heart.

Already the maanôd, gatherer, had brought over his metail kuatiz --small brass pot -- and antler-hafted knife to begin processing the ground nuts. Soil still clung from digging them up. They should be cleaned, at least somewhat, before being cooked. Asokw Mgezo anticipated collecting turkey drippings to enhance the treat to come.

Author's photo

Asokw Mgezo'a uassahla *saki* uigôdamiui ali agma ôitsokadôzik Olitôguezo gatahôzo -- Cloud Eagle became *quite* happy as he assisted He Who Speaks Pleasantly prepare -- the skibô for cooking. Kyâs'hútâ finished his bego smoothing (he didn't want to accidentally scrape off *too* much... there is such a thing as being too perfect). Uncle then came over to see what Olitôguezo and their nbizonhouad were doing.

Their *naturel docteur* still had si'si'kuak on his mind. "K'nananhi namitô mahom'a, si'si'kua -- Did you happen to see a grandfather, a rattlesnake -- pôzidziui dali -- over there, -- atali k'meskôôb skibô? -- where you found the skibô?" -- he inquired of the successful gatherer.

"Ônda -- No, -- ônda debaskhodigan'ua na mahom -- no sign of that grandfather,"-- Olitôguezo answered. "Kaguesa kisi ôdauiui dali? What is over there?" Cloud Eagle asked. "Kaguesi abaziak... -- What sort of trees..... -- d' pasodaui? -- are nearby?"-- Both the harvester and Kyâs'hútâ understood that Asokw Mgezo wished to increase his awareness of the environment in which skibô might be most commonly discovered... the vegetative varieties the plant is likely to be found among. Olitôguezo described the various plant growths in the neighborhood of the skibô he had discovered, as far as he could recall. The predominant tree species were maahlakusak -- black ash trees,[164] -- with a few ôgemakok -- white ash trees ('snowshoe frame trees') -- close by.

Kyâs'hútâ's face lit up at the mention of the ash trees. The references to rattlesnakes and ash trees had triggered his recall of an almost forgotten legend. "Yah," (meaning "No"), he first said in Iroquoian, and then switched to both the Abenaki Ônda and the French *Non* to make certain he was understood. "Yah onhga, Ônda pazego, No one, ike's geds'henlyes...-- is likely to find..." -- he maintained, again starting in Kaanauagiui -- Kaanauagi speech -- and then, thinking hard, switching to Alnôbaiui. "No one is likely to find a rattlesnake among a grove of ash trees," -- was the import of his words. "O'hôô," Cloud Eagle readily agreed, aware that ash trees have powerful medicine. "Nia agemagôuô laghsód'ha -- I well remember my grandfather, -- ("my grandfather" in Kaanauagiui, which Asokw Mgezo and Olitôguezo understood), -- "telling me the story of the ash tree and how good it is against those poisonous serpents."

As he spoke a faraway look came over him. He gazed dreamily toward the southwest, toward what *les Anglais* were calling "New-York Province," and the Mohawk Valley homeland of his relatives. Though he had been, himself, born at Kahnauagé,[165] the mission town at the north, in Kibek, his people were originally from the Mohawk Valley. Once settled in at the Québec Kahnauagé the migrants, while harkening to the harangues of the Black Gowns, did not disown their relations who remained in the Mohawk Valley. They visited back and forth, at times trading, to the discomfiture of the French, Canadian furs for British and Dutch-made trade goods. Kyâs'hútâ had visited the original, New-York Kahnauagé on occasion himself, the first time when he had been quite young, as young as his nephew Walks Softly was now.

Walks Quietly had been busying himself with the roasting turkeys, favoring his wounded leg with the support of a stick. He no longer needed Cloud Eagle's astahigan, which was longer and heavier than he required. The stick was msakuad'a, a big stick, though shorter than the spear. Hearing the older man mention "ahstauenónyareh -- rattlesnake," -- and "laghsód'ha -- my grandfather"-- he slowly approached. He suspected that lohsót'ha'eh -- his uncle -- was going to launch into a story. Whatever it might entail, he was interested, especially if a *traditional* narrative.

---

[164] Designated *Fraxinus nigra,* collectively "brown ash." *Western Abenaki Dictionary,* Volume II, pp. 16 - 17.

The white ash, *Fraxinus americana,* is "ô'gemakw, snowshoe wood," wood for snowshoe frames, *Ibid,* p. 17.

[165] *Abenakis & English Dialogues,* p. 52 and p. 209. "Caughnawaga, (Iroquois) for *kahnawake,* at the falls, from: *ka,* where, *ohnawa,* current, swift current, falls, cascade, and *ke,* which marks 1° the duality and plurality; 2° the presence of a preposition, which, in many instances (in the Indian languages), is represented by the termination," p. 209. Caughnawaga is at the foot of the St. Lawrence River's extensive Lachine Rapids. Iroquois migrating to the proffered French missions, particularly to Kahnauagé, were also largely from the *original* Kahnauagé, "At the Falls," located at an eastwardly rapids/falls on the Mohawk River.

He smiled to himself as he noticed Uncle's eyes dart briefly, furtively, about. Such a glance was an ingrained habit back at the mission village. The would-be Story Teller was ascertaining that neither a Black Gown nor one of their spying *donneures* was present. If one of them was, the Story Teller would hesitate, because the relating of a mythic Iroquois tale, considered *"païen"* by the missionaries and their most devoted acolytes …would bring on dark looks and a glum lecture on what is truly proper.

However, Génh -- Kaanauagiui for *Here*, -- there was no Black Robe, and if any of the warriors present were all that churchly, no one was demanding that they listen. Quite the contrary, the resolutely 'pagan' Ô'banaki medauinno "Odsad'h Auegs -- Cloud Eagle" -- was listening to Kyâs'hútâ with interest, with inviting anticipation. Olitôguezo also seemed quite interested. As for the latter's spiritual inclinations, there was no crucifix hung as a pendant on his necklace of wampum beads. The pendant was instead a scallop shell daubed with the 'païen' image of a "yogen'nolen dsi'ténha -- a rain bird,"-- i.e., the swallow, a traditional Abenaki life-affirming emblem.

Walks Softly had not been the only one of those busy around the cook fires (or cleaning recently-discharged gun barrels) who had become cognizant that Kyâs'hútâ was leaning toward relating an atookuakun. He would put it in his own language as "Yo-dogénhtih gada'ãtis, A sacred talk." One of the recently successful turkey hunters, Ôlebmôuzo, "He Lives," The Survivor, sauntered over, carrying a large piece of elm bark upon which rested several slices of steaming nahamaiya.

"Génh, Lagenohá'a -- Here, My uncle,"-- he invited, offering the platter first of all to Kyâs'hútâ, "Uncle" being older and on the premise that he was going to tell a rarely-heard story. After Kyâs'hútâ had taken what he wanted, Ôlebmôuzo passed the platter to Cloud Eagle and the other two. Asokw Mgezo suggested that the five of them relocate to the central location between both cook fires, where Kyâs'hútâ could be more easily heard by those attending to skuedaal -- the fires. -- The Kaanauagi *raconteur* sat down in the most central place between them, sitting on a conveniently outcropping rock that was cushioned with thick moss. Ôlebmôuzo, twisting off a drumstick from one of the roasting turkeys (he had bagged it himself), sat close on one side of him. The young hunter was of mixed Kaanauagi / Ô'banaki heritage and was fluent in both languages. When the Story Teller's grasp of Alnôbiaui faltered, He Lives could translate for him without having to resort to French. Walks Softly settled in on his uncle's other side, the better to hear the tale and to also assist in interpretation. Kyâs'hútâ munched on pieces of tasty nahamaiya, sipping fresh herbal tea from a tree-burl cup, virtually masticating on what he was about to say.

He began by alluding to his revered maternal grandfather, who had been a great keeper of Gahnyen'kehàgä traditions, ladsyénhayens -- a councillor, -- and a shaman… From his first visit to the original Mohawk Valley Kahnauagé Kyâs'hútâ retained a vivid memory of him, especially upon seeing him gahéhadakonh -- in a ripening field --

among maize, beans and squash, wearing a spirit-face mask (woven of corn husk fronds), blessing the growing Three Sisters, driving bad influences away with his singing and his propitiations. By fasting, praying, donning his "medicine" regalia and appealing fervently for the Spirit World's help, he had transformed himself into the virtual essence of that Benevolent Spirit: "Good Harvest" dsinikâyen -- itself. -- Kyâs'hútâ had been deeply impressed. He remembered well the "medicine staff" that his grandfather had supported himself with, ceremoniously carved and painted with the colors of the Sacred Cardinal Directions: oneguénhdaleh' -- red, -- genlá'gen --"light color," white, -- odsînegual -- yellow, -- and gahòndsih --"dark color," black. -- It had all been so interesting!

Returning to the Québec Kahnauagé, he had participated in the rituals of the Church. But was puzzled as to why the friars disparaged his people's ceremonies. Even today he was still struggling with that question… but said little about it to the missionaries in view of the good work they were doing in keeping Kahnauagé free of the curse of alcohol. He appreciated that they were effective in keeping brandy away from the mission, and, furthermore… were diligent in banning the fiery drink from any place where native people gathered, irrespective of whether they were Iroquoian or Algonquian.

A cooperative muzzleloader models a corn-husk 'spirit-mask' and traditional regalia to portray Kyâs'hútâ's rLohsót'ha (grandfather), a revered Iroquois shaman. Authors' photo depicts 'Grandfather' appealing to the Spirit World… so that the 'Three Sisters' (corn, beans and squash), cultivated by the women, will grow abundantly and well.

14. Oh niodyélenh néh Éhas' Gélhiteh Auiyo Ononhgua' Gadeliyos Ahsdauenónyarlehogonha (Gahnyen'kehàgä[166] Iroquois)
Odzikaui Ô'gemakw aligek Oli Nebizon apci Sisikuak
--Why the Ash Tree is Good Medicine against Rattlesnakes --
(Abenaki Alnôbaiui)

"Ô'ahón'nise'génha -- A long time ago,"-- Kyâs'hútâ intoned, with Ôlebmôuzo echoing "Kuena anegi -- Long ago,"-- without attempting to interpret the Iroquois equivalent for "time" (getting to the point more quickly). "É't'hoh kèn'ne Ló'ngue' --There was a man."-- A man, *Alnôba* -- An Ordinary, a Native man, -- whether Iroquois or Algonquian not specified. He had a family... "Ló'neh nog dehniksá'eh -- A wife and two children."-- While the husband and father was away, probably hunting or fishing, "Ahsdauenónyareh ôagadaueyà-donh lonón'ha' uigiuôm -- A rattlesnake came into their lodge."--[167] Kyâs'hútâ used the Abenaki *uigiuôm* for lodge rather than the Iroquois *ganónhsa'* because, as he might have explained, everyone knew what it meant. Most Iroquoians know it, "*even* the English" understand it. Knew it so well that new arrivals, fresh from Europe, often employed the term when speaking to Iroquoians --or to Siouans such as the Catawba, -- glibly assuming it to be part of a common "Indian language." Through trade it was fast becoming a term known to everyone, along with other common trade - fostered Algonquian words like "moccasin," from *mkezen*, and "sachem" or "sagamore," for a chief, from *sôgemô*.

"Ne ónyareh uagélioh --The snake killed -- ake' nihsdenha nog egsa'okónha' the mother and the children." When the husband and father returned, finding his spouse and little ones poisoned to death by the serpent, his grief was violent. "Desas'hs'hénd'honh -- Weeping, -- laonha gheli'honyénih dsi Häuen'néyw -- he appealed to the Master of Life."-- For revenge, and for a means of preventing such reptiles from killing others.

"Häuen'néyw --The Master of Life, -- ala Ktsi Manitou -- or Great Spirit, -- gadahonh'siyóhsd'ha' -- heard him,"-- and gave him permission to turn into a tree, "dsi dyo'nhahdón'don ne nahòten -- the branches of which -- agénha'ge' gón'nis

---
[166] P. 121, *One Thousand Useful Mohawk Words:* David Kanatawakhon Maracle, Audio-Forum, 1992. Maracle defines Gahnyen'kehàgä as meaning "Mohawk nation." However, insofar as 'Mohawk' is from an *Algonquian* term, a pejorative from the era when various Algonquian nations were at odds with the Five Nations Iroquois, the present author takes it upon himself to provide the "Mohawk" people's *own* definition of Gahnyen'kehàgä: "People of the Land of the Flint." Glossary, p. 277, *Hail! Nene Karenna, The Hymn,* Bruce A. Burton, 1978, Security-Dupont Press, Rochester, NY. Professor Burton spells Gahnyen'kehàgä as Ganienkehaga.

[167] Pp. 127 - 128, "The Ash Tree," *Legends of the Iroquois,* Told by "The Cornplanter," "From Authoritative Notes and Studies," William W. Canfield, A. Wessels Company, New York 1902.

aen'nagónh nog kayènguileh -- would make bows and arrows"-- with which his people could kill such enemies. "Néh Gélhiteh ígen' Éhas' -- The Tree is the Ash."-- "Néh óhondeh óneldeh -- The green leaves," -- placed in a circle around those who sleep... form a barrier through which the reptiles fear to crawl. The bruised leaves can be made into a poultice, drawing venom from a sufferer. The bark, pounded and brewed, makes a medicine that drives delirium from the victim.

Anyone who approaches the tree to avail himself of those boons should ask permission of the éhas, saying, "O our friend, your brother needs your help. He has met the venom-fanged one whose bite is the sting of a poison arrow. He knows not what except to turn to you, his noble brother. The stab of the forked-tongue is deep! Eyes will close in the long sleep if you do not help." Taking fresh leaves for a poultice and stripping bark for the medicine-brew, you should say: "I'ih gheka'leôah'de ise, lagdsí'eh --I wound you, my brother," -- continuing with words, the effect of which are; "But elders speak of your goodness and of your disdain for the rattling-tailed one."

"Na Ho -- I'm done,"-- Kyâs'hútâ concluded, satisfied that now everyone under-stood his contention that you were not likely to encounter an ahsdauenónya_rleh, that is, a si'si'kua, among a grove of ash trees.

Author's June 1st photo of guanak ô'gemakw'a -- a tall ash tree, -- near his home. In the spring ash trees leaf out later than other trees, as can be seen by the almost fully leafed out trees in lower half of photo, young maples only half as tall as the soaring ash.

It was pleasant to listen to the trilling of song birds roundabout as everyone maintained a respectful silence, absorbing Lagenho'-ną -- Uncle's -- story. Cloud Eagle kept quiet, enjoying He Who Speaks Pleasantly's nahamaiya - drippings flavored skibô.

Though... pondering, he wondered about the tale's murderous si'si'kua. The snakes, in the normal course of events, do not deliberately prey upon human beings. People, even small children, are much too big for them. The purpose of their si'zi'uanak --rattles -- is to give fair warning... their way of saying "Gwôzoda! -- Keep Away! " -- What had probably happened was that the reptile had been a hungry one... In pursuing azi auaasiz -- some animal, small -- such as a chipmunk or "alezauad -- gnawer"-- (mouse), the fleeing rodent had scurried near the ganônhsa' of the unfortunate woman and her children, especially if *into* the wigwam, where the humans would have panicked upon seeing the suddenly slithering skog. Their shrieks of alarm, their terrified behavior ... the woman may have picked up something and attempted to strike at the rattler, -- which would have panicked the fork-tongued one in turn, provoking it into striking out in self-defense.

Had it all been a tragic misunderstanding?

Asokw Mgezo compared Kyâs'hútâ's tale with the atookuakun concerning Kullos'kahp's creation of the first people. The first man and woman, the ancestors of all Alnôbak today... had been sculpted from *ash* trees. The Hero may have restored to human form the Alnôba... who had been a man in the first place! And *his wife,* as well, restored to life!! Subsequently she had borne their children. The little ones had been brought back as well!

Alnôbai mina...-- Born again...-- Thanks to Ktsi Manitou... Great Spirit is merciful, *so beneficial..!* Cloud Eagle reflected, feeling contented as he savored the nahamaiya - flavored skibô. His patients were healing nicely under the balmy spring sun. He added the comment that, to ward off illness, especially "gebedzôla[168] -- it's a closed nose," -- everyone should partake of the brewing herbal tea. Though the early afternoon weather was beautiful, the spring nights were yet quite chilly. Have some, particularly because one of his ingredients consisted of "uaôizôuadsapkassig[169]-- all-yellow little roots," -- called by the Pastoniak 'goldthread.' The delicate, thread-like roots are good for treating colds and fever.

Also good against colds are coltsfoot blossoms. He had seen many when digging up mozilalo -- moose's tongue -- tubers. The equally medicinal leaves of coltsfoot would appear later. Noticing some blossoms nearby (similar to dandelions) he declared "Ôlaui, ibi nikuôbi...-- However, right *now..."* -- and demonstrated, picking a few within reach, and ate them. The medicinal flowers can be eaten raw.

---

[168] What in English is called a 'head cold,' gebedzsôla, p. 186, *Western Abenaki Dictionary*, Volume I. "Gebedsôla**s**" (note the **s** added to word-final position) *also* indicates a seashell, pp. 186 - 187 *Ibid*. The **s** in word-final position on gebedsôla*s* is likely a diminutive, a contraction from siz, indicating small, because the aperture, the "nose," so to speak, on a mollusk is generally smaller than an adult human nose.

[169] *Western Abenaki Dictionary*, Volume II, *Coptis groenlandica*, p. 171.

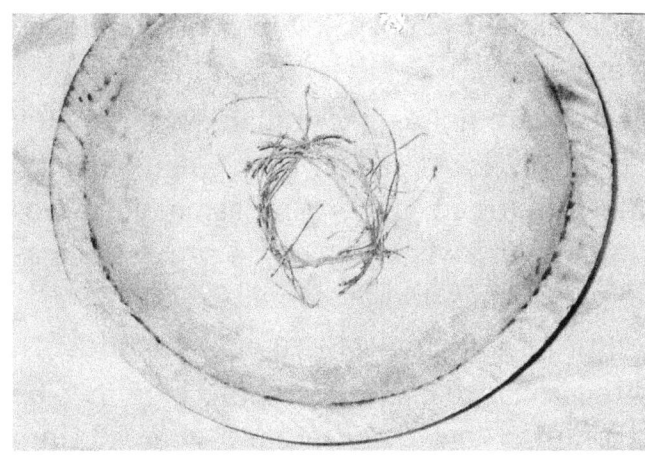

To the left: Author's photo, May, of wreath of goldthread roots, in abaziiya kuat --wooden bowl,-- preparatory to simmering for good nebizon.

On the right: "Moose's tongue" tubers and leaves on birch bark (among coltsfoot blossoms).

Appreciating all the good medicines placed, in some instances, within leisurely arm's reach of wherever one happens to be, Asokw Mgezo couldn't understand the contention of the Black Robes that their *Dieu* is "Askaminnouid'a auani gagôuigo ta guôguen -- a God who is angry and jealous." -- Or is it those grim Pastoniak manitstelak, ministers, who make that assertion? Dôniyo... -- Whichever -- both claimed to be guided by that same auighigan, whether termed *La Bible* or Up Biblum. **Guôguena?** -- ***Jealous?*** -- Kagui'ua? -- *What of* ? -- Gagôuigo? -- *Angry?* -- Kaneua ôdzikaui? -- But *why?* -- It seemed to him that such negative passions shouldn't be attributes of *dômô* Askaminnouid, *any* Eternal One, whatever name the deity has. Kisikauo and other elders asserted that the Ktsi Manitou that Alnôbak traditionalists believe in is the source and spring of everything that is ***good***. In contrast, such a bleak, negative emotion as guôguena is known to be one of the glaring faults of that insinuating troublemaker, **Madahôndo,** the *Bad Spirit*. The Christians, claiming their god to be a "jealous and angry" one... seemed to have mixed Him up with their *Diable..!* It was, therefore, hardly surprising that they had brought so many disasters with them from Agômenoki, the Land on the Other Side.[170]-- Such as all the strange, terrible sicknesses that now afflicted the People. The constant wars... Hardly did one conflict end when another was breaking out. They asked to meet with councils of chiefs,

---

[170] The term for Europe: *Western Abenaki Dictionary,* Volume II, p. 132.

negotiating treaties, and then, soon after, their signed and sealed pledges could be regarded as scraps of pizeuadoik pilaskol -- worthless paper. --

Pakaldam -- Of course, -- the Plac'môniak were not as bad in that respect as the Iglismôniak... Probably because the fewer Frenchmen here, on this Great Island... needed the help of the Alnôbak warriors against the more numerous Pastoniak. It was well that the French needed the Alnôbak so much! Otherwise they might prove to be as arrogant and as zahagedzaa -- greedy -- as the Iglismôniak and Pastoniak.

The more Cloud Eagle lidahôzi pamômiui kinaui kagôsal -- thought about such things -- the epidemics, the threat posed by the zahagedzaa *Anglais,* the gloomier he felt. Realizing that his mind was slipping "alômiui ôlkamiga -- into a low area" (into depression), -- Asokw Mgezo squared his shoulders. He resolved to think in more positive terms. Remembering his inspired synthesis, earlier, whereby his recall of a *La Bible* story -- the shaman Mozes on *Mont Sinai,* -- enabled him to reconcile the contrasting versions of Kullos'kahp's creation of the First People... he smiled, savoring the taste of skibô.

Asokw Mgezo could also taste, somewhat, the coltsfoot blossoms, which led him, in turn (ruminating positively), to contemplate the benefits of that particular plant. Pmi niben paiyab -- When summer came, -- the herb's yellow flowers would be long gone. Kaneua! -- But! -- Abundantly replaced by the broad, wonderful leaves of that herb, providing even more of its nebizon. Guina baami! Much more! Mazipskoik medicine practitioners such as the elder medaulinnoskua Nbizonhouo M'Sadokues, Kisikauo, Wise Woman, himself, and others availed themselves of several abundantly-growing patches that flourished, here and there, around Sôgemô Ôauanoleuo's castle.

Dreamily he envisioned one particularly abundant patch... a place that he and Ôeoandamsko resorted to quite frequently. When they harvested the leaves, they sometimes took (there being so many at that particular place!) more than they needed for their own use. Arranging the leaves into layered pads, they gifted them to other Mazipskiak as they walked home. Tribal members, probably mezi'ua Alnôbak --all of the (Native) People, -- had a great use for summertime coltsfoot leaves. It involved burning dried-out leaves and then using the fine white ashes to sprinkle on freshly cooked food. The ashes constitute an extremely healthy kind of ziuan -- salt. --

Sea salt, brought from the ocean by Plac'môniak traders, was, in contrast, coarse-grained and expensive. That commodity is best used to preserve meat and help cure freshly skinned hides. Before the coming of the Auanock to Mazipskoik the People had reduced the leaves to ashes with fire-heated soapstone bowls. Once metal kettles and pots became available, those utensils were used, placing the leaves deep in the pot, thus avoiding the loss of the delicate ashes, which could easily be blown asunder by the slightest breeze, when transferring to food or to a storage container.

Dahôlauikhôzo'a piayô -- A picture came -- to Cloud Eagle. He was surprised that he recalled it so vividly. He had approached the abundantly fecund patch with the afternoon sun behind him. Kizos was so direct that, as he bent over to begin picking leaves, he took special notice of his shadow on the vividly illuminated vegetation. That image, considered unimportant at the time… had for some reason been tucked away in his mind as something worth retaining.

Author's photo

Longing for home, which they should reach after a few days steady paddling, another image surfaced in his mind's eye. *Agma* 'ua -- Of **Her**. -- He could imagine what she was doing right now, most likely. Agma ao tali akikônal --She would be in the fields, -- along with other women, seeding the freshly turned earth, planting beans and skamonal --maize kernels. -- Agemôuô piuesid kuahliui -- Their little one nearby, -- where she and the other women could keep a close eye on her. They would be singing lullabies and lintouôganal'ua môsandzôgan ta kinôbauôgan -- songs of love and courage -- as they worked. Would she be wearing that new blouse recently made from the bolt of print cloth they had acquired..? It was edged with white lace, with mkui zilkial -- red ribbons -- around the cuffs, collar, and hem. Would she have on her new red calico dress..? He envisioned her wearing those fetching garments …he so much enjoyed seeing her in them, even working in the fields. The soil underfoot being so freshly upturned, she wouldn't be wearing her finely beaded moccasins, worn on social occasions. Instead she would have on her workaday caribou-hide footwear.

Phyllis Notôuo Larrabee, dressed in typical Abenaki regalia, 'as Ôeoandamsko.' She is using a 'dibble stick' to poke holes in soil for planting adebakual ta skamonal --beans and corn (kernels).--

Author's photo, taken in Kikas -- Field - Making Moon -- (May), Cabot, VT.

Another pleasant image, he recalled from the previous year, came to him unbidden. He was looking into the maskua dautigan, birch bark container they had started putting berries in. Birch bark articles, usually, are fashioned inside-out. The white outside bark winds up on the inside of the item, making the exterior brown. On that particular day nibena -- last summer -- they had harvested two kinds of berries simultaneously. The Pastoniak, he remembered, call one variety "blackberries" and the red ones "raspberries."

That is not what the People call them, however. Rather than name them according to their color (or from *raspis,* for the raspberry) the Ô'banakiak go by the berries' tactile nature. They're called pezaguedamenak, which signifies how ripe they can get. Pezagudamen means that the berry is "thick (as a liquid), soft and slimy." 'Pezaguedamenak'[171] is, specifically, applied to blackberries, but the appellation for raspberry is similar: zegueskimen, "soft, broken-up berry." The day having been so bright, the red and black berries had contrasted markedly against the white interior of the container.

---

[171] *Western Abenaki Dictionary,* Volume II, p. 38. Botanical name: *Rubus alleghaniensis.* Blackberry *bush* is pezagudamenakuam.

The white bark became *pesakôlala uôbi* -- *glaringly* white -- when they looked into it. A pleasant recollection, o'hôô, yes, (he almost smacked his lips thinking of those berries) but what, in addition to the association with Wise Woman... had brought about that recollection? Glancing around, it came to him. Ahaa!! It's the warrior's paint his fellow band members are wearing,

Author's photo

especially!... those from Mazipskoik and Odanak. Mkui -- red, -- uôbi -- white, -- ta mkazaui! -- and black!-- Minaguiba --Though, -- considering that he was along more as a healer than as a combatant, he tended to think of his own paint as more ceremonially benign, more peaceful. Not as warlike.

Though it would be late summer before those berries became ripe again, he had no feelings of regret because they weren't available just now. A waste of emotion. He had dried-out berries with him, in his bmiôgan -- trail food. -- Mixed in were pessimenal[172] -- currants, -- satal -- blueberries, -- and ômuaimenal -- "shad bush" or serviceberries.

As Asokw Mgezo dreamed of home, he felt relieved that agma ta agma ôauidziatidzik[173] -- he and his brothers -- had emerged safely from the obnoxious war. Or were fairly safe... there was yet the possibility of running afoul of a party of Muheconnuck or Maguak scouts who didn't know that the Anglais *armée* was now in full retreat. But they should be all right as long as they remained alert. Kept their ears as well as their eyes open ali tsaga kinamek ta kitamek -- as if looking and listening --

---

[172] *Ribes sativum,* red currant, *Ibid,* p. 96. Currant bush is pessimenakuam. *Ibid,* p. 35 for serviceberries.

[173] Indicates "those who are brothers together," not necessarily meaning familial siblings. As in the English "brethren," fellow church members, labor union brothers, members of fraternal societies, etc. *Western Abenaki Dictionary,* Volume II, p. 52.

ôadsi meskauamek si'si'kuak -- to detect rattlesnakes.--

As members of the mômôui'ua ôidkauinnoak -- company of companions -- settled in for the remainder of the day, there occurred low-toned (rather inaudible, even if you were only a few feet away), conversations between individuals here and there.

Satisfied that everyone was doing nicely in the vicinity of the skueda that Olitôguezo was cooking his skibô over, Cloud Eagle wandered closer to the other fire. He wanted to see how everyone was doing over there. As he drew closer he could catch snatches of conversation between two warriors who were often seen in each other's company. The nbizonhouad knew they were cousins, half- Abenaki Osôgenak --Algonkins -- from Canada. He and Wise Woman had entertained them when they had arrived in Mazipskoik as part of the present war party. They were enjoyable company, each blessed with a quick sense of humor, frequently ribbing each other. Even when there seemed nothing to say, when everyone was silent, you could detect traces of sardonic humor in their faces, their eyes twinkling with bemusement.

The jocular pair acted like brothers but were actually first cousins. They were closely related to the Attikamegak, Algonkins well to the north, and to the northeastern Inniuk, also Algonquians, called by the French *les Montagnais*. Had one called the other Kuôgunas-? And had the other had responded by addressing his cousin as… C'hila-? The appellations were not flattering. "Kuôgunas"[174] can be understood as meaning 'prickly,' indicating someone who bristles, is easily offended, reminiscent of one of the words for the porcupine, *"Spiny* One, Kôgw". "C'hila" is similar, indicating one who is perennially cross… grudging, ill-tempered.[175] Yet, far from being offended, the exchange only seemed to make them chortle all the more. Their names were Maigamo and Salom. 'Maigan' indicates the wolf, related to the Abenaki môlsem, among the Algonkins of the vast Kibek territory, especially of the area around Abitibi, a council fire village of that people.

When first becoming acquainted at Mazipskoik, Cloud Eagle and Ôeoandamsko had been puzzled by Maigamo's name, together with his hailing from the **north,** in Kibek. He had mentioned his town of origin as Abitibi. "Maigan" has a ring similar to "Mahican" (from 'Maahicander') the Dutch word for Muheconw,[176] singular for a member of the Muheconnuck nation, such as T'songeba. While both terms involve Algonquian language-family affinity, they have markedly different meanings. A Muheconw is someone "of the Rising and Falling Waters," a reference to the tidal nature

---

[174] Reference Chapter XI, Nagako Ta Mozis, Chief Henry L. Masta's *Abenaki Indian Legends, Grammar, and Place Names,* pp. 35 - 42. For 'C'hila' also.

[175] Related to Cilao, "he is bad tempered, peevish, easily angered." *Western Abenaki Dictionary,* Volume I, p. 146.

[176] Ultimate source for the popular designation of **Mohican,** as in James Fenimore Cooper's early 19th century *The Last of the Mohicans.* The currently fashionable 'Mahican' is from the colonial Dutch "Maahicander."

of Hudson's River, said waterway constituting the heartland of the Mohican Nation.

In contrast to the wholly Alnôbaiui nature of Maigamo's name, Sa̧lom is Abenaki-accented French, a baptismal name, from 'Saint Jerome.' Though Salom wore a crucifix as a necklace pendant, one with two crossbars, a 'Cross of Lorraine,' Salom wasn't especially churchly. The medicine couple soon learned that he perceived his cross as representative of the *dragonfly*. Anciently evocative of Ma̧nitou, the four-winged insect is "free and active," very quick... traits essential to a warrior.[177] It signifies oda̧môgan -- the dragonfly (*or* the pipe), -- ...denotes *mahom*, a *grandfather* entity, flitting back and forth between the material and spiritual planes.

Salom was interested in anything the couple said when they recalled traditional legends and alluded to the Oligo Mkui Ô'udi. Listened with as much respect as the plainly "païen" Maigamo. Sometimes he, like his cousin, would volunteer stories and commentary from Attikamegak or Inniuk sources, especially when such narrations were similar to Ô'banaki lore. Occasionally they made insightful but witty comments relative to the tales. The cousins attained heights of hilarity when they recalled legends about the rollicking Inniuk demigod Kua̧kua̧dzec -- Wolverine. -- Kuakuadzec is obviously the same universally Algonquian figure as Kullos'kahp, but various of the stories about him, the tongue-in-cheek, deliberately comical ones, are even funnier, Kuakuadzec routinely getting himself involved in absolutely outrageous situations.[178] Predicaments that were very funny, in the re-telling, of his (self-inflicted) travails and misadventures.

At the present juncture Asokw Mgezo inadvertently couldn't help but harken to the cousins' murmured banter while scrutinizing the margin of the camp. He happened to notice Maigamo's shadow, where the warrior's deer and kôgw-hair roach, festooned with two heron feathers, was outlined. Naturally, what a shadow ever does is outline a shape. However, for the first time Cloud Eagle noticed a feature "reflected" *inside* the shadow. It was Maigamo's necklace of pale shell beads! Just a coincidence. The reflected "necklace" was actually a tiny, somewhat curvaceous twig lying athwart Maigamo's neck... that is, the shadow's neck. A pattern of coltsfoot blossoms within the shadow could also be seen as large yellow beads embellishing the shoulder strap of the warrior's bandolier bag. One blossom even looked like it might be a bright gold or brass earring hanging from Maigamo's left ear.

---

[177] P. 104, *Silver in the Fur Trade, 1680 - 1820*, Martha Wilson Hamilton, 1995, Chelmsford, MA.
[178] To be found in *Wolverine Creates the World*, "Labrador Indian Tales" collected and retold by Lawrence Millman. 65 stories from the oral history of the Inniuk Nation. Capra Press, Santa Barbara, CA 1993.

Bemused by this observation, Cloud Eagle wondered… a message from Spirit pertaining to Maigamo? If a message… he certainly couldn't understand it. Kisi pizeuadoo -- Its nothing. -- Another objective was forming in his mind as he tuned into the cousins' joshing banter. If the young men weren't particularly engaged at the moment, the medauinno hoped to recruit them in harvesting more greens and herbs.

Author's photo

They were indeed rather idle, finishing off the remains of the agasksw --woodchuck, -- madeguas -- hare, -- ta mikoak -- and squirrels -- they had bagged earlier, tsadzabenamek mekuedsazigan -- sharing the roasted meat -- with others. Had finished cleaning the fusils they had harvested the game with.

When they called each other C'hila and Kuôgunas Asokw Mgezo assumed the appellations were facetious nicknames applied to each other. What was puzzling was that sometimes 'C'hila' labeled his cousin with that name, and "Kuôgunas" referred to 'C'hila' as… Kuôgunas! The nicknames were not hard and fast… were interchangeable. In the course of gathering additional greens or herbs before night fell, the nodsipelouad[179] would, he expected, get to the bottom of it. He didn't want to be minôbeskiatta… -- too inquisitive…-- But was curious. He suspected that there was an interesting story behind it all.

Cloud Eagle did, indeed, elicit an interesting story --very interesting -- from the cousins after he had recruited them to help him gather more medicinal herbs and wild greens, making a sortie back to the area where he had met the returning turkey

---

[179] A doctor: "One who treats ill persons therapeutically." *Western Abenaki Dictionary,* Volume I, p. 373.

harvesters. Not that all three collected... one kept watch, firelock at the ready; there could be enemy scouts lurking about. Also to bag a worthy game animal that might wander near. The cousins, fairly whispering, told the story of their vivacious (then young and newlywed) grandmother / great aunt Soliôn -- Alnôbaiui for Juliette,-- an Odanak Ô'banaki. And her older... *problematical*... husband, the Abitibi Algonkin Kuôgunas. Called C'hila, as well, names evocative of "prickly," ill-tempered. Asokw Mgezo was surprised, even shocked, at their revelations.

Cloud Eagle first led the cousins toward where he had met the turkey-hunters earlier. He thought he had noticed an abundance of ôinozak, wild-growing leeks, in that area. When listening to T'songeba and Pepôkuan relate their thumbnail sketch of Muheconnuck / Suônniuk history (confirming the Auanock to the south had also adopted the nahamak-harvesting trick of posing as cowbells-tinkling kaozak)... had quite forgotten about the leeks. Remembering presently, his interest was renewed.

Though they would not have to venture very far, they should be prepared for action lest they fall afoul of enemy scouts. With the exception that the medauinno left his new acquired musketoon behind. Despite its short barrel, it would be too heavy, too clumsy, lacking a carrying sling. He wanted to keep both hands free for gathering, relying on the cousins for protection. They were experienced fighting men who could be depended on.

As they strolled toward the presumably abundant ôinozek -- place of leeks, -- they crossed a low area...made up of brown reeds and old, flattened aquatic growth. Snow melt and spring rains had flooded the area shortly before. New greenery had not yet appeared. Save for one species, which thrust tentative leaves and white flowers among winter-ravaged reeds from the previous year. Asokw Mgezo halted, kneeling down. O'hôô, Yes, useful medicinal flowers! They were pagakanihlôg, bloodroot flowers.

The band's *naturel docteur* was quite impressed with these particular pskuasauônal[180] -- flowers, -- in herbal terms. It was not only the flower (the blossom) that interested him. The medicinal value includes the leaves and roots. An ironic feature of the plant... is that she can be said to be "two spirited." Negative and positive contained within the same species. While the leaves and roots can contribute to your health, aid you against sickness... the blood-red sap of the stem is toxic.

---

[180] *Western Abenaki Dictionary,* Volume II, p. 151. Dr. Day spells flower 'peskwatawa,' "it is open," plural peskwasawônal. However, the present author has eliminated the **e** of pesk and changed his **w**'s to **u**'s to reflect the non-labial freckltle (minimal movement of the lips) mode of 17th and 18th century Ô'banakiak speech, believing such e's and w's came to be used more often as original vocalizations gave way to the louder, more extensive mouth-movements of the European way of speaking. As colonized Abenaki people, routinely interacting with *Québécois* and Anglo-Americans, perforce absorbed more French and English... they were influenced in the way they articulated Alnôbaiui. Nonetheless, here and there the original, minimalist way of speaking is reflected in print as late as the 20th century. A case in point is Dr. Day's spelling for "water snake flower," *Scutellaria galericulata.* To wit: Nebiiskog pskwasawôn, p. 151, *Ibid.* Note the absence of the **e** (in what would be otherwise spelled 'pesk') in "pskwasawôn."

Cloud Eagle found this to be fascinating. Why did Great Mystery provide medicine in the leaves and roots and yet… determine that the sap should be poisonous..? Of course, the leaves (and roots) should be used to a limited extent. Use too much and *they too* will prove toxic.[181] The youthful nbizonhouad at this moment could be called maṇdokôzid, "one who sits and reflects, a conjurer, he thinks." He was silent, pondering.

Author's early spring photo of medicinal pagakanihlôg -- that which bleeds, -- a wild flower, which can be noticed along sun - drenched streams recently in flood. Blood - red stem sap can also be used as a dye for decorating basket splints, snowshoes frames, games, buckskin garments, &c.

Ah, o'hôô, as "armament" of self-defense?? Intended to *protect* the useful plant? The early flowering blossoms, white with yellow centers, have allure, are beautiful. And therefore can attract the attention of herbivorous auaasak, which would meander over to eat the blossoms and leaves. Perhaps crush the roots as well. The blossoms are no doubt necessary to attract insects and foster pollination. The sap in the stem is toxic to keep herbivores from eating the plant… pagakan-mkuigen, blood-red colored, to warn the animal against eating more after a first nip. Warn the auaas that *its own* blood will turn bad if it keeps on eating. Could that be it? And yet, for human beings, for the Alnôbak, even the sap is useful. It can be used as dye to color basket splints and decoratively redden dressed skins… Some are so bold as to daub some of the sap on their skin as ceremonial paint. Not much, acoui, of course. Had he heard there are warriors who deliberately looked for pagakanhilôg -- in season, of course, in ôskiziguan -- early spring, -- to use as war paint..? To demonstrate how bold they are, emphasizing their willingness to confront danger.

---

[181] **Caution!** Before the gentle reader is inspired to attempt to extract medicine (for a variety of ailments) from bloodroot roots, the author would advise experimenters to reference *Earth Medicine - Earth Foods* (Plant Remedies, Drugs, and Natural Foods of the North American Indians) by Michael A. Weiner, Macmillan Publishing, New York, 1972. See pages 77 and 114.

Kisikauo, Nbizonhouo M'Sadokues, Ôeoandamsko, and Asokw Mgezo, not only in their capacities as olinebizonoho môsônledoak -- good medicine practitioners,-- but simply as -- ôli nsatouinnoak -- prudent, careful people,-- didn't recommend using the sap directly on one's own skin.

The cousin named Maigamo, 'Wolf,' joined *le homme de médecine* in collecting pagakanihlôg roots and some of the leaves. Salom in the meanwhile hid himself in a nearby copse of trees, keeping watch, fusil held ready. Where the bloodroot grew was routinely inundated, a wetland, though quite dry underfoot at the moment. The area could be termed akikôn, a field. The place afforded absolutely no cover for the two should enemies appear.

Maigamo and Cloud Eagle discussed both the negative and positive attributes of the plant as they bent to their work. 'He is Wolf' thought he remembered someone saying that pagakanihlôg môskebala -- blood-root sap -- is (or ought to be?) an ingredient in springtime insect repellent. Should be harmless if applied to your skin as it would be diluted, mixed with other elements, such as fresh pine sap. Against such absolutely tiny insects as mosquitoes, it *should* remain powerful enough... even though mixed with other ingredients.

Asokw Mgezo allowed that he had heard something similar, and may well have smeared on insect repellent containing bloodroot sap when he had accepted repellent concocted by others. He intended to consult Kisikauo or medaulinnoskua M'Sadokues about the matter when finally back at Sôgemô Grey Lock's 'castle.' The two could have spent the rest of the afternoon harvesting leaves and roots of the flower, there were so many of them in this sun-drenched expanse. Lategua, negemiui -- Hundreds, easily. -- However, the pair became increasingly apprehensive, periodically looking around to make certain enemies were not approaching. Their location was too exposed. Presently the nodsipelouad straightened up, saying "N' uadsônôbena ôami --We have enough."-- Time to move on, find that place of ôsôna ôinozek -- abundant leeks. -- He and Maigamo both extracted their odamô pouches, putting down tobacco while murmuring thanks to manitou'ua pagakanihlôg -- the spirit of that which bleeds. -- They signaled to Salom, moving on. Cloud Eagle knew that he should have lit his pipe, taking a contemplative puff or two, and passed it on to Maigamo in saying oliôni. However, he would feel better about doing so when they were among some trees. Not so obvious to lurking foes. Would address the manitôu'ua pagakanihlôg again when thanking other vegetative spirits. Leaving the slough, climbing a gradual slope, they spotted another species of fresh greens: upstart ferns, so-called "fiddleheads." Nhloak nauadsiak -- The three paused. -- That the growths are in the process of *becoming* masozial, ferns, is apparent. Recalled when his family, making their way west and north, the English called this pale-stemmed kind "bracken fern."[182] Words that were non-existent in Alnôbaiui, containing the consonants R and F. Is he right about that? Whatever they are called, the tightly curled tops are edible (though they should be cooked first). Those topmost parts, before they unfurl, are quite welcome siguanasin -- when spring arrives. -- The Pastoniak call them 'fiddleheads,' which translated into Alnôbaiui, is rendered as 'alipodôzigdebal.' "Debal" describes heads, of course. Alipodôzig means "that which one rubs back and forth," indicative of a curious stringed instrument of the Auanock,[183] whether French or British.

Author's photo

The trio -- actually the pair, Salom remaining watchful -- broke off the 'heads' from the cluster before them, putting them in their ash-splint basket. There were seventeen in the clump. Not many. They looked around for more, Asokw Mgezo thinking they might find another kind, the darker green sort. A species the Pastoniak used the term 'cinnamon' in connection with, which are just as abundant as these… in some places more so. They moved on, winding among trees as they climbed a hill.

Ta sogata dabi! --And sure enough! -- The nbizonhouad spied some of the greener alipodôzigdebal. These are known as 'ostrich fern'[184] because the mature fern resembles the feather of a foreign bird. Harvesting the tightly curled heads, they found many that were hidden. These were uncovered by fingering aside old leaves from the previous autumn. They lingered long enough to fill the ash-splint basket, and then, quietly murmuring oliôni, putting down odamô, moved on. Thicker woods were ahead, affording more cover. They were getting close to where the nahamak hunters had succeeded in getting their nguedôz nahamak -- six turkeys. -- *Ahaa!* Then they espied ôinozek -- the place of leeks. -- There were indeed many of them. The *homme de*

---

[182] Petersen Field Guides, *Edible Wild Plants,* pp. 232 - 233, "Bracken, pasture break," *Pteridum aquiline,*
[183] *Western Abenaki Dictionary,* Volume II, p. 432. Alnôbaiui for the violin, and can also describe the harmonica.
[184] *Petersen's Edible Wild Plants,* pp. 232 - 233, ostrich fern (also cinnamon fern), *Petretis pensylvanica.*

médecine had been half hoping that they might run across additional skibô, but so far had not seen any. Still, they might yet… taking a somewhat different route back.

Author's photo of cinnamon fiddleheads in ash - splint basket. A cluster of fiddle - heads can be seen to the right of basket, as yet unpicked. These still feature their distinctive brownish 'paper' wrapping which lends them the folk name of cinnamon ferns. It is the fully grown, full-fledged fern that is called the ostrich fern due to its resemblance to the large, prominent tail feather of an ostrich. The actual feathers were used, at the time of our story, to festoon the hats of men and ladies, including the headdresses of Native American chiefs.

Nhloak -- [The] three -- felt much more comfortable as they settled among the leeks, surrounded by numerous trees on all sides. Nonetheless Maigamo, this time, stood guard, keeping a careful lookout, while Jerome and Asokw Mgezo found short sticks to dig with. The two bent to their task of harvesting as many of the ôinozak tubers as would fill their remaining containers, the skin and mazôn nodal -- hemp sacks. -- The cousins would change places when Salom grew tired of digging. Or perhaps their nbizonhouad would keep watch, next, borrowing a fusil while both cousins "C'hila" and "Kuôgunas" harvested.

After Salom had been digging for a while, he paused and exhaled emphatically, as if growing weary of the tedious work. He is Wolf smiled and spoke to him, very quietly (including, as much as he could, the first two attention-getting expressions); "*Haw, haw, Kuôgunas.*" continuing to whisper the following: "*Zauitôzo, d' kia?,* Tired of working, are you?" Salom smirked at this, factiously replying: "*K' ôakasômkuad kuazikha nigidziboôd,*[185] *idzia!* --Your few words make me bristle, cousin! -- *Ônda, niak ônda zaui!* --No, I am not weary! -- *Ônda, n' alokaô nspi kesitahônsôngan'ua kighaui Nokemes Soliôn!* -- No, I am working with the zeal of our heroic Grandmother Juliette!"--

---

[185] "Bristle" in the sense of nigidzsiboôd: "he who's hair or fur stands on end," p. 365, *Western Abenaki Dictionary,* Volume I, and p. 178, *Ibid,* Volume II.

15. Sissa Maskauloha ôadsi Okemes Soliôn
-- Lavish Praise for Grandmother Juliette --

The cousins chuckled good-naturedly over this exchange, provoking Cloud Eagle's curiosity. "Okemes kia lôdouô'ua aiyagô aobba *gezôuado*[186] p'hanem --The Grandmother you speak of must have [been] *quite* the woman," -- he observed, straightening up. "Kagui kisi agma -- What did she [do] -- nada oliha k' gelôzi kassiui oligo'ua agma? -- that makes you speak so well of her?"--

Maigamo and Salom looked at each other, smiling broadly. "Agma oskidhla nspi Mahom Kuôgunas! -- She put up with Grandfather Prickly One!"-- they both blurted out at the same time, laughing. "Agma'aob kighahuadui! -- She was heroic! -- N' ualdamôbena, *n' ualdamôbena* --We know, *we know,* -- Niona **waldamôbena** d' niona askauitôzik ôadsi kuesihamek n' kitsiiak! --We **know** we're supposed to respect our elders! -- Kaneua agma'aob tsibagôba! -- But he was awful! -- Kia uadsônô ônda kiuidahôzuôgan tôhné madsi! --You have no idea how bad! -- Kisi odsikaui niona lôbedalemôbena! -- It's why we laugh! -- Niona meska kuaguahlimamek -- We find it astonishing, -- ônsagaagh -- amazing, -- nada n' uadsônôbenoob kinaui madsigoid ôadsi Mahom'a -- that we have had such a bad man for a Grandfather."--

"Askuatta n'nihlôdsik d' kassi oligid! --Yet we **ourselves** are so nice!"-- quipped Maigamo, and both laughed again at this latest witticism.

"Kisito k' uadsônôba pazego madsi Mahom -- Do you have one bad Grandfather, -- ala nizuak? -- or two?" -- Asokw Mgezo asked, thinking of C'hila, the other name. "Ibi pazego -- Just one,"-- Salom answered. "Pazego ligen dabi -- One is enough. -- Bahami ndaki dabatta! -- More than enough!" -- he added ruefully.

Their lookout, even while keeping watch, began to explain. "Pmi nôkskua, Nokemes Soliôn kezidaldambanik ali pitta olgio -- When a young woman, Grandmother Juliette was considered to be very pretty. -- Kezidaldambanik olinôguezo -- Was considered good looking, -- *ta* pitta ôauôdam -- *and* very intelligent.--

Glancing up briefly, Salom chimed in. Though it is deemed impolite to interrupt someone who is talking, the harvester wasn't really interrupting. He knew that Maigamo was supposed to be keeping watch, not conversing. He was allowing their lookout to concentrate on his duty, rather than become conversationally distracted. 'He is Wolf' understood.

"Agma gezaldamab'ua ôla klamiozuôgan -- She was fond of good amusements,

---

[186] "Quite," as a term of routine emphasis, can be translated as saki. However, 'gezôuado,' in the above context, more specifically indicates someone who is "worth a lot, valuable, dear: is important, esteemed." *Ibid*, Volume II, p. 200.

kôdak ali tkasmimek[187] -- such as swimming -- lintômek, ta pmegamek -- singing, and dancing. -- Kuaskuai ôdsikaui agma nibaoab Kuôgunas onolemaldamen -- Exactly why she married Kuôgunas is uncertain,"-- Jerome continued. "Saki maasa agma

Author's May 4th photo of wild ôinozak -- leeks, -- photographed with soap - stone pipe and buckskin odamôinoda -- tobacco's pouch. -- Both items are shown because such are typically employed to express gratitude toward the plants. Note crumbled tobacco on the pouch, from odamô raised and cured by the author the previous year. Tubers of four up - rooted ôinozak, near pipe bowl ('Cloud Eagle's' digging stick laid across stalks) have been cleaned to photograph more clearly. Also in photo is an *olômpskw'a* -- a *bud* -- of trillium, above pipe, pouch, and stick. A few new - born tentative fiddleheads, just barely starting out in life, are also present, hardly visible in photo. One can be seen where an old stalk crosses under pipe stem. Another can be glimpsed on the extreme left. Tiny fiddleheads so minute that many of them can be discovered only by fingering aside leaves of the previous year's autumnal leaf - fall.

---

[187] By becoming familiar with the basic grammar of Alnôbaiui, the equivalents for *fundamental* nouns, etc., in English, such as up, down, hot, cold, loose, solid, good, bad, &c. one can gain insights into how Native American words were originally formed countless centuries ago. One can see at a glance that tkasmimek, swimming, begins with tka, *cold*, as its prefix. Swimming involves cold, because the temperatures of Northeastern waters are (usually) colder than the air immediately above. In the Abenaki world-view to engage in swimming is not only a matter of immersion in water, but can be said to involve *cooling off*. Reference *Abenaki Legends, Grammar, and Place Names*, p. 35, Chief Henry L. Masta 1932.

ôaualemegueziab ôadsi agma kuôgunaskid -- Quite early he became known for his cross and jealous nature."--

"Agma aob doz'ua Ô'banakiak Ntami[188] Sôgemô Llobal, ac'hi -- She was the daughter of Abenaki Head Chief Llobal, too,"-- Maigamo added. Though at the moment he had his back turned, scrutinizing all around, he could hear Salom perfectly.

"Kaneua 'nidôbenna' C'hila ônda ogezaldamenab ôadsi dômô uiagôuzouôgan --But our 'friend' C'hila didn't care for any kind of pleasure-making"-- Salom recalled. "Agma aob pitta ozigi nspi agma nizuiididzi'i uedladakauôgan... He was very unhappy with his wife's manners" -- saying (in words to the effect of) "...it would be so much better to leave, ta lagukannôbena li Abitibi -- and move to Abitibi."-- Salom continued on about how Soliôn didn't like the idea of going so far away. She knew that Kuôgunas was motivated by nothing more than baseless jealousy. However, she loved him -- no one knows why, -- and didn't balk. They reached Abitibi without incident.

"*Kaneua* adali aobanik ôskinnoak dali ac'hi -- *But* there were too many young fellows there also, -- kassi agemôgik sôgaui[189] -- so they left quietly, -- adodzi alemakannomek nopaiui alômi kpiui -- traveling further into the forest, -- where they were unlikely to encounter anyone else... where C'hila could have Juliette all to himself. Ala kassi agma *debidahôdam* -- Or so he *thought*.--

They built a wigwam and settled in, safely and privately ensconced in the trackless forest. But even there, Kuôgunas was uneasy. He feared that someone might wander up to their lodge while he was away hunting, quite unexpectedly, and that "someone" would be a young man, not only younger but better looking than himself. So one day he claimed; "O kamôdzi saagad, n'akuamalsiô -- Oh, it's too bad, I'm unwell-- nia gizi'ônda nadialmek -- I can't go out hunting."-- It was at this juncture that the affectionate Soliôn showed how resourceful she could be."Kamôdzi saagad, It's too bad, *N' kigizi* nadialiô! -- *I can* hunt!" -- she said. --"K' aguedzatô yudali, You stay here." Soliôn set out right away. And did quite well! Every morning, for days, she would go

---

[188] In Chief Masta's *Abenaki Grammar,* Masta translates Chief Llobal's status as Head Chief without using dup (or deb), the equivalent for head. Ntami actually translates as *first*. The First Chief, the Paramount Chief. P. 390, *Western Abenaki Dictionary,* Volume I. "Ntami: First of a series."

[189] Chief Masta's story, or "legend," about Soliôn and Kuôgunas is not repeated here word for word, is only paraphrased, the present author having added his own quite original (culturally insightful) embellishments. Of special interest is Masta's employment of sôgaui to express **travel** or traveling, which invokes the image of the **crayfish** (or of how a crayfish moves)... the Alnôbaiui equivalent for lobster, crab, or crayfish being sôga, p. 231, *Western Abenaki Dictionary,* Volume II (plural sôgak). The suffix 'ui' indicates like, similar to ...crayfish-**like**. The simile invokes the ability of the camouflaged crayfish, prey to various predators such as raccoons, to travel invisibly from place to place along the streambeds of the rivers and brooks that they inhabit. An Anglo-American version would be "to get away ...like a snake in the grass." Kuôgunas paranoia motivated him to bring Soliôn to the Algonkin Council-Fire town of Abitibi, and then, because there were "too many" young men there who might take an interest in her, quit Abitibi for the deep woods quietly, *stealthily* (crayfish-like) without attracting attention. Traditionally it became routine... for whole columns of native people to travel so on wilderness trails... silently, watching, listening, every sense on the alert against ambush or any kind of surprise.

Soliôn set out right away. And did quite well! Every morning, for days, she would go out. Soliôn had reason to be happy. Kuôgunas, noticing her satisfaction, became fretful, became restless. Abruptly, he proposed that they return to Abitibi. But Juliette laughed at the idea. Refused, declaring that she liked it where they were. This made C'hila / Kuôgunas even more suspicious. "O'hôô -- Yes,"-- he said, in words to the effect: "could be that you're having pleasure with someone." "O ni! Kaguesa ôanudaminauôgan! -- Oh my! What silliness!" -- Soliôn laughed. Her disdain convinced him that they should remain where they were... for the time being.

"Niona d' mezenamek psigia pabômiui moôuin -- We're getting to the part of the story about the bear,"-- Maigamo couldn't keep himself from scornfully interjecting.

Jerome continued: The couple remained where they were, and in that time a boy was born to them. They named him Ôualôba, because he was handsome and resembled his mother.

"Agma ao nmitôgues -- He is my father,"-- remarked Salom. C'hila's health remained 'poor.' He couldn't do any hunting. While Juliette went out, Kuôgunas remained at home and took care of the infant. Soliôn, however, seemed to thrive despite the added burden. She had to nurse the infant, continue hunting, roast the meat, scrape and tan the hides... Her pleasures were few. But she was courageous, agma melikasanin kizigenak nspi ôli alokauôgan -- her efforts met with success. -- Agma aob ôiagiui -- She was jovial.--

16.   Idômbaui Moôuin -- [The] Friendly Bear--

"A'hem!" Maigamo pretended to clear his throat. He wished to add something. "Kia acouiba dablodôzigô na Nokemes ao Ogauinno'a --You should mention that Our grandmother is a Bear Clan person."--

"Kadata, pitta zôbi -- Indeed, very true,"-- Salom nodded. "Nokemes ao Ogauinno'a -- Our grandmother is a Sleeping Person (i.e., a Bear Clan member).--
Salom continued with words to the effect that C'hila's health seemed to improve... he waxed indignant, acting strangely. "K' neguicinô yudali, saba -- You stay here, tomorrow, -- *nia* alosôdzi nadialmek -- *I* will go hunting,"-- he announced emphatically. Grandmother attempted to dissuade him, saying that he should take care of himself so as not to get worse. But he left in the morning... wasn't gone long. He brought back a great deal of meat and proceeded to roast some of it. Baked bread and even made gravy. An appreciative Juliette remarked, licking her fingers, their repast had been the best yet in that place. Kuôgunas didn't mention what kind of ôios they had eaten until she inquired as to what kind of animal it had been.

"Ennagani -- Well dear," -- he replied saying (in effect): "It's the flesh of your friend, the bear. You *didn't imagine* I could get him, eh? One day I followed you. Saw you pick up a stick and strike a hollow tree. A bear came out! You and the moôuin played together so long I had to leave in order to look after our child. I'm telling you: this gambol won't be repeated. "Ônda nspi ôada moôuin -- Not with *this* bear."--

Grandmother was so shocked and aggrieved that she couldn't do otherwise but weep and wail. Being Ogauinno, of the Bear Clan, it was as if she had eaten the flesh of a close relative. Ogauinnoak of course don't hunt bears... and this moôuin had been particularly friendly, brightening her time alone in the forest with its playful antics.

When she had collected herself somewhat she said: "Niak pizeuadoo li kia anegi yo -- I am nothing to you after this." -- She was still so outraged that she determined to leave C'hila... child and all, leaving him to take care of the baby by himself..!

"Ôadsi Tabaldak'i ôizuôgan -- For God's sake," -- Kuôgunas pleaded, "tôniba kizi n'dôlli nanaualmôn kedmôgi Ôualôba nspi nia? -- how can I keep poor Ôualôba with me?"-- The infant was still a nursing baby. Grandmother looked at their little boy and started weeping again. "I'll never leave you, dear child," she cried. "K'-d-aidzi ôaidsiui nspi k'nonon[190]--You'll always be with your mother,"-- she reassured her tiny son. Turning to Kuôgunas she wiped her eyes and glared hard at the wretch, saying words to the effect of: "Well, then, *C'hila,* we will go away from here. But as soon as we get out of the woods, Ôualôba and I will go to my father, to my parent's lodge. K' kisito olestôuadinô? -- Do you agree? -- Ôhôô? Ônda? --Yes? No?"-- "O'hôô --Yes," said he (because he had to). To be sure, Grandmother and her baby olitonbanik li Alsigôtekw-ok -- made it to the Empty Camp River - place (the mission town of Odanak / Saint Francis)[191] maôuitôzo -- all right.--

---

[190] Nonon is the Ô'banaki equivalent for the European 'momma,' p. 378, *Western Abenaki Dictionary,* Volume I, enunciated with N's instead of M's in keeping with the traditional habit of minimal mouth movement. *Also* present in (Abenaki - related) Woodland Algonquian is 'mama' (or variations thereof) *not necessarily* as juvenile for "mother (familiar, son or daughter speaking)," p. 378, *Ibid.* In the Glossary for *Sacred Legends of the Swampy Lake Cree,* James R. Stevens, McCelland & Steward, Ltd., 1971, we find listed O Ma Ma Ma, "a goddess, the earth mother from whom all spirits were born," p. 16. Going further, back to the beginning of all recorded languages, in the *Earth Chronicles* series by archeo-linguist Zecharia Sitchin we find the apparent origin of the term in ancient Semitic *Akkadian*... in the name of a top-ranking "Anunnaki goddess." She fostered motherhood, creating *Adamu.* "Adamu" can be translated as The Man. He was a cross between the Anunnaki 'gods' themselves and earth-born hominids. A hybrid, like his mate *Tiamat* (the later Eve), were bred so that their progeny could perform work demanded by the gods. Her 'divine' name, or epithet, was originally Ninti, but changed to Nin**mah** (author's emphasis) once having engendered the Adamu (apparently by Lord Enki's wife Ninki). "Later on she was nicknamed **Mammi**, the source of the universal Mamma / Mother," p. 163, *Genesis Revisited,* Avon Books, 1990. Knowledge about Ninmah / Mammi, Adamu, Tiamat, etc., is derived from *extremely* ancient clay tablets inscribed with cuneiform markings. These diluvian tablets were uncovered by archeologists in the Near East going back to the 19th century (a few found as early as the 18th century). Orientalists such as Sitchin have been able to interpret the cuneiform script because two yet-living tongues, Hebrew and Arabic, evolved from Akkadian roots. The scribes of Akkad extensively recorded key information from Annunaki-inspired Sumerian originals.

[191] Though Chief Masta refers, in English, to the Québec mission town of Odanak as "St-Francis," in his Alnôbaiui original, he wrote "Alsig8tekw," referring to the Empty Camp River... interpreted, usually, as the Empty *Cabin* River, on modern maps the French-derived St. Francis River. After the prefix **Alsi** we have **gô** (or **kô**), a contraction of **kôn**, camp,

Asokw Mgezo stood up, and as Salom paused, the *homme de médecine* asked if he was getting tired...a hint that he might change places with his cousin.

"O'hôô, Yes, n' kedegok d' tsidanosô -- my knees are getting stiff."-- Rising from his leeks container, he picked up his paskhigan. Maigamo turned, propping his fusil against a tree, and knelt down. Wielding Jerome's digging stick, he, speaking quietly, continued the latter's narration about their grandparents. Cloud Eagle had assumed that when Okemes Soliôn left Kuôgunas that would be the end of the tale. However, there was a bit more.

Their nbizonhouad was slightly taken aback that the sad story continued. The possessive C'hila wasn't done yet! He had gone to the Tribal Council of the Osôgenak, the Algonkins, and complained that Soliôn had no right to leave him, presenting himself... as blameless! The Algonkin chiefs in turn, knowing Juliette to be the daughter of *Abnaquies* paramount chief Llobal, demanded that an assembly be convened between themselves and the Odanak chiefs. In earlier times, before the advent of the French (especially of the missionaries) a separation between husband and wife would be no one's business but their own. But now there were certain lagidamuôganal --laws, -- governing affairs as private as marriages.

The new rules cited by the Algonkin counselors seemed to concern only a woman's role in a marriage, however. Two of the quoted provisions specified that "p'hanem'a couidebad kuzilauiô *ta kitauô* agma nisuiididsi -- a woman must respect *and obey* her husband." -- The other rule that Maigamo recalled was: "P'hanem couidebad ônda pabagihla uigiuômo'ua agma nisuiididsi -- [The] woman must not leave the domicile of her spouse."--

"Uigiuômo'ua *agma nisuiididsi??* -- The domicile of **her husband??**" -- thought Cloud Eagle. The old way, as traditionalists such as himself understood it, is that the woman, *the wife,* owns the wigwam (if anybody can be said to own it at all). If a couple splits up, it is the husband who vacates to other quarters. However, according to the regulations of the Auanock, whether French or English, the men... own **everything.** Including the women *themselves!* An exception was *les Anglais'* Queen Anne. Who, at all events, inherited the throne on the strength of descent from her father.

Salom couldn't resist chiming in with the observation that ôadsi kôniôsi -- for a moment -- it looked as if war would break out between the Algonkins and *les Abnaquies,* should the Tribal Council of the latter support Soliôn's divorce from her tyrant husband. Aodouôgan! --War! -- Asokw Mgezo was stunned. And between such

---

level" of a structure, p. 150, *Western Abenaki Dictionary,* Volume II, combined with *zig*wagen, 'it is empty,' p. 128, *Ibid.* A translation of Alsikôntegw, *Clam*-camp river, a site for fresh-water mollusk harvesting--?? It may be a combination of both Clam (Shellfish) Camp River *and* Empty Camp River. Alstegw means "clam river, oyster river, shell river," p. 37, *Ibid,* Volume I. All hunting and fishing camps are abandoned, therefore empty, from time to time. A mollusk (clam, etc.) is als, plural alsak.

close allies! Intermingled allies at that... the marriage between C'hila and Soliôn was not unusual between the two peoples. The *Canadien* Algonkins had given over vast tracts of land as hunting territories to the Ô'banakiak, in view of so many of the latter being exiles, Ô'banakik territories further south having been usurped by the *agressif Anglais*.

Fortunately Juliette's father, Sôgemô Llobal, rose to the occasion... by stepping down. He withdrew from the deliberations of the Council in view of the fact that Soliôn was his daughter. This may have encouraged Algonkin councilors to speak up, testifying to Kuôgunas absolutely paranoid jealousy and Juliette's devotion to him, both loving and resourceful... in spite of it. One who had done her best, only to be rewarded by the wanton murder of the playful, very friendly moôuin.

Cloud Eagle was relieved to hear about the positive outcome... wiser heads had prevailed, despite (what he saw as) the influence of the Black Gowns. According to their rules, a couple, once married, could not separate, no matter how bad one mate or the other became. It made no sense. Especially when taking into consideration that the friars themselves... weren't supposed to take wives. They didn't have, or weren't supposed to have, any personal experience in such matters. Kizi askua kedaga nanisaôi-tahônsôngan pabômiui louôuzouôgan'ua Plac'môniak -- It's yet another baffling quandary concerning the customs of the Whitemen.--

Asokw Mgezo didn't think it necessary to remark that he saw in Mahom Kuôgunas stubborn refusal to accept the separation a shadow cast by the Mkazaui Pitkôzonak. He assumed that the cousins also understood why such an alien, rigid regulation was accepted by the Tribal Councils at Abitibi and Odanak (though adroitly ignored, in the present instance, to grant freedom to Juliette). Went far to explain why 'He is Wolf' remained a *païen* traditionalist. Why Salom, despite his baptismal name, preferred to think of his Cross of Lorraine as signifying odamôgan, the dragonfly... rather than emblematic of the holy torture edifice. If Christians chose to view his pendant as representing Sazo's dreadful punishment post, that was all right with him. However you considered it, it was a mystic symbol, either way.

The salubrious outcome of the separation proceeding, coupled with the absurdity of such a procedure having to be endured *at all,* was a large factor in developing the cousin's sense of humor, their nbizonhouad suspected. The sardonic side of their wit, especially.

"Niona uadsônôbena ôami -- We have enough,"-- the young medauinno announced, straightening up again. He extracted his odamôgan, putting the stem and soapstone bowl together (commonly separated when not being used)... silently placing tobacco in the bowl. 'He is Wolf' rose, volunteering his own scallop shell - contained hot coal to light the odamô. Time to thank the Ôinoz Manitou and the Spirits of all the edible greens and medicinal herbs they had harvested. The medauinno and Maigamo bent a knee again, Cloud Eagle taking a few puffs, exhaling gratefully. He raised the pipe aloft, saluting the Four Winds. Then passed the odamôgan to Wolf, the bowl held in his left hand, of course (your left arm being closer to your heart). Maigamo drew on it two or three times, likewise reverently lifting the odamôgan to the Four Directions. Salom quietly put his paskhigan aside (though well within reach), and knelt down, accepting the pipe when his cousin was done. Taking his turn, completing the rite, he, like his relative, had been sure to include the Bloodroot Manitou (as per the example set by their medauinno) when expressing his gratitude. The trio was silent for a moment, lost in contemplation.

Then they arose, Asokw Mgezo and Maigamo picking up the containers they had been filling, Wolf retrieving his fusil. He used the paskhigan's sling to carry the weapon over his shoulder. Turning toward camp, Jerome stepped out, alertly scrutinizing the way ahead, holding his firelock at the ready. Cloud Eagle walked between the cousins, Maigamo frequently turning to look behind them, guarding their back trail.

"Neuautamen kiôua kezaldamek ôadsi k' Okemes Soliôn -- [I can] understand your appreciation for your Grandmother Juliette,"-- their *naturel docteur* murmured as they made their way downslope. He deemed it unnecessary to comment on the base perfidy of Mahom Kuôgunas.

Pausing, Salom looked around carefully, and spoke in extra - low tones: "Adodzi d' pita kagini -- There are very brave, -- saki kinaôi okemesak gottliui n' Osôgenak alôgomômak -- quite amazing grandmothers among our Algonkin relatives -- ac'hi -- also."

Maigamo whispered that they would speak of them when safely back in camp. Just now it was best to suspend conversation, keeping a lookout for game, remain alert to detect lurking enemies.

Making their way through the area where they had harvested fiddleheads (though avoiding the exact same route), they passed cautiously over the slough of flattened reeds where 'Those that Bleed' were flowering, jumping over the brook. In that exposed area they spread out widely... Asokw Mgezo refrained from heading toward the sibosiz --the stream, little (the brook), -- until Salom was safely across and among the trees. Jerome, once behind cover, turned and kept watch while Cloud Eagle crossed, Maigamo remaining in concealment on the far side. He ventured to join them only after their *homme de médecine* was also well among the trees. Then the first two watched to make certain that enemies wouldn't ambush Wolf as he crossed the stream.

They noticed small game, here and there, as they approached camp, such as a pakesso or two abruptly thundering away, and *some* sort of running auaasak crashing away, as loudly as deer... which proved to be gray squirrels, last year's carpet of autumn leaves being now so crisp. The only creature that provoked Jerome into jerking up his fusil was naguibaguihla, an "under leaf bird,"[192] -- a woodcock-- that burst skyward quite near them. Salom restrained himself, the flier streaking away too quickly for even a snap shot.

They knew they were nearing camp, in addition to their familiarity with the terrain, when they heard, not far ahead, an emphatic *"gobble-gobble"* ring out, but could detect no turkeys nearby. The source was soon apparent. Cheerfully rising from concealment was young Nespokusino, 'He Dreams of Someone.' He was holding, "at the ready," Asokw Mgezo's newly acquired musketoon. He had his arrows quiver on his back, agma atôbi kuahliui -- his bow nearby. -- Before leaving with Jerome and Maigamo Cloud Eagle had asked Nespokusino to (eventually) stand sentinel, whereby he might both guard the camp while watching for any game that might wander near. While their medical man didn't want to burden himself with the heavy firearm while collecting greens, at the same time he preferred that it not lie totally unused. Lending it to "Dreams of" until he returned was his utilitarian compromise. Allowing the youngster to keep watch with it… a wise move, as the ôski migakauinno, not yet possessing a fusil of his own, would be especially interested in handling the firelock. Might gain experience in firing and reloading it ahead of when he acquired his own. Would serve as a sentinel / still hunter who could be expected to be especially *well-motivated* on this balmy, sunny day.

Ôazuaui alômi kôn -- Back in camp -- the three gatherers reported on their sojourn while they distributed their bounty among the company. The fiddleheads were committed to a kettle and smaller pots freshly filled with water. The leeks would also be cooked as part of the evening's repast. Cloud Eagle attended to the wounded, inquiring, seeking to determine if any of their bloodroot ingredients should be used right away. Kept until later? Whether the leaves should be boiled and bruised to make poultices, applied immediately… or later, used eventually.

When He is Wolf and Salom settled down at one of the two campfires, they did so deliberately and not randomly, their nbizonhouad would later realize. At the campfire they gravitated to, tidbits of smoked turkey and fried namasiya, fish - flesh, were offered by Ôiguahlo, Whistling Swan. A member of the morning's nahama-hunting party, that afternoon he had gone fishing. Had done well, using different methods depending on the 'feel' of intriguing sections of the creek. Here he had used a trident nodamaguôngan -- fish spear.[193] -- There he had employed c'hauapeniganatagw -- hook and line. -- Among the namasak caught were many skog-alaôanmek, snake - resembling [ones]. -- Nahômoak, "They go with the Current"[194] fish. That is, eels. Two of them, skewered on a lengthy spit, were being smoked over the fire. Whistling Swan

---

[192] *Western Abenaki Dictionary,* Volume II, p. 454.
[193] *Abenakis and English Dialogues,* Chief Joseph Laurent, p. 48.
[194] *Ibid,* p. 39.

had converted it into a smudge fire by allowing the (already modest) skueḑa to die down, feeding it damp material.

As Jerome and Maigamo settled in, greatly appreciating Ôiguhalo's generosity, looking forward to the fiddleheads and ôinoziya now cooking, their medauinno could see that the cousins were in a more somber mood. Or were they simply a bit wearied from the day's multifarious activities? Remembering Salom's parting remark about brave grandmothers among the Algonkin side of their heritage, he sensed that they were waxing reflective, taking into consideration what they were about to relate.

After a while, having rested and eating pieces of delicious nahômoiya, the cousins recover their voice. Their *homme de médecine* pays close attention as, fired up, now on an 'ancestral ' story - telling "roll," the cousins can't refrain from speaking of amazingly courageous, heroic grandmothers, **great** - grandmothers, -- on the Algonkin side of their intertribal family. Osôgenak -- Algonkin -- women who escaped from Maguak captivity during the 1600s, when Dutch-armed (and later English-armed) Iroquois raiders wreaked horrifying devastation in Canada. They are tempted go on for hours about their resourceful great-grandmother Mali, called Takuanipihisizko,[195] Rainbow Girl, (when young) in her Atticamegues Nation dialect. She was named after Saint Marie when baptized as a convert, both to give her an adult name and to inspire her to be mindful of the example of the mother of the holy Sazos. Ôskigo menagezoik -- Younger listeners[196]-- learn much about (or are acutely reminded of) emergency survival woodcraft as they listen, sometimes asking for clarifications. Such youths, it must be said... waited patiently for the Story Teller to pause, to take a sip of refreshing mint tea, or some such need, before venturing to inquire.

The cousins wish also to speak of their remarkable great-aunt Malgelit. Christened after Saint Margaret, she was also known as Ininäḑsko -- Caribou Woman[197]-- in Atticameguesui. However, the hour having grown late, the company finally 'falls out,' taking to their bear skins and blankets for the night. They face extensive paddling down Wood Creek to the wide lake on the morrow. A hopefully uneventful *voyage* north awaits the triumphantly returning fighters as they leisurely wrap up the evening, taking to their bedrolls.

Not all take to their blankets or bearskins at the same time. A few continue to linger by the fire, staring at the slowly dying flames... mulling over what they have

---

[195] For the Algonkin word 'Rainbow' reference the Index, p. 144, *Indian Crafts of William & Mary Commanda,* David Gidmark, 1995, Stackpole Books, Mechanicsburg, PA.

[196] Menagezoik indicates listeners in the sense of "Those seeking stories," p. 1, *Green Mountain Oracle* No. 1, by George Larrabee and Tomas Azarian, 1987, published by Three Hoots Press, Woodbury, VT, c/o author.

[197] To interpret 'Caribou Woman' the author has taken the Osôgena (Algonkin) word for caribou, ininätik (which is caribou in the **plural**) deleted the ik pluralization, making it singular, added **sk** to indicate female, the word-final o serving to indicate it's her name, replacing **ua,** the suffix of skua, female. Source (for caribou, by itself): *The Indian Crafts of William & Mary Commanda,* p. 27.

heard. Others step into the woods to answer 'calls of nature,' at the same time checking to ascertain if any danger threatens, while one or two (as the mood seizes them) taste again remaining tidbits of smoked nahômoiya and well-roasted nahamaiya.

Morning dawns at long last. Breakfasting briefly, everyone (except the wounded) begins to load the canoes... until driven to shelter by a sudden spring shower. As they huddle, idle conversations begin anew. Their *Suônni* recruit, murmuring to T'songeba (both not far from Cloud Eagle) expresses puzzlement.

Asokw Mgezo has not been listening carefully... his thoughts are elsewhere. In fact he has been dreaming about home, Ôeoandamsko, and their Little One. For some reason -- he didn't know why, and it wasn't important, was only idle daydreaming... he was envisioning Wise Woman (very young then) when she, coyly, had presented him with a model of a wigwam. A small conical wigwam, floored with bark, covered in buckskin. She had provided its interior with a tiny floor mat of woven grass and a fireplace with a tripod over it. *Their* future home, she was suggesting... She was accepting him as her husband! It was a very pleasant memory.

Author's art work depicting the teen-aged 'Courteous Girl' (the future Wise Woman) with her new-made model of a wigwam... a broad hint to Cloud Eagle that they should start building a full-sized real one, their future home... *soon.*

Portrait by the author is of Ms. Sharon Powers, "Wigwam Woman," of the *Totem'ua Siômo*, Clan of the Hawk, an Abenaki band of northern Vermont.

17. 'Pepôkuan,' Suônni Migakauinno, Nadodemaua Kinaui Liuizuôgan'a --"Firelock," [the] Shawnee Warrior, Asks about a Certain Name --

Pepôkuan, having heard that the surname of the M'Sadokues brothers has something to do with rainbows, avers that, in his grasp of the Mazipskoik / Odanak Abenaki dialect, *managuôn* indicates a rainbow, not *msadokues*, the latter another word for *azeban*, the raccoon. Their nbizonhouad silently agrees, saying nothing, having heard that the brothers dislike that interpretation. Is it a family totemic name, disavowed by converts because of its' animalistic *infidel* "ancestral" implication? 'Msategues'[198] also indicates a Person from the Big River (more popularly known as the Long River), the Connecticut, the brothers' older relatives having indeed, like Cloud Eagle's and Ôeoandamsko's families, forged northward from the Massa'tzosek section of that famous stream.

The young medauinno clears his throat, seeking the attention of his Suônni and Mohican compatriots. Worried that bad blood might develop between "Firelock" and the M'Sadokues brothers if Pepôkuan speaks too loosely, especially by linking the Abenaki pair to *msadokues*, "high-rumped creature," raccoon, their *médecine homme* decides that he had better speak up. He notes that the 'Msategues' interpretation, with a French inflection rendered 'M'Sadoques' (the brothers' usual habitation being at Odanak, the priestly mission), may be something that is *not spelled out*, but is *understood* to indicate a family of... *Many Talents* like the many colors of the rainbow... who ancestrally *hail from* the Big River to the south. And indeed, as at least even T'songeba has learned by now, any individual M'Sadokues you can name is a multi-talented person. Fine craftsmen, great hunters, the women too, doing fine quillwork and beadwork, melodious singers also... you name it. Of course Cloud Eagle can't *swear* that he's absolutely right... it's just something heard rather vaguely, indirectly, the medauinno not being a resident of Odanak.

Before they can probe the question any further sunlight bursts upon them. The storm is passing... reduced to fleeting clouds above and some drizzle in the distance. Time to get going! The companions bestir themselves and start for the canoes.

Then they see a brilliant rainbow arching close by..! The multi-colored arch glows not far from their camp and the nearest height of the Taconics Range. Everyone pauses, gazing in awe. A good omen! Cloud Eagle is tremendously pleased. His impression is that it is *a reply to Firelock*. Turning toward T'songeba and Pepôkuan, he quietly remarks: "Daka k'ozidauauôgan --There [is] your answer." -- A shining answer

---

[198] Reference p. 336 for msadokwes, "big rump animal," (raccoon totem?) *Western Abenaki Dictionary,* Volume I. P. 338 for msategues / Msadoques, p. 339 for msitegwes, "big river person," *Ibid.* The question is Dr. Day's.

"Ozidauauôgan li Pepôkuan --The answer to Firelock."--

Photo by the author.

given by the ever-helpful Grandmother and Grandfather Spirits themselves! What a wonderful start for the new day! The companions embark, their gear stowed "on board," and shove off, paddlers stroking enthusiastically. Even the wounded are smiling, especially since they don't have to paddle, can lean back and take their ease. *Capitaine* Pmauikho calls out, ululating a paddling song. All voices rise in melodious harmony. As the company progresses downstream, between songs there is an exchange about old stories concerning "misi nebes aôahônedoak -- large lake monsters"-- …thought to dwell in the depths. They *used* to be seen further north, in the widest, deepest part of the lake. However, no one has seen them lately. A Mazipskoik term for one is mskog'kuedmos, an expression consisting of big, compounded with skog, snake, hence snake-like, with the suffix indicating out of sight… something seldom seen.[199] Asokw Mgezo recalled, back when the People had been numerous and flourishing, about the wondrous creatures (whole *swarms* of them), who had been **allies** of the Ô'banakiak! They had swum *alongside* when fleets of great war-canoes set out against enemies to the west. Were surviving creatures still … their friends today? He wondered. Certainly hoped so! Kaanauagihnono companions mention an old Iroquois tradition about a similar creature, which might be described as an "underwater panther." In fact of an entire submarine *human*-like population down there… Nok ā'rleh -- But again, -- yah gāne'kah'ens ôu'adkāht'ho -- seldom seen. -- Especially these days, as far as was presently known. Cloud Eagle suspected that, nonetheless, such talk was making everyone quite curious. Are some glancing into the depths as they paddle..? The conversation reminded him that he should throw some odamô in the water when, a day

---

[199] An historically extant description, from Alnôbaiui, the Abenaki language, of Lake Champlain's reputed gigantic, dinosaurian lake creature popularly known today as "Champy." Two were detected on sonar recently.

or two further north, the *voyageurs* passed that small island, most of it a large up-thrust rock, widely thought to be the final form of Odzihôzo. Another one of the Great Mystery's creative forces, that entity, "He who made Himself from Something," is said to have gouged out the terrain that is now filled with water, known as Pitaubagw, 'The Water Between.' Between the mountain ranges to the east and west, piled up from where the lake is now. Though the manahan looks small, composed of utterly inert rock …we shouldn't be fooled, Asokw Mgezo had been advised. It *could be*, though outwardly rock, that Odzihózo still keeps watch, is very conscious, and appreciates being acknowledged... Should be rendered due respect, given the mighty work he accomplished in the Dawn Time... of such great benefit to everyone today. Odzihózo is certainly no one to disgruntle, to anger as you paddle, blithely ignoring him. One should take into account that, if miffed, he is quite capable of calling up a raging storm... something you don't need when paddling kuatsemiui kaskâk nebes -- out on the wide lake.-- Tossing a little odamô overboard -- or skamontahigan, cornmeal, if you're a woman,-- isn't much to ask, the aspiring medauinno judged.

In view of their calm paddling weather maôuigan -- in fact, -- it would be a good idea to do so *right now,* he thought. And in view of the glorious managuôn lebagiadigan -- rainbow benediction -- that had blessed them as they had embarked. *He,* especially, should show appreciation, and put down his paddle, momentarily, to dig into his odamôinoda.

Apparently Maigamo and Salom perceived that the talk of great underwater creatures, of strange underwater *people,* for that matter, was too vague a subject. Decided to speak of another heroic great-grandmother of yesteryear, another who, though enduring great suffering, had, with great resolve, escaped from baleful enemies. The operative word here was apcikozitsik, enemies, not Maguak. Since the cousins had told much of Okemes Mali's ordeal the evening before, quietly referring to her Maguak captors by nation, it was understood that the captors of the now-introduced Okemes Malgelit, she having been Osôgena (Algonkin) would have been Maguak also.

The previous evening, after the companions, all Algonquian of one tribal identity or another, grouped around Ôiguahlo's eels-cooking smudge fire, had been listening to the cousins for a while, their brothers around the other skueda, engaged in discussions of their own (likewise nibbling on tidbits from the day's hunting and fishing), took notice of the earnest narration going on around the other fire. There seemed to be two story-tellers holding forth over there, the half-Osôgenak cousins. Their conversations lapsing, the curiosity of Uncle Kyâs'húta and other Kaanauagihnono became aroused. Sauntering over, they were likewise treated to portions of Ôiguahlo's most recently smoked nahômoiia, eel flesh. In the meanwhile Jerome or He is Wolf continued, adroitly avoiding any employment of 'Maguak' or 'Iroquois,' substituting the handy generalization of 'apcikozidsik' instead. They had a mind to 'keep peace in the valley,' passing on important ancestral history while avoiding anything that might cause friction between present-day allies.

Uncle Kyâs'húta, Walks Softly, and the other newly-arrived listeners hear the last half of the cousins' remembrance about Okemes Mali. The cousins' intention to also speak of Okemes Malgelit fades as the evening waxes neigh. Their voices almost hoarse, they promise to speak of that grandmother on the morrow, reputedly a large, formidable woman not known as Ininädsko, Caribou Woman,[200] for nothing....

Changing the subject, bruited about from canoe to canoe, about legendary creatures of the lake, Salom and Maigamo launch into what they have heard about great-grandmother Malgelit / Ininädsko, narrating from one boat to the other. That is, when the canoes are close enough to each other so that conversation can be made without shouting. At times the birchen flotilla drifts apart, and the cousins suspend their narration until everyone draws closer again. At one point their narrative segues into song, kedaga libiamek lintouôgan -- another paddling song, -- as they literally sing the praises of their resourceful and courageous Okemes Malgelit. Of any native women outwitting enemies, attempting to make their stanzas rhyme or alliterate, in either Ô'banaki or Osôgena accents (whichever dialect lends itself best), with the measured rhythm of their paddling. Their creativity in turn inspires uiagaldôzik lintouôganal --joyful songs -- from others, lyrics resonating in Kaanauagihniui as well as in Algonquian vocalizations.

The day's paddle brings the band of brothers to a point where Pitaubagw can no longer be considered 'riverine,' definitely no longer qualifies as 'Wood Creek,' -- that designation lies behind them, -- to the south. There is a pass here, quite strategic on colonists' maps, where a combined English / Maguak force, under a Captain Jacobus de Warm, hoping to seize control of the Champlain Valley, built a fort in 1690.[201] De Warm could not maintain his ambition, abandoning the stone structure after little more than a month. However, some of the two-foot thick stone walls were still there, at present, on the north side of the passage (between today's Crown Point, NY and Chimney Point, Vermont)... utilized by a contingent of French at the moment. There were still more Whitemen on the peninsula across from de Warm's old fort, regulars and Québecois *milice* both. The companions landed at a likely spot on the south side of the peninsula, setting up camp not far from French tents. In view of any location along the southern part of the lake being in danger (somewhat) of Mohican and Maguak raiders, it seemed good policy, especially for the sake of the wounded, to camp near the Plac'môniak. If such marauders attempted a surprise attack French and *Canadien* warriors could come to their support, and quickly. They heard Canadiens refer to the spot as *Pointe de la*

---

[200] We find in the Index of *The Indian Crafts of William and Mary Commanda* the Algonkin word for caribou -- (actually, in the plural), ininätik. Which the present author has modified to the singular, introduced sk to represent female, and ended with an o to indicate it is "Caribou Woman's" formal name.

[201] P. 59, *The French Occupation of the Champlain Valley,* 1609 - 1759, Guy Omeron Coolidge, 1938.

Chevelure, a designation having something to do with *hair*... Québec Province defenders, counter-attacking against *Anglais* probes such as de Warm's expedition... had taken scalps here..?

The weather holding fair, the campsite proves salubrious, that evening members of the company exchanging smoked game, from yesterday, for Québecois cheese, bread, and tobacco. Asokw Mgezo, Chief Pmauikho, and Kyâs'húta, however, become aware that they should keep an eye peeled, should, to a degree, monitor such exchanges. Among the Whitemen are *armées* - trailing traders, "sutlers," selling various merchandise to *les troupes*. Pernicious blandi and various *liqueurs* included. The latter fact is unwelcome news, not only to Pmauikho and Kyâs'húta, to their *homme de médicine,* but also, especially, to T'songeba and Pepôkuan. They haven't trekked north to join their Ô' banakiak cousins, evading the jin and rum purveyors of Fort Orange... in order to fall prey to Canadien brandy peddlers. Not that they have any problem in resisting such *coleporteuers,* but... dislike even being around habitual roisterers, near ôuigesmouinnoak -- drunkards. -- However, no alcohol-related problem arises that evening, even though they are visited by a few Québecois. Maigamo and Salom keep to their word in regaling the band about Okemes Malgelit.[202]

As the band of brothers strike camp the following day, preparing to launch, discomfiting news reaches them... of an outbreak of sickness further north, in the Ô'banakiak villages near the mouths of the Winooski and Lamoille Rivers... and at Mazipskoik too? They hope it isn't true, but are not surprised. With so many Auanock, Strangers, coming and going along the lake, it is something, unfortunately, to be rather expected. Cloud Eagle puts down yet more odamô, praying fervently.

On their return to Mazipskoik (others having disembarked previously), their welcome home is subdued. They find the community wrapped in grief... *O'hôô,* Yes, another horrible illness has infected the People. Sad to say, **pitta** ozigiui -- ***very*** sad, -- Wise Woman's and Cloud Eagle's new-born girl baby is among the fatalities. However, the grieving parents, comforted by the paramount medaulinnoak, Kisikauo and Nbizonhouo M'Sadokues, are greatly encouraged by something that occurs when they participate in a ceremony at the fishing camp on the south shore of Missisquoi Bay. The two medicine elders call upon those who yet venerate the Old Ways, who are present... to participate in a pipe ceremony along the shoreline.

---

[202]The stories of Okemes Mali, along with that of Grandmother Malgelit, are elaborately detailed in Book II, a continuation of the present work.

18. Nalaôiôi'a nspi Meḍaului-Kagini Mikinakol
-- A Ceremony with Spiritually-Powerful Turtles --

Rather than form a circle in an inland clearing, Kisikauo asks the participants to stand in a half circle facing the water. As the men (with the women and girls forming a protective half circle behind them) pass the pipe from hand to hand and speak of their hopes and fears …they notice, out in the bay, close by, that their half circle is now complete. In the water is a half moon of aligedaidzik -- "jumpers,"-- snapping turtles… *mikinakol -- **turtles!*** -- That so many turtles are not there by accident is evident from the fact that the mikinakol, treading water (or standing tiptoe on the shallow bottom), are ***facing them***. They have arrived… to complete the circle! Mikinakw represents Mother Earth herself. The most fundamental totemic affinity group of the Ô'banakiak is "descended" (so to speak) from Mikinakw (and of the neighboring Iroquois as well).

Looking on in amazement, the young parents grasp the portent of the turtles' participation. Their presence is ***pitta*** zôgelizo olômauôgan -- ***very*** strong evidence -- of the reality of the (normally invisible) Spirit World. Souls of those who have gone before, discarnate relatives, have (in all likelihood) motivated the turtles to attend the ceremony in order to complete the circle, the 'Hoop of Life.' That was Kisikauo's prayer when he asked the participants to form only a half circle on the beach.

In addition to the turtles who attended the pipe ceremony, shortly afterward Ôeoandamsko sat with **Nbizonhouo M'Saḍokues**, an aunt of the M'Sadokues brothers. Okemes Nbizonhouo, a spiritually powerful "medicine woman" herself, an associate of Kisikauo, was comforting the bereaved young mother… when an aligedaid appeared. Crawled close to the women… and stopped. Seemed to listen… -- approvingly? -- to what they were saying. And… could it be? Was perceived to be definitely smiling!

The import that Wise Woman and Asokw Mgezo draw from the ceremony is that the babies they had thought were lost to illnesses… are not lost. Their tiny bodies had not been able to resist the disease. Therefore their spirits had retreated to whence they came. But if the bereaved couple wished, they could try again. And so it proved. They did try, and were blessed with the births of a healthy son and an equally healthy daughter, Olôbao and Oliuôgasku'sizo. The spirits of the babies had attempted to achieve physical life before. Again invited, they tried once more. Circumstances being more favorable… this time to stay.[203]

---

[203] The unexpected "Ceremony with Medicine-Turtles" described above was not simply dreamed up out of whole cloth by the author. It is extrapolated from an actual experience that occurred in 1991 while attending a gathering of members and friends of the Abenaki/Sokuakiiak Nation of Missisquoi at the old State Fish Hatchery facility on the south (Vermont) shore of Missisquoi Bay. The men had formed a half-circle on the shoreline to pass a ceremonial pipe from hand to hand, taking turns to praise the Great Spirit and give voice to their concerns. Looking out over the bay, we saw a half-circle of turtles' heads raised from the water (apparently snapping turtles, judging from their size)… and facing in our direction! Our circle was now whole.

"…an aligedaid appeared. Came close to the women… and stopped." Listened in (so it seemed) to their low toned, murmuring discourse. Listened approvingly, its decision to join them …itself "talk," a message. Especially when it could be seen that the turtle …was smiling.

Author's photo.

19. Pedegimôdzi'ua Oladiali ta Namaskan Lakamiguezo
-- Return of the Good Hunting and Fishing Family --

The hunting family reaped more good fortune after catching the tmakua (if the reader will recall), the author, detailing Asokw Mgezo's and Olôbao's sacrament of putting down odamô, his discussion of Alnôbak menfolk's cultivation of tobacco, which in turn introduced the new, colonialist - derived resource, wild honey… elaborating on aboriginal ceremonies, of "medicine practices," and Cloud Eagle's strenuous endeavors, when younger, on the war trail.

Bringing the flat-tail carcass back to solid ground, the family established their camp for the night, cutting poles to erect a shelter of birch bark, unrolling the sheets hauled along. Olôbao and his medauinno dad quickly gathered firewood while Oliuôgasku'sizo and her mom skinned and butchered their prize. While collecting combustibles Asokw Mgezo and son also cut and trimmed two slim saplings, using buckskin thongs (packed along for the purpose) to fashion a hoop to stretch the tmakuaua -- beaver skin -- on. Their skueda blazing sufficiently, the family dined on portions of tmakuaiia, beginning with the heart, liver, and kidneys. Cloud Eagle, being the oldest present (though not much older than Wise Woman) eating first. Their adiak were also fed, rewarded for their good service thus far. Given dried meat brought along… they were denied any of the present tmakuaiia. An old, time-honored tradition dictates that dogs shouldn't be fed flesh from such fresh-caught creatures as

---

The appearance of the turtle on land, coming up to listen in (apparently) to a conversation between two women in attendance, is not imaginary either. The women were the late Mali Keating (nee M'Sadokues), an actual Abenaki Medicine Woman, and Notôuo, "Good Talker," the accomplished poet Phyllis R. Larrabee. School teacher Brian Long of Eden, VT (an editor of the present work) was also present, and counted seven turtles participating in the ceremony. A flight of …*seven*… geese were seen shortly before the turtles appeared. The Clan of the Hawk has its name from… **seven** hawks seen circling overhead when the name was decided on.

abagôloak lest the spirits of such animals become offended. In addition, once the skin and flesh is stripped from the bones, oskanal -- the bones, -- should be deposited, in the instance of aquatic creatures, back into the environment from whence they came. In justice returned to the water that had been their home in life. There must have been instances, though, where such a bone, because of its particular quality or shape, was retained for a special purpose. The blade of the original "pkalagenigan -- crooked knife,"[204] -- that had been a beaver incisor... springs to mind.

Having dined, including tasting portions of delicious beaver tail, Beautiful Girl and Olôbao proposed that they do more hunting... investigate the upstream part of the nebes. What might be there? Cloud Eagle, nodding his agreement, suggested that they take their amiskuôganal, ice-chisels. There could be another beaver lodge, or, quite likely, moskuasek, muskrat habitat. Their father would follow at a distance, his firelock ready.

With his fusil poised and ready; he would be hunting as well. While the siblings looked for beaver sign or moskuasouiuazessak -- muskrat lodges, -- their father would, while keeping an eye on the teens, alert against danger, remain on solid ground where he might spot non-aquatic auaasak... anything from a rabbit to a moose. He also didn't want to be too far away from Ôeoandamsko, who remained in camp, scraping fat and tissue from the now-hooped tmakuaua. Asokw Mgezo had one of their dogs with him, the oldest, best-trained one, who could be relied on not to run about recklessly, spooking game away before its master could take aim. The others remained in camp with Wise Woman, under control and in position to warn her of danger.

Oliuô gasku'sizo also brought along, since hers wasn't big, was light-weight, a bone-pointed nodamaguôgan -- fish spear. -- Not of the trident type, but single-bladed, with a barbed point, drilled to attach a line, the other end secured to the spear shaft. The point can be inserted into the hollowed-out forepart of the shaft. When skewering a fish, the namas might pull away a certain distance, taking the point with it. But the line, playing out at length, would keep the barbed point (and the fish) attached to the shaft.

Handsome One and Oliuôgasku'sizo didn't find another beaver lodge, but did find muskrat uigiuômal and even smaller muskrat feeding 'stations.' Pausing to listen as well as look, they detected slight movement in one of them... and, in an instant, became "ôiunitahamôdak, those who strike around," circling the rodent's shelter in high excitement, nailing the dodging moskuas with their ice chisels. Olôbao brought their victim back to camp to be skinned and otherwise processed. There might be other muskrats near, but the commotion of getting the first one would have sent them into hiding. Oliuô gasku'sizo, deciding to try her nodamagu ôgan, continued on, finding a likely spot where the feeder brook came in. Having brought along a piece of buckskin,

---

[204] Pkalagenigan, literally tool for taking off, "peeling by hand," p. 213, *Western Abenaki Dictionary,* Volume II. Pelaghagenigan, "peel by hand instrument," is also listed, p. 213, *Ibid.*

she knelt on it to keep her knees more directly out of the snow (even though she was wearing caribou-hide leggings). Presently she spotted a plump skotam, trout. When it meandered close enough… she lunged, skewering it.

The family ate well that evening, Beautiful Girl demonstrating great patience by persisting as an ahômauauinno -- fishing person, -- not quitting until she had skewered four skotamak in all. Though the latter three didn't prove quite as big as her first one "ôikailid -- the very fat one."--

Lakamiguezo -- [The] family -- had still better luck the next day after breaking camp to head back to where the rest of Chief Grey Lock's hunting band were camped by the Riviére Missisquoi. They rose early, breakfasting on shreds of tmakuaiia ta moskuasiia, and set out. They had heard môlsemok, wolves, howling in the distance the evening before, but thought little of it, such serenading being a routine feature of the wilderness. About half way back to the river they discovered that the pack of howler-canines were now much closer than the night previous. Fortunately Cloud Eagle and Olôbao were in the lead, alert for game, the medauinno's firelock at half-cock and the youth holding his tôbi in one hand and an arrow in the other.

They sensed some sort of commotion off to their right. Suddenly deer burst into view, plunging desperately through the snow, as if being pursued by Madahôndo, the Bad Spirit, himself! Asokw Mgezo immediately raised his paskhigan, flipping off the frizzen boot and thumbing the hammer back to full cock. Handsome One notched his arrow, raising the bow. The two froze, standing stock still as the nolkak raced closer. The deer were running blindly, in their terror unaware of nizuak nadialouinnoak -- the two hunters. -- Howler-canines were after them, having discovered a herd's winter 'yard.' The pair aimed for the nearest deer as they passed in front of them, Cloud Eagle aiming at the second closest one, assuming that Olôbao would aim for the nearer of the two. Asokw Mgezo fired just as Olôbao released his steel-bladed tiskuôdi. The abrupt roar of the firelock, together with the equally abrupt barking of the family's adiak, scattered both the shocked wolves and deer in all directions. The targeted nolkak had gone down, Handsome One's deer struggling briefly until he ran up and shot another arrow into him.

The family thought that they had done well in getting a flat-tail and a moskuas the day before, but bagging the two deer (who didn't know what hit them) was better yet. Cloud Eagle reloaded while Wise Woman and Oliuôgasku'sizo came up, their adiak hauling the toboggan. The family paused, forming a circle while father and son extracted tobacco from their odamô pouches… time to give thanks. Asokw Mgezo put together his soapstone pipe (traditionally pipe-stem and bowl are carried disengaged), lighting it with a hot ember from their seashell protected fire-starting kit. Man and boy took a few puffs, raising the odamôgan, each in turn, to the Four Directions (also to the sky and to the earth) mildomek oliôni, giving thanks… mother and daughter protecting

Author's photo of "Oliuôgasku'sizo's (putative) plump trout" and fish spear, with line attached to bone point (the latter nearly invisible on the snow).

Property of the author.

them while they did so with the greater spiritual power of their feminine natures. They also put down tobacco to commiserate the spirits of the deer. The family arrived at Chief Grey Lock's camp while it was yet early, feeling well satisfied with their sojourn to the moskuasek… that was now a renewed beaver habitat.

Let us listen in again on a "round table" discussion between the chief, *Québecois* visitors La Bluetté and Besogne, together with Cloud Eagle, Ôeoandamsko and company centering on Abenaki language, culture, and history. In the course of give and take, first around the outside campfire and later inside A'lôn's wigwam, skog, the word for snake comes up.

It was inspired by the presence of instruments for the winter game *Su ha!* also known as "snow snake," three examples of snow snakes themselves having been noticed standing in the snow between lodges. The 'snakes' are debarked, straight saplings with somewhat of an upturning at their "heads," resembling the heads of snakes, hence the name. For the game the 'skogak' must be hurled down a lengthy, very straight furrow in the snow customarily made either by dragging a log or by asking a boy to volunteer. The ôskinnos, boy, " young person, small," a male (the feminizing suffix skua being absent), eagerly throws himself down on his back, sticking up both feet, and two men (or older boys) each grab an ankle and drag him to create the channel. The ôskinnosak regard it as grand fun, as play, clamoring for the 'privilege'… Once that is done, the players bring forward their 'snakes,' the contestants and their friends wagering who will win, displaying prizes, and the game can begin. The 'snakes,' having been thrown underhand to their furthest extent, are not simply taken out of the way, clearing the channel for the next competitor, but are placed upright in the snow (*alongside* the channel), to mark the furthest that the last snake reached, thus keeping score. The last sapling thrown that reaches the furthest… wins.

20. "Tsebahado Kezidalouôganal'ua Mahom Si'si'kua -- Different Views of Grandfather Rattlesnake"--

Originally, among those who wished to play "Su ha" once there is sufficient snow, the "snakes" were made every year beforehand. There was a tradition, still practiced by some, whereby the 'snakes' are burned to keep them from reviving, coming out of hibernation, with springtime's warmth. La Bluetté and Besogne, begging to differ, declare (with all the courtesy that they can muster), that the custom is absurd. The skogak are not real snakes! ...are merely lengths of wood. The chief and company have to agree... to burn them every spring and make new ones in the autumn is a waste of time and effort. Chuckling, Wise Woman and Asokw Mgezo, strong traditionalists though they are, agree also. Burning the sticks is an ancient custom still observed only in more remote places. Most likely is done to impress credulous, naïve children.

The discussion turns to real snakes, especially si'si'kuak, rattlesnakes, the only poisonous serpent known in that part of Ô'banakik -- Abenaki territory -- and seldom seen as far north as Missisquoi. Grey Lock and A'lôn, having originated in the Mohican-allied cantons to the south, agree with the Lenapéuk / Mohican belief that "Kicimahom Si'si'kua -- Great-Grandfather Rattlesnake," -- is to be greatly respected. In contrast to the attitude of the Iglismôniak, who commonly wax hysterical at the sight of a si'si'kua (however passive "Grandfather" might be), either fleeing in terror or undertaking to kill him. In contrast, their Ô'banakiak brethren to the East, near the ocean, show no fear. Demonstrating *ktsi kagini*, **great** courage, they actually grab the serpent with bare hands, one hand behind the head, preventing the snake from striking, and the other grasping the squirming body toward the tail. Then the migakauinno *bites* into the reptile, stripping skin from its back *with his teeth,* drinking the snake's blood.

Moreover, the warriors claim that they do this, Ôauanoleuo explains, "when they are weary," and need potent si'si'kua blood "to refresh themselves..!" The chief laughed as he said this, wondering if it was actually the practice anymore. He was of the opinion that today it's rarely done, for the simple reason that there are, probably, no longer many si'si'kuak in those parts. Between such warriors drinking their blood and frantic Pastoniak, Iglismôniak in general, killing them on sight ...si'si'kuak have become -- most likely -- quite rare in that region. He Who Fools Them and A'lôn agreed with Cloud Eagle and Ôeoandamsko that their cousins, the Muheconnuck, are right... Mahom Si'si'kua should be left in peace. When seeing one, "Grandfather" should be addressed with deference. The snake gives fair warning, shaking the si'zi'uan on its tail, making it easy to avoid him. This is to be respected. One's attitude should be to live and let live. If they don't bother *you,* one has no reason to attack *them.*

While the gifts of the two Québecois were greatly appreciated, it was feared that the sugars they brought, -- a rare treat -- could induce an epidemic of naaiahlauôgan,

Author's array of three "uazôli skogak -- snow snakes,"-- made by himself, essential items for playing the winter sport of Su Hą. The two 'snakes' on the left are made from maple saplings. The one on the right is a willow sapling. They have musket balls forced into cavities in their 'heads' to give more weight 'up front' when launched. Knobby-headed middle stick features a naturally occurring cavity that required a minimum of excavating to insert musket ball.

Author's photo.

"down flowing," diarrhea, among the band (*especially* at that time of year). Particularly the following morning when everyone ought to be packing up, starting out. Their digestive systems unaccustomed to so many sweets, this was no time to be afflicted with "the runs." In this Wise Woman and Asokw Mgezo heartily agreed with the chief. Together they advocated, circulating from one lodge to the other, that before retiring everyone make a beverage from odamô, diluting it, pulverizing the shreds even more than usual. Rather than the tobacco, in this instance, function as a *spiritual* medicine, an attribute of the nicotine should serve as *physical* medicine, fortifying digestive tracts against the effect of bowels-loosening sweets. Other herbs should be used as well, Ôeoandamsko and Cloud Eagle averred, questioning band members to ascertain what relevant herbs they possessed. If fellow Alnôbak didn't have enough, the medicine couple dug into their own supplies and gifted them. Among their hoard, particularly important against diarrhea, were dried berries from "cones," (clusters) of zalônak, staghorn sumac, *Rhus typhina*.[205] Said berries should be steeped to make a tea. The

---

[205] "A tea from the berries is drunk as a remedy for diarrhea," p. 111, *Folk Medicine of the Delaware and*

berries had (by now) lost much of their potency this late in Falling Boughs Moon -- February. -- However, their nebizon should still be fairly effective; used as a *preventative*... rather than as a curative. The latter would require fresher, stronger sumac-medicine. In addition, as they traveled downriver, everyone knew the location of stands of zalônakuamak, sumac trees, where their supplies of the berries could be renewed. Though the autumn-reddened leaves of the trees (good to mix with tobacco in making killinick) were now long gone, the 'cones' still clung to their branches, imbued with the strong cold-defying spirit also possessed by nibimenakuam --'my switch' berry bush -- ("high bush cranberries") as well as by partridge-berries and wintergreen berries. Those unharvested zalônak clusters might still be good.

Assembling in the dawn, the band stripped birch bark from wigwam frames and secured them to the loaded toboggans. Ôeoandamsko and Cloud Eagle scrutinized the company. Everyone seemed healthy...no indication of "down flowing." All had imbibed the recommended nebizon... *Mamedauigen!!* -- *Excellent!!* --

Macigek'ua Auighigan Pazeguen -- The End of Volume One -- (but *not* the end of our story). Further chronicles of Chief Grey Lock, Cloud Eagle, &c., are continued in Book II, including narratives of courageous heroines Auani Poleuabanik odsi Mimôt'hôdaôaui Apcikozidsik -- Who Escaped from Fierce Enemies.--

As an incentive for the reader to obtain Volume Two, either through purchase or by borrowing a copy from the local Public Library, the author has provided a preview, excerpting pages from a chapter (elaborately extrapolated from <u>brief</u> notes by 19th century historian Francis Parkman, who drew his sketches from French Colonial sources)... which involves the escape by a great-grandmother, christened after Ste. Marie, one *Mali* (long before she became a grandmother) as related by Cloud Eagle's two assistants, the half-Abenaki, half-Algonkin cousins, Maigamo and Salom.

Though a captive, she is temporarily left alone in Oneida territory[206] and decides

---

Related Algonkin Indians, Gladys Tantaquidgeon, Anthropological Series No. 3, Pennsylvania Historical Commission, Harrisburg, PA, 1977.

[206] Mali was momentarily left to herself after slipping away with a party of Onondagas, the warriors of which had captured her years previously. They had released her in the custody of a Mohawk chief, the peace-making Kiodsaton -- who had himself been captured by vengeful Algonkins and taken to Canada. But rather than being tortured to death as per usual, he had instead been spared, *feted,* and won to the cause of peace..! The agreeable Onondagas had enabled Mali to be brought safely back home. However... the war faction of the Maguak had violated Kiodsaton's brokered peace between the Five Nations Iroquois and the Algonkins and the French. Pretending to have "come in peace," wishing "only to trade"...they thereupon attacked the Canadian bands (during the winter) and, killing her husband and one of her children, the Maguak had with great brutality captured Mali a second time.

to make a break for home, far-off Canada, even though bereft of any means of sustenance at that bleak time of year. It is late winter / early spring; no knife, no fire-starting kit, etc. She nonetheless bravely starts out, but soon despairs of making it all the way back through the dense wilderness, and, convinced she is going to starve to death, or become the prey of an emerging and *hungry!* bear (or other wild beast) decides to "end it all." She makes a noose out of her woolen waist sash, tying the other end to a handy limb. However, the impromptu noose, its fibers much worn (an item she has been wearing prior to having been captured)… breaks. She tries again; again it breaks!

Deciding that her time is not yet, she plugs onward. Later, famished, weak from hunger, she sees a turtle emerging from the mud. She kills it with a rock. Finding a 'knife' in the form of a narrow, sharply pointed stone, she accesses its meat, and, discovering various combustible materials, starts a fire by rubbing sticks together, roasting the oios, the meat. "Chowing down," it is sufficient… for the time being.

Her situation improves markedly when she spots a group of Iroquois hunters before they see her, and later comes upon their recently vacated camp site… where she finds a forgotten tomahawk! She has more luck when she comes upon an unguarded canoe on the shore of an Adirondack river… moreover a river flowing northwest to Lake Ontario! Toward home! In the meanwhile she also repairs her waist sash with interwoven withes and strips of fresh bark, which will become crucially useful later. The canoe contains paddles, enabling her, when she thinks about it, to formulate a plan whereby she can utilize the tomahawk, the canoe, and the lengthy sash, one end tied to a thwart, to enable her to catch as large an animal as a nolka (*or* possibly an elk or a moose <u>calf</u>… providing the latter weighs only as much as an average-sized deer).

Kuaskuitaha Nolka nspi Kemdnôb Alni-Tmahigan -- Killing a Deer with the Purloined Tomahawk --

"Then she saw them! Nolkak, kinamek tali agma! -- Deer, looking at her! -- Naska'ua agemôuô! --Three of them! -- She tensed, stroking more slowly. This is it! Guani'ua Kahalaki! -- [the] Moment of Truth! -- She paddled toward them, quietly, carefully. She trembled slightly, her sense of anticipation growing more and more acute. At first she paddled straight toward them, praying that they would remain where they were, wouldn't go bouncing off into the woods, the white undersides of their tails flung up in alarm. They remained in place, apparently fascinated by the sight of her. They had never seen such a strange apparition in all their lives.

Drawing closer, she gave the paddle an almost indiscernible flick with her wrist, redirecting the craft from its trajectory straight at them to a point off to one side. After that she ceased using the paddle, knowing that the craft now possessed enough momentum to make it to the shore. She wanted to absolutely minimize any of her movements, approaching as quietly, as subtly as possible. She avoided direct eye contact… didn't look straight at them -- could tell exactly where they were out of the corner of her eye. Direct eye contact might make them nervous… they might gain an inkling of her lethal intention if they locked eyes. She deliberately looked away as she stepped ashore, drawing the canoe up. She beached the canoe lightly, just enough to keep it in place. Fortunately the discharge of water into the lake had none of the current of the fast-flowing river. She had at first considered leaving the hatchet in the canoe, but then decided to carry it lest something unexpected occur and it became necessary to defend herself. She hid the weapon, holding it behind, out of their sight, away from them. She didn't want her quarry to know she had it. One can assume they didn't know anything more about tomahawks than they knew about the life and loves of Grandmother Moon, but she wasn't going to take that assumption for granted. Allay their natural paranoia as much as possible.   She looked dead ahead, gazing at the forest in front of her as she stepped inland, pretending to ignore them. The nolkak kept their single-minded gaze fixed on her, following her with their eyes as she strolled evenly toward some unknown objective. But she wasn't walking straight away, into the depths of the woods. Her path curved… she was circling, bringing herself between them and the lake. Her course curved so much that, turning their heads to keep her in view, they now had to shift their entire bodies.

 Finally she was exactly opposite them, the lake to their backsides. Now she began walking toward them. She strode softly, closer and closer… slowly bringing the hatchet around. She was facing them, but still refrained from looking at their eyes… gazed past them, beyond them. Still they stared at her, hypnotized, mesmerized. No indication of alarm. Such a strange being. *What* is it? What's it doing?? It had come from the lake, unaware of them, apparently, and now was returning. *Why?*

 Then 'it,' whatever 'it' is… was definitely getting too close. They began to inch to the right and left, tails beginning to twitch, thinking that they might have to run… were getting ready to run. Which is what she wanted. She wanted only one of them -- that would be plenty. The one that, panic-stricken, would take to the water. The volume of nepi it would have to plow through should slow it down.

 The middle one looked to the left, then to the right, couldn't make up its mind which way to go, tail flicking nervously. Now she was **much** too close, and all three bolted, the rightward one fleeing to the right, the more leftward one leaping to the left. Now she charged, tomahawk raised. The middle one pirouetted with a breathy snort, whirling completely around, and plunged into the lake, only his head above water.

 As he splashed in she ran for the canoe as fast as she could, swiftly depositing the hatchet inboard and shoving off. (He? She? It wasn't easy to tell which was which, the bucks having shed their antlers during the winter, making them all resemble does at this time of year.) She grabbed the odahôgan and dug into the water with all the strength she could muster, driving after the frantically swimming nolka. The canoe dipped and swayed from her exertion, but then she straightened it, knifing into her prey's spreading wake. Again and again she dug in, as his head bobbed above the water, drawing along his right side, parallel to the middle of the canoe, where she knelt. She grabbed one of his ears with her left hand, shifting her weight to keep from capsizing. With her other hand she swept up her waist sash, the section she grabbed having been tied into a noose, the knot for it a 'slip knot,' the other end secured firmly to a thwart. With a swift, desperate motion she looped the noose over the animal's head; jerked back powerfully. She drew the slip knot *tight: tighter!* The hapless creature was now bound to the rocking canoe, thrash about as he might. Then she snatched up the tomahawk…

…bringing the blade slicing into the spinal cord. She avoided cutting into her noose at the same time; a near thing. The nolka convulsed, knocking against the bark hull …then went limp. Okemes Mali downed the hatchet and hauled her prey higher, gripping tightly, straining for dear life. Might the tattered, oft-repaired sash yet break? She could lose the deer! All her strenuous effort useless, swirling down, down, out of sight…

Addendum

In looking over his finished manuscript, scrutinizing the art work (all done by the author) and the 35mm photographs, the author-illustrator studied how well his drawings coordinated with his narration. He did find some missing information. In his drawing on page 118, depicting some of the animals, birds (and one reptile, mikinakw, turtle), among the auaasak invited to witness Kullos'kahp's creation of the first human beings… he saw that his text failed to mention the names of a few of the birds -- and one mammal -- *depicted*. Given that his *overall* narration loyally cites the Abenaki names for any animal or bird mentioned in the text, he will here mention the names of the animal and birds shown in the drawing but not mentioned in the text… so that the reader can be fully informed.

The etymology of the name of the bird at the bottom of the drawing, the Canada jay or "whisky jack," is especially interesting. *Whisky* jack? Do they, somehow, have something to do with whisky..? They are also called "moose birds," frequenting the company of mozak. (Latin designation is *Perisoreus canadensis*.)

In the upper left hand corner can be glimpsed an onlooking *bison,* called a pziko* in the Abenaki language. Further over, perched among the antlers of the aiyôba magôlibo -- bull woodland caribou, -- is a raven, which, in Abenaki, can be called either ktsi mkazas, great black person, or ponki mkazas, northland black person. "Ponki" is an abbreviation of 'pebonki,' winter-land (northland).

Perched among the antlers of the alhla magôlibo, female woodland caribou is kokokhạs, a great horned owl… The name is also used for the barred owl (the larger owls). Their name is obviously onomatopoetic… it sounds like their 'hooting' call. When you think about it, so does 'owl' in English. Though much abbreviated.

Below, looking on over the back of the alhla magôlibo, can be glimpsed the head of a great blue heron, kaskó, from *kaskạ*, wide, an allusion to the *wide,* usually marshy waters from which they get their living. The Alnôbaiui word for the crane is the same, for the same reason. Next to the moôuin, below the muzzle of the aiyôba uôboz, bull elk, is uôbtegua, a wild goose, in this instance a Canada goose. The name begins with an abbreviated form of uôbi (or wôbi), white, and may allude to the white 'patch' on the bird's cheek. We can discern river, *tegu* (from tegw) in the name also, wild geese frequenting waterways.

Between the bear and azeban, raccoon, is maanamaguas, "fish gatherer" (or catcher), an osprey. Maana, "gather" is in the initial part of the word, and 'fish,' namas, is apparent in the following syllables … nama(gua)s.

*Page 36 of Chief Joseph Laurent's 1884 *Abenakis and English Dialogues*.

Addendum continued

Now we come to the jay. It is **keskedzagua**, a 'rubbish bird.' Not that the bird *is* rubbish; **keskedzagua** derives from the fact that it *collects* 'rubbish'… that is, they snatch, in the vicinity of people, man-made food sources, discarded edibles which people regard as crumbs or whatnot, some of which may be bits of larger meat, earning the bird the nicknames of 'camp robber,' venison hawk, and 'scatter hoarder.' "Whisky jack" derives from the European settlers' clumsy attempt to pronounce the Algonquian term, likely from the plural form **keskedzaguak**, as usually we see more than one of them. 'Keskedzagua' denotes 'rubbish collector,' but when the Euro-Canadians attempted to get their tongues around the word, their tortured attempt converted **keske**dzagua into 'weski' (later, presumably in print, it became 'whisky'). The 'jack' derives from the pluralization of (the final syllable) of "jaguak," originally pronounced *dzaguak*.

The author usually avoids the traditional 19th and 20th century spellings of Abenaki words that involve 'j,' Gordon Day, Ph.D, explaining in his pronunciation guide, *Western Abenaki Dictionary,* Volume I, page XV, that "…j is an apico-alveolar affricate pronounced between resonants like the dz in English adz: *mijo* 'he eats something' is pronounced as though it were *midzo*," etc., &c. Understanding that the above is language that (for the most part) only professional linguists can comprehend, being so much gobbledygook to the rest of us, the author has decided to 'cut to the chase' and employ 'ts' or 'dz' in place of the archaic j **to begin with,** a more phonetic spelling, thus making things easier for the gentle reader.

In his pronunciation guide Dr. Day explains that when he does use a j that *really is* a j (as in 'jay') he employs a capital J so that the reader will know the difference *even if* it is in the *middle* of a word. Another problem with J (as in 'jay') is that the old-time Abenaki speakers had difficulties with it (due to their minimal mouth-movement way of speaking) if the J is in word-initial position. Thus, Joseph becomes 'Sozap,' Jesus becomes 'Sazos,' and so on. The j of 'Kinjames,' a European monarch, from the English King James, they had no problem with because it is in the interior of the word. As the author noted in his Author's Preface, quoting from *The Indian Crafts of William & Mary Commanda,* the Algonquian language (including Abenaki) "is a splendorous thing," and it is "unfortunate that the Indian languages are so inaccessible to non-natives." Hopefully the author's books will give the reader a head start on understanding Algonquian, and will be impressed by both the poetry and the *sophistication* of Abenaki speech. For example, the names of creatures are invariably *accurate,* describing their calls, appearance, or functions quite knowledgably… unlike in English, whereby the 'fisher' **does not fish** -- doesn't like even getting its feet wet (though will swim if absolutely unavoidable). Butterflies: do they have anything to do with butter? No! And are not always "buttery" (i.e., yellow).

Addendum continued

For confirmation of the accuracy of descriptions of wildlife that form the basis of Abenaki names, let us look to the *roots* of words as documented in Dr. Days' *List of Selected Roots,* pages XXVI - LXXI, *Western Abenaki Dictionary,* Volume I. Here we find the possible basis for the word for the otter, which is onegigw (p. 410). On page LVIII of *Selected Roots* we find oniga- which indicates "carry, portage." Does carry, especially *portage,* have anything to do with the "life style" of otters? We usually think of the term 'portage' in connection with humans carrying, on their shoulders, canoes to places of calm water between stretches of fierce rapids or waterfalls. Do otters function in much the same way? Not that they carry anything on their shoulders. But when you consider that otters are *aquatic* animals, who get their living by snatching, very quickly, fish or frogs, do we detect a portage-like pattern? In what sort of streams do otters catch their fishy sustenance… in fast water or in calm water, in pools? Fish usually hover calmly in pools, watching for food to descend to them from upstream. If you approach stealthily you can see them 'hanging in there,' patiently waiting. Traveling from *pool* to *pool,* passing by fast water to reach calm water… as if "portaging," without a boat, without paddles… but isn't an otter quite boat-like? They have 'paddles,' -- their webbed feet. Their bodies are much like boat hulls… elongated, streamlined. An otter even features a 'rudder' of sorts… his streamlined tail. Therefore it is likely that there is a close affinity between the terms oniga- and onegigw, otter. Also in the commonly understood words for "carry or portage," onigan, and onigas: "portager, a carrier," page 410.

The 'fisher,' so-called, brings us to a similar expression. The word is olanigw. We see in the first syllable the equation for 'good,' ola (other common variations are oli and ole) which implies that the animal is *good* at something. Could it be good at hunting, moving rapidly from place to place, tireless, relentless, as it chases squirrels across branches or springs after rabbits and chipmunks, etc., on the ground..?

Let us examine, now, the Alnôbaiui etymology for an *inanimate* object… the knife. 'Knife' is a word that all English-speaking people know, of Anglo-Saxon origin according to *Webster's Dictionary*. The instrument is called nsakuagw in Abenaki. But how do those syllables equate to what we understand about knives..? We know that a knife, the blade, must be sharp. Examining the word syllable by syllable, consulting Day's *Selected Roots,* p. LVII, we find nsa… meaning 'careful.' The second part may be from another Abenaki word which can apply here… kôgw, porcupine, from "***prickly***," and meaning, *possibly* (keeping in mind that we're using European letters here, as opposed to the spoken word) "Careful… it's sharp..! [Like a] porcupine's quill." Other knives, more specialized than the common knife referred to above, the bark-peeling knife and 'crooked knife,' are spelled out on page 115.

Bibliography

New Familiar Abenakis and English Dialogues, Joseph Laurent, Abenakis Chief, Leger Brousseau, Québec, 1884. Global Language Press Reprint, http://www.language.press.com. P.O. address:
Suite 613-1755 Robeson St, Vancouver, V6G 3B7, British Columbia

Western Abenaki Dictionary, Dr. Gordon M. Day. Mercury Series, Canadian Ethnology Service, Paper 128, 1994. Volume I: Abenaki to English. Volume II: English to Abenaki. Canadian Museum of Civilization, Hull, Québec

Alnôbaôdwa: A Western Abenaki Language Guide, J. E. Brink, Gordon M. Day, 1990

Language of the Abnaquies, Rev. Sébastian Râle, Collections of the Maine Historical Society, Volume IV, 1856, Augusta, ME

Abenaki Legends, Grammar, and Place Names: Chief Henry L. Masta, 1932, Victoriaville, Quebec. Bowman Books reprint, Greenfield Center, NY 12833

French-Abenaki Dictionary, Rev. Joseph Aubrey, circa 1700. Abenaki-English, 1995, Chief Stephen Laurent, Odanak Reserve Museum, Odanak Reserve, Québec

Native New England Cooking, Dale Carson, Peregrine Press, 1980, Old Saybrook, CT

The Wampanoag Indian Federation, Milton A. Travers, Christopher Publishing House, 1957. Boston, MA

One of the Keys Wampanoag Indian Contribution, 1676 - 1976. Milton A. Travers, Dartmouth, Massachusetts Bicentennial Commission, 1976, Dartmouth, MA

New Hampshire Nature Notes, Hilbert R. Siegler, Equity Publishing, 1962, Orford, NH

Dictionary of Native American Terminology, Carl Waldman, 2010, Castle Books, NY

The History of the Five Indian Nations Dependent on the Province of New-York, 1727, Cadwallader Colden, Facsimile Reprint 1980, Cornell University, Ithaca, NY

One Thousand Useful Mohawk Words, David Kanatawakhon Maracle, 1992, Audio-Forum, Guilford, CT

Pageant of the Gun Harold L. Petersen, Doubleday & Co. Garden City, NY, 1967

Roots, An Underground Botany & Forager's Guide, D. B. Elliot, 1976, Chatham Press, Greenwich, CT

Edible Wild Plants, Peterson Field Guides, 1977, Haughton / Mifflin, NY

Bibliography Continued

Wilderness Harvest, Alyson H. Knap, Pagurian Press, Ltd., 1979. Toronto, Canada

How Glooscap Outwits the Ice Giants Retold by Howard Norman, 1989. Little, Brown, & Co., New York, Toronto, London

Glooscap and His Magic Legends of the Wabanaki Indians Kay Hill, 1963, McClelland & Stewart Ltd., Halifax, Nova Scotia

Hail, Nene Karenna. The Hymn, Bruce A. Burton, 1978. Security-Dupont Publishing, Rochester, NY

Legends of the Iroquois, from 'Authoritative Studies and Notes,' as told by "The Cornplanter," William W. Canfield, A. Wessels Co., New York 1902

Silver in the Fur Trade, 1995, Martha Wilson Hamilton, Chelmsford, MA

Wolverine Creates the World Labrador Indian Tales, Retold by Lawrence Millman, 1993. Capra Press, Santa Barbra, CA

The French Occupation of the Champlain Valley, 1609 - 1769 Guy Omeron Coolidge, Harbor Hill Books, 1938, Mamaroneck, NY

Folk Medicine of the Delaware and Related Algonkin Indians Gladys Tantaquidgeon, 1977 Pennsylvania Historical Commission, Harrisburg, PA

Secrets of Mayan Science / Religion, Hunbatz Men, Bear & Company Publishing, 1990 Rochester, VT 05767

What Language Is (And what it isn't and what it could be), John McWhorter, 2011. Gotham Books, New York

The Earth Chronicles (Series), Zecharia Sitchin, 1976 – 2007. Bear & Company Publishing, Rochester, VT 05767

Slave Species of the Gods, Michael Tellinger, 2005. Bear & Company Publishing, Rochester, VT 05767

New Englands Rarities Discovered, John Josselyn. Massachusetts Historical Society Facsimile Reprint. "First printed at *London* in the Year 1672 and reprinted at *Boston* in 1972 by the Massachusetts Historical Society"

INDEX

Abenaki - Ô'banaki: The eastern direction, from Ô'ban or **Aban**-aki, the *Dawn* Land. When applied to a person, it means a person of the East of Algonquian affinity. When referring to the Abenaki *people,* the animate plural 'ak' should be added as a suffix: Ô'banaki*ak*. French-accented versions are *Abnaquies* or Abénakis 1, 16-17, 24, 35, 43, 51, 53, 55-56, 58-59, 61-62, 64, 66, 68, 70-74, 77-78, 81-84, 86-88, 91-93, 96, 99, 103-107, 109, 111, 113, 116-117, 121-124, 128, 133-134, 136, 139, 143-144, 146-147, 152, 154, 156-157, 160, 162, 163-164, 168-169, 173, 175

Abenaki Stories - Ô'banaki Ôtlokôganal 1, 14

Abitibi - Osôgena (Algonkin) Council Fire town in Canada 144, 147, 155, 158

Adirondack Mountains - 62, 176

Agauamuk - Agawam People 56

Akkadian - Akkad, ancient empire following Sumer 63

A'lôn - (from Saint) Hélène, Chief Grey Lock's wife 4-6, 8, 12-16, 19, 21, 23, 25-28, 34, 61, 173

Algonquian - Usually refers to the widespread Algonquian *language family* 4, 54-55, 56, 84, 89, 106-107, 127, 129, 131, 136, 145, 165-166

Algonkins - The *specific* First Nations people of Canada, in their own language Osôgenak 129, 144, 147, 154, 157-159, 161, 166, 175

Antler - Askan 66, 117, 132

Anunnaki - Those Who from Heaven to Earth Came 63

All Mighty Power - Nônguic'hi-Ntatôgw 29

Amulets - 73

April - Makuônikas, Red-Boiling (Maple Sugaring) Moon 45

Arbor - 58, 61

Arrow, arrows - Tiskuôdi, tiskuôdial 37, 74, 89, 91, 93, 106, 109, 113, 115-116, 122-123, 129-130, 137, 160, 171

Arrowhead Bird - Seguanihla, Pileated Woodpecker 64

Artist - Nodsi-sezouigad 3-4

Aubery, the Rev. Joseph - Missionary to the Indians, compiler of circa 1700 *French-Abenaki Dictionary* 99, 104, 116

August - Tmezôuas, Cutting Moon 52

Autumn - Taguôgw 46, 60, 80, 118, 123, 150, 153, 159, 175

Awashonks - Euasaunks, Woman Chief 54-55

Bad Weather - Madsekisegad 3

Ball Game - Pabaskuhamauôgan (Lacrosse) 13

Bark - Ualaga 52, 58, 65, 93, 115, 120, 102, 137

Basket - Auanoda (Woody Bag) 50, 123, 151

Basswood - *Tilia americana*, Wigebimezi (Bast Tree) 80

Bats - Madagenihlasak 28

Beads - Mozôbial 2, 58, 74, 82

Beans - Adebakual 68, 75, 134, 141-142

Bears - Moôuinak 51, 59, 61, 87, 108, 112-113, 116-117, 156-158, 161, 176

Beavers - Tmakuak, Tree Cutters, Abagôlak, Flat Tails, Auadnakuazidsik, Wood Carriers, Makuabid (a beaver in the sense of "Red One Who Sits") 29, 35-43, 115, 119, 170-172

Beaver Lodge - Tmakua Uigiuôm 40-41, 44

Beaver-Stabbing Instrument - Tmakua Astahigan (Trident) 36, 40, 42

Beaver Stick - Kaskaamaakw - It is wide, broad (surface of pond) stick found there, having been used for food by beaver 36, 41-42

Be still! - Zôgenauigi! 35

Beeches - Ôadsoimiziak - Highland Trees 31, 120

Beef - Kaoziia 20

Bees - Ôauilômuak (Wasps) 56

Bible, The - *La Bible,* Up Biblum 55, 57, 113-114, 119, 140

Birch (Tree) - Maskuamozi 48-49, 102

Birch Bark - Maskua 6, 10-13, 15, 48-50, 102, 139, 143, 166, 169

Birch Tree Sap - Maskuamoza Ôskidakuon 12

Birds - Lidooak "They that fly." Can include Bats 28, 64, 92, 111-113, 115-117, 119, 121, 124-125, 137

Birds - Sipsak (Small birds, songbirds, recently birds in general) 63, 116

Bison - Pziko, animate plural pzikoak 217

Black Flies - Gigue'ds'ze'gibsak, Little no-neck ones 44, 76

Black Partridges - Meskagôdaghlak (Spruce Grouse) 61

Black Robes - (also Black Gowns) Mkazaui Pitkôzonak 20, 23-26, 30, 57-58, 69, 75, 113, 133-134, 139, 158

Bloodroot - Pagakanihlôg 148-149, 160

Bobcats - Uigôdiak (No Tails, also Lynx. Pezoak - Wild Cats) 35, 117

Bobolink - Nebesicogeleskok, Pond Blackbirds 64

Bon Appétit! - Ôigapuôgan! 14

Bone hide scraper - Oskan pelagakhigan 6

Bone - Oskan 66

Boston, City of - 9

Boston Harbor - 55

Bostonian - Pastoni 10, 15-16, 25, 54-57, 66, 71-72, 76, 78, 80-81, 87, 91, 105, 107, 113, 124, 126, 128, 139, 140, 142, 150, 173

Bourgeois 24

Bow, long - Tôbi kuena 36, 74-75, 93, 109, 115, 122-123, 129-130, 137, 160, 171

Bowl - Kuat (also Pot) 27

Brandy - Blandi 57, 69, 167

Bread - Abon 20, 75

Brother - Idzia 40, 59

Buck - Aiyôba - Male Deer, Male Ungulate 44, 117

Buckskin (Deerskin) - Nolkaua 7, 29, 58, 66, 73, 119, 122, 130-131, 153, 170

Bull Frog - Agebalamo (a cousin) 58

Cache (Stash) 19

Cæsar Besogne - La Bluetté friend, assistant 6, 8-13, 15-16, 20, 22, 24-25, 27, 173

Cakes - Abônak (from Breads) 19-20

Camp - Kôn 1, 70, 102, 107

Canada Jay - or 'Whisky Jack,' from Keskedzagua(k), Rubbish Bird(s) 218

Canada - Kanada 18, 24, 71, 77, 83, 102, 107, 129, 133, 161, 176

Canadiens 3, 5, 22-23, 24, 28, 81, 84, 89, 91, 93, 103, 109, 127, 129, 133, 158, 168

Cane Sugar - *Canne* Zogal 6, 10, 19

Caribou hide - Maglibôua 10, 143, 172

Caribou, Woodland - Magôliboak 12, 15-16, 18, 29, 116-117, 162, 167

Carlson, Dale 19

Catamount - Pittôlo - Very Much Tail (also Cougar, Puma, Mountain Lion) 35, 80, 103, 117

Caughnawaga - Kaanauagihnono (Iroquois allied to French) 4, 81-83, 129, 131, 133-135

Ceremony - 54, 57-58, 62-63, 67-68

Chestnut Stew - Uôbimen Pagasôbôkôn 19, 27

Chickadee - Kejegigilhasiz 63-64

Chief - Sôgemô (Guide, Pathfinder) 1, 12, 17-18, 53-54, 59, 62, 68, 75, 78, 92, 112, 121, 128, 136, 140, 151, 157, 174-175

Children - Auôsizak 9, 67-68, 71, 114, 136, 138

Chipmunks - Anikusesak 66, 138

Chocolate - Tsôkaulat (from Nahuatl: *Chocolatl*) 8, 75

Christian - 24, 27, 30, 55-56, 75, 84, 87, 114, 139

Church - (Usually Catholic Church) 75, 134

Clan - Moiety, Affinity Group 61

Clay Pot - Mazalôpskw Kuat 6

Cloud Eagle - Asokw Mgezo (a Person of Spiritual Power, 'Medicine Man') 26-32, 34-35, 37-43, 53-55, 57-58, 60-63, 67-69, 71, 73-75, 77-78, 80, 82, 84-93, 95-108, 111-113, 115, 119-124, 126-128, 130-134, 138-142, 145-153, 158-160, 162-164, 167-175

Club - Gualôm (club), Migakaigualôm, Fighting Bat 40, 73

Coffee - Kapi 5, 8, 75

Common (Native) People - Alnôbak 12, 23, 26, 33, 46, 49, 54, 57, 63-64, 71, 74, 77-78, 80-83, 87, 89-91, 94, 98, 100, 103, 109-110, 113-114, 119, 136, 138, 140, 148, 169, 174

Common People's Way - Alnôbaiui 4, 16, 18, 43, 46, 61, 63, 83, 105-107, 121, 145, 147

Compagnie - French for company 24

Connecticut River - Kuenitegw, Long River 54, 56-57, 69

Cooking - Zogelozuôgan 21

Corn (Zea maize) - Skamôn 50, 68, 134, 141-142

Council Fire - 65

Council - Podauazeuôgan 53, 57, 76, 78

Council House - Podauazeuigamigw 65, 67

Crackerjacks - Maple syrup-dripped popcorn 19

Craions - Crayons 4

Crows - Mkazasak, Charcoal Colored Ones 39

Crucifix - *Le Crucifix* 75, 84

Cultural Genocide 59

Dancers - 58-59, 63

Dawn Land - Ô'ban Aki 70, 111

Day, Gordon M., Ph.D. - Compiler of *Western Abenaki Dictionary,* I, II 72, 163

Dead Water - "A reach," Mskitegua (or 'Scodoqua') 25

Deity - *Dieu,* Niuaskw, Niuaskouôgan 23, 26, 139

Deerfield, Massachusetts 57

Deer Island - Nolka Menahan 55

Deer, Whitetail - Nolka 12, 110, 117-118, 128, 145, 159, 172, 176-178

Delaware - Word used for the Lenapéuk Nation, derived from first governor Lord De La Warre, from whom Delaware Bay and Delaware River take their names 174

Deniz - Denis, Azôn-Badise's cousin 16, 26

Diable - French for Devil 24, 84, 140

Diarrhea - Naaiahlauôgan, "Down Flowing," 78-80, 90, 92, 173-175

Doctor - Nbizonhouad, *naturel docteur* 106, 109, 144, 146, 148-150, 160, 163

Dog - Adia (obsolescent), alemos (contemporary). Dogs, obsolescent plural: Adiak, contemporary plural: alemosak 35, 41-42, 51, 75, 83, 97, 99, 170-171

Donators - *Donneuers*, Donnéak 20, 24-27, 69, 133

Drinking utensils - Odzesmimek auakôganal 21

Drum - Pagholigan 22, 24, 26, 58, 61-64, 69

Drummers - Pakholidak 61, 63-64

Drumming of Grouse - Neguanapozin 62

Ducks - Kuiguigemok (specifically black ducks, but *can* mean ducks in general) 66

Dutch 25, 70, 78-81, 87, 90, 99, 102, 109, 124, 126, 133, 161

Eagle - Mgezo 49, 86-87

Easter - *Pâques* 75

Eating - Mohômek 21

Eels - Nahômoak: They Go with the Current 160, 166

Elders - Ktsiiak 15, 53, 55, 58, 86, 109, 114, 120, 140

Elk - Uabôz (White Rumped) 29, 35, 117, 176

Eliot, Reverend John - 55

English, the - Iglismôniak, *les Anglais,* (Dyol'hensha'geh in Mohawk) 1, 4, 10, 12, 16-18, 33, 54-57, 65, 71-77, 79, 82-83, 85, 90-93, 96-99, 102, 106, 108-111, 116, 122, 124-128, 133, 136, 138, 140, 143, 147, 150, 153, 157, 160-161, 166-167, 173

Englishman's Way - Iglismôniui 17, 55, 65, 99, 105

Epidemic - 71-72, 140

Fans - 58

Feast - 56, 62

February - Piaôdagos 8, 29, 30, 35, 175

Female Birds - Skuahlak 61

Fence - (Beaver-stopping barrier) Pemelodigan 41, 44

Fiddleheads - Alipodôzigdebal 149-151, 153, 160-161

Field - Kikas and Kikônal, Fields (plural), 13, 58, 62

Firelock - Paskhigan, *fusil*, musket (long gun) 1, 11, 37-39, 73-74, 76-77, 80-82, 86-87, 89-91, 94-100, 106, 122, 125-127, 147, 151, 157, 160, 171

Flicker Person - Guelegueno, Olôbao's uncle 57

Fishers (Fisher 'Cats') - Olaniguak 51, 87, 111

Fish(es) - Namasak 20, 28, 33, 53, 68, 111-112, 119-120, 123, 160, 170, 172

Fishing - Ahômauômek (Act of Fishing: Namaskan). Fishing Place: Pmômanosek 43, 70, 76, 85, 123, 127, 157, 160, 169, 171

Fleuve St. Laurent - The St. Lawrence River 71

Flies, Black - Gigue'ds'ze'gibsak - No-Neck Ones, little - 44

Flies, House - Odzauas (Plural Odzauasak) 56, 120

Flies - Plac'môniak Odzausak, Whitemen's Flies (Honey Bees) 45-46, 49, 50-51

Fork - Nimatguahigan 14

Fort George -18

Fort Orange - Colonial name for Albany, N.Y., from Dutch regime - 78-79, 87, 91, 100, 107, 126, 128, 167

Fort Saint Anne - 46

Fort Saint Jean - 65, 69, 103

Four Winds, the - A Native American way of indicating the (Sacred) Four Directions of the earth (the Cardinal Directions) 58, 103, 135, 159, 171

Fox - Ôkuses 35, 116

France - Plac'mônki, Whitemen's Land 65, 79, 114

Frenchmen - Whitemen: Plac'môniak 3-4, 20, 33, 51, 57, 65, 70-71, 74, 77-85, 87-92, 97, 100, 103-106, 113-116, 119, 122, 129, 133-134, 140, 145, 150, 157-158, 163, 166-167

Fur Hat - Osuadagen Asolkuôn 1, 2, 5, 29

Furs - 3, 56, 65, 74, 95, 110, 116, 119, 133, 145

Fur Trader - *Coureur de Bois* (Runner of the Woods) 57, 69, 77-78

Game (Sport) - Papuôgan 13, 43, 56

Garden - Nebizonkikôn (Medicine Field) 43-45, 48, 51, 68

Gathering Song - Makagamoldinek Lintouôgan 22

Ginseng - 65, 104

Good Forest, the - Olakuika 29, 30, 63, 93

Good Morning (also 'I'm glad to see you,' if afternoon) - Paakuinôguzian 4

Good Red Road - Oligo Mkui O'udi (Spiritual Path) 54, 69, 86, 145

Gookin - The Reverend Mister - 55

Goose, Wild - Wôbtegaua or Uôbtegaua (Geese Wôbtegauak) 217

Grand Chief - Ktsi Sôgemô 17

Grandfather - 118-119, 173

Grandmother - 118-119, 147, 152, 156, 177-178

Great Grandmother - Ktsi Okemes (plural: Ktsi Okemesak) 44, 112

Great Sailing Ships - Kitolagol 46

Great Spirit - Ktsi Manitou (Great Spirit), Ktsi Maneniuiô (Great Mystery), Ktsi Kagôssal'Misiui (Great Creator), Ktsi Niuaskw (Great Deity) 23, 27-28, 30, 95, 111, 114-115, 118, 136, 139, 148

Greetings - Pahakuinôguezi (to someone you haven't seen for some time) 21

Grey Lock - Ôauanoleuo (He Who Fools Them) Pial-Azôn (*Pierre-Jean*) 1, 7-8, 11-12, 16-17, 21, 24-25, 27, 34, 59, 78, 128, 140, 149, 172-173, 175

Grey Lock's Brother - Malalamet 26

Ground Nuts - or Indian Potatoes: - Apenak (also Skibô, in the sense of "can be eaten raw.") Can also mean testicles 77, 98, 105, 108-110, 119, 132, 137-138, 140, 144, 151

Gun Barrel - Zôbôlagezo 5

Half Moon - Pabasôgizo, 'a tall hunter,' 20, 22, 24, 26, 30, 58

Handsome Lake - Seneca spiritual revivalist 9

Hare - Mataguas (also means Rabbit) 146

Hawk - Siômo 1-2

Head Breaker Club - Baskhôdebahigan 73

Hedgehog - Old New England folk name for porcupine 51

He Dreams of Someone - Nespokusino 122-123, 160

He Lives (the Survivor) - Ôlebmôuzo 134, 136

He Makes Himself from Something - Ôdzihózo 49

He Produces (or He Makes) - Kisikauo, Paramount Medaulinno at Missisquoi 69-70, 87, 93, 140, 149, 168

Heron - Kaskó (also name for the Crane) 217

Hesitant, Delaying Person - Turtle Clan Member: Pelauinno 61

He Who Goes Ahead - Pmauikho, War Chief 83-86, 88-92, 100-102, 106, 108, 121, 128, 165, 168

He (his voice) Sounds Nice - Olitôguezo 128-134, 144

He Who Walks Softly - Sken'nenhahson'adsi'ile, young Kaanaugi scout / fighter 81-84, 90, 93, 95, 129, 133-134

Hide - 61, 73, 92, 110, 124, 155

High Bush Cranberries - Nibimenal 7-8, 10, 12, 175

High Bush Cranberry bush - Nibimenakuam 7, 12-14, 16, 175

Hoosic River - Tributary of Hudson River 25

Hudson's River - 91, 107, 126, 145

Hummingbirds - Nanatasizak 45

Hunters - Nadialuinnoak 11, 56, 74, 110, 120-122, 130, 134, 147, 150, 160, 163, 171, 176

Hunting - Nadialmek 9, 49, 56, 70, 74, 80, 85, 106, 110, 123-124, 126-127, 129, 155, 157, 160, 170-171

Ice - Pkuami 67

Ice Chisels - Amiskuôganal (for breaking into beaver houses) 35, 40-41, 170

Iraq - 63

Iroquois - Five Nations (Mohawk, Oneida, Onondaga, Cayuga, Seneca) 24, 81, 83, 127, 129, 131, 133, 135-136, 161, 166, 175-176

Isle La Motte - 46

Jean-Baptise - Azôn-Badise, Grey Lock's son, Ôski Nikola --Young Nicholas,-- Migakadoso --Fighting Man, little -- 4-5, 15-16, 18, 26, 59

Jesus - Sazos 20, 75, 158, 161

Jonas T'songeba - Expatriate Mohican member of Chief Pmauikho's war party 78-81, 84-89, 90, 101, 106-107, 121-122, 124, 126-128, 167, 144, 147, 163, 167

Keeper of the Game - Nanaualdad'ua Auaasak 30, 34

Kennebec River - 17

Kettle - Akogw - 21, 51, 65

Kiodsaton - Mohawk chief who -- too briefly -- brought about a brokered peace between the previously contending Five Nations Iroquois and the French and Algonkin Nation of Canada 175-176

Killinick - It's mixed: Certain dried leaves and flower petals mixed with tobacco, 31-32, 103, 175

King James I - Kinjames, Sakso (Abenaki accented *Jacques* from French for James) 16-17

King James II - 70

King Louis XIV - *Le Roi Louis XIV* 65, 79

King Philip - Metacom or Metacomet 54, 55, 110

King Philip War - 9, 55, 128

King's Broad Arrow - 95

King William's War (after King William III of Orange) 71, 74

Kisikauo - Paramount Medaulinno at Missisquoi 69, 70, 139, 140, 149, 167, 168

Knife - 37, 39, 48, 66, 73, 77, 80, 96, 98, 106, 114-115, 131-132

Knifemen - (or Cutthroats), T'sauguaqock 54

Knockers - Nôbasasak, Woodpeckers 64, 120

Kuôgunas - (Interchangeable with C'hila): "Prickly One," (perennially dissatisfied one) 144, 147, 152-159

Kullos'kahp - Man from Nothing (Spontaneous Man), or "Elder Brother," (Mi'kmak word) 49, 111-119, 130, 138

Kyâs'hútâ - Gahnyen'kehàgä Iroquoian for 'Fire on the Mountain,' an older Kaanauagi warrior with Pmauikho's band, uncle of Walks Softly 129-138, 167

La Bluetté - The Artistic Farmer 3, 5-8, 10-16, 20, 22, 24, 27, 38, 173

Lake Champlain - Pitaubagw -- the Water between-- 25, 62, 65, 69, 71, 76, 101-102, 121, 165-166

La Marine - French Navy and Colony *troupes* of *Ministère de la Marine* 65, 78, 83, 94, 100

Lamoille River, upper - Ointegak -- (Bone) Marrow Waters -- 26

Lamoille River, lower - Mskiteguak (or "Scodokuek") -- Dead (Still) Waters -- 25, 26, 167

Late Summer 'Eating Moons' - Midsouôgankas 52

Laurent, Joseph (Chief) - Language Educator 56, 60, 63, 68, 72, 85, 92, 104, 107, 116, 160

Laurent, Stephen (Chief) - Son of Chief Joseph Laurent, 20th century translator of the Reverend Aubery's French - Abenaki Dictionary into English 70, 99, 104, 116

Leeks - Ôinozak 147, 150-153, 158, 160 -161

Lenapéuk - (Ordinary People) Delaware Indian Nation 127, 174

Lieutenant Louis Le Mercier - 78-80, 82-86, 88-94, 100-102

Lightning - Padôghi (Thunderbolt) 63, 67, 114-117

Lilies, Trout - Uzôuataual, Skotam - Mozilalo (Moose's Tongue) 43, 139

Liquor, hard - Akubi 24-25

Little Pine Trees Place - Koasok 57, 69

Little Pine Trees People - Koasak 54, 57, 69

Loaves and Fishes - Abônak ta Namasak 20

Lodge - Uigiuôm (Wigwam) 9, 12, 16-17, 69-70, 92, 109, 114, 119, 136, 138, 154, 157, 170, 172, 174-175

Longhouse - Kuena'tagigamigw 65, 68

Louisa Sackett - Bride of Sakso 9

Maigamo - Algonkian for He is Wolf 145-146, 149, 152-155, 157-161, 166-167, 175

Maine - District of, 56

Male Birds - Nôbahlak 61, 62

Malgelit - Algonkin for (Ste.) Margaret, otherwise known as Ininädsko, Caribou Woman 161, 166-167

Man - Sanôba 13, 66, 75

Manure - Pakikôgan 51

Maple (Tree) - Senômozi (Rock Maple) 45, 47, 52, 78, 174

Maple Sugar - Senômozimlases (Rock-Maple Molasses) 6, 10, 19

Marie-Charlotte - Mali-Sallot, A'lôn's and Grey Lock's daughter 16, 26

Martens, Pine - Apanakesak 51, 87

Massachusetts - Mäsa'dzosek (or Massa'dzosek) Great Hills Place 4, 9, 15, 54-55, 59, 74, 105, 124, 126, 128, 163

Masta, Henry L. (Chief) - 20th century Abenaki Language Educator 61, 113, 144, 154, 156

Master of Life - Tabaldak 29

Medicine - Physical medicine, *nebizon* (the word stems from **mineral** water) 33, 54, 68-69, 71-75, 84, 92, 102-104, 134, 136-137, 139-140, 146-147, 149, 174

Mesopotamia - 63

Molasses - Melasses 6, 10

Mink - Moskuas 29

Mint - 69

Miracle - *Miraculeux* 20

Missionaries - *Missionnaires* 24-25, 33, 69, 134

Mission - St. Francis, Odanak 72, 84

Missisquoi - Mazipskoik, "Place of Flint" (meaning place of *chert*), Mazipskiak: (Chert-Place People) 27-28, 45-46, 56, 69-71, 83-84, 101, 113, 121, 140, 144, 164, 168, 173

Missisquoi Bay - *Le Cul de Sac* 69, 76, 168

Missisquoi River - Mazips'tegw 65-66, 171

Mittens - Meldzasak 2

Moccasin - Mkezen 23, 72, 76, 78-80, 123, 136

Mocha - 6, 10, 12, 75

Mohawk - Maguak (Abenaki translation: "They Defecate in Fear"). Called by French '*Aniez*' 15, 18, 71, 76, 78-79, 81-82, 86, 93, 95, 102, 127, 129, 133-134, 136, 143, 165, 167, 175

Mohicans - Muheconnuck 4, 26, 71-72, 76, 78-79, 81-82, 86, 92-93, 95, 102, 107, 122, 124, 126-128, 144-145, 147, 163, 167, 173

Mohican Way - Muheconnui 81

Mont Royale - Montreal, Canada 46

Moon of Moose Hunting - Mozokas (March) 11

Moose - Moz 12, 21, 29, 31, 112, 116-117, 170, 176

Moosewood - Striped Maple 19

Moth / Butterfly - Mamidzôlo, nickname for daughter of Cloud Eagle & Wise Woman 31, 35

Mother Earth - Nigaues Aki (*Our* Mother Earth) 23, 28, 68, 168

Mother - Nigaues, *My* mother 44, 57 (also as Nonon, Abenaki accented 'Mama') 156

Moose meat - Moziya 11

Mosquitoes - Peguesak 76

Mother Tongue - *Langues Maternelle* 10

Moses - Hebrew biblical figure 114-115, 140

Mount Sinai - Legendary biblical mountain in the Sinai Peninsula 140

M'Sadokues - (Ancestral) Person from the Big River (the Connecticut) 149, 163

Mskog'kuedmos - Big, huge, snake-like creature that is seldom seen (today's Lake Champlain dinosaurian creature popularly known as "Champy") 164

Muskrat - Moskuas 30, 34, 113, 171

My (or Our) friend - Nidômba 4, 110

My (Our) grandmother - Nokemes 14

My switch - Nibizi 12

My switch berry - Nibimen 13-14

My switch berry-bush - Nibimenakuam 13-14

Narragansett - 54, 68

Natick - Praying Indian town 56

Naturels, Les - The Naturals (Native Americans) 10, 24

Naval Stores - 65

Nbizonhouad - Abenaki name for a medical aide, or doctor 144, 146, 151, 158, 160

Nbizonhouo M'Sadokues - Medicine Provider of Big River Forebears, aunt of the M'Sadokues brothers 168

Necessaries pouch - Couidebal pitôgan (or "bandolier bag") 66, 82, 85-86, 90, 106, 145, 153

New France - *Nouvelle France* 69, 77

New Leaf - Pilaskw (Paper) 3

Nicola - "Nikola," (Nicola with Abenaki accent) Son of Chief Grey Lock 27, 94-96, 98, 104

Nicotiana rustica - Tobacco 2

Nicotiana tabacum - Tobacco 3

Nickommo Ceremony - 54

Northampton, Massachusetts - 57

Nipmuck Nation - of Massachusetts, 12, 54, 57

Odanak - Plural for town*s* in Abenaki language. Specifically Christian mission village with the (primarily) French town of St. Francis across river 105, 113, 143, 147, 157-158, 163

Oneida Nation - One of the original five of the Iroquois League of Five Nations, whose ancient territory was the next west of Mohawk territory 175

Old, ancient - Negôni, negônia (older) 15

Olôbao - Handsome (One), son of Cloud Eagle & Wise Woman 29, 34, 36-37, 39-40, 50-54, 56, 58, 60-61, 63, 68-69, 71, 169-171

Osprey - Maanamaguas, "Fish Gatherer," plural Maanamaguasak 218

Our land - N'd'akinna 4, 77, 109

Ours - Le Sieur Nicholas de Saint, Colonel *du Milice* 18, 22

Owl - Kokokhás, the Great Horned Owl or Barred Owl 217

Ô'auksuauni - (or Hawkswawney) Festive time following autumn hunt 56

Ôligouôgasku'sizo - Beautiful Girl, Daughter of Ôeoandamsko & Cloud Eagle 31-32, 37, 39-40, 69, 71, 170-172

Ôualôba - 'Pretty One,' infant son of Soliôn and Kôgunas 156

Païen - Pagan 24, 27, 32, 134, 145, 158

Paint - Sezohiga 4, 67, 73-74, 84, 135, 143, 148

Parkman, Francis - Popular 19th century historian whose theme was 'The Romance of the American Wilderness' 175

People of the "Flint" (actually Chert) Place - Mazipskiak 56, 61, 70, 84

Pepôkuan - Name of an expatriate member of He Who Goes Ahead's war band, and a way of saying, in the Shawnee Nation dialect, 'Firelock,' from Explosion Instrument (a gun)… 106-107, 121, 124, 126-128, 147, 163-164

Person of Spiritual Power - Medaulinno (or medauinno, shaman, *'homme de medicine,'* medicine man, so called. A *Woman* of Spiritual Power is Medaulinnoskua) 27, 36, 40, 53, 60, 64, 69, 70, 72-73, 75, 84-85, 88, 90, 92, 115, 130, 134, 140, 146,

147, 149-151, 158-161, 163, 165, 168-169, 171

Pigeon - Pelaz, Wild Pigeon, Passenger Pigeon 15

Pilgrims - 54, 110-111

Pioneers, Military - *Pionniers* (the French word) 102, 109

Pipe Bag - 58

Pipe - Odamôgan, Smoking instrument. Also name of dragonfly 31-32, 58, 104, 145, 153, 159, 168, 171

Pipe Tomahawk - Combination hatchet and smoking pipe 80, 103-104

Place of Flint (meaning Chert) People - Mazipskiak 56, 61, 84

Planet Nibiru - 10th planet of solar system (assuming Pluto to be a *planet,* the 9th, rather than the 'planetlet' of the 'official' astronomical Establishment) 63

Plymouth Company 17

Plug-Bayonet - Kebahigan-Metsetsakw 77

Pmauikho - 'He Goes Ahead,' Abenaki Chief of Scouts, War Captain 83, 88-91

Pocumtuck Confederation ("River Indians") 54

Popham, George 17

Popham's Fur Trading Station - 56

Porcupine - Kôgw: Spiny One. Also Mandaôsw or Môndaôsw: Slow One 51-53, 58-60, 62, 68, 117-118, 128

Portage - 68

Pot, small - Kokuiz 21

Pounders - Lôbatahigasak: Woodpeckers 62

Powder, gun - Peza 5, 73

Prayer - Aiyamihauôgan 27, 74

Prayer House (Church or Chapel) - Aiyamiha'uigamigw 58

Praying Indians - 55, 57

Princess - *Princesse,* Plincess, Ktsi Sôgemôsku'sizo (Great Chief, female, small) 17-18

Puritans - 55, 74, 111

Québec - Kebek / Kibek, Canadian Province and City 69, 98, 133, 135, 144, 156, 167

Québec Governor Vaudreuil 15

Québecois - Resident of Province of Québec 27, 36, 38, 50, 71, 147, 167, 173

Queen Anne's War 25, 71

Raccoon - Azeban 1, 51, 163

Rain Dance - 63

Rain - Zogelôn 46, 50, 58, 62, 65-68

Rainbow Girl - In Algonkin language: Takuanipihisizko. Otherwise known as Mali, from Ste. Marie 161, 166-167, 175, 178

Rainbow Salmon - Managuôn Mskuamago, Olôbao's Uncle 43, 59

Rain (Bringing Birds) - Zogelônihlak (Swallows) 62, 134

Raleigh, Gilbert - 17

Rapids of Chambly - 65

Rattles, ceremonial - Si'zi'uanak 21-24, 27-28, 58, 60, 75, 130, 138

Rattlesnake - Si'si'kua, Abenaki name: 59, 130, 133, 136-138, 144, 173

Rattlesnake - Iroquois name: Ahsdauenónyalrehogonah 136-137

Raven - Ktsi Mkazas, Great Black Person, or Ponki Mkazas, Northland Black 217

Red Boiling Moon - Makuônikas, April, Maple Sugaring Moon 11

Red-Winged Blackbird - Mkui-Oleguan Kogeleskua 21

Rivière La Chute - 103

Rivière Richelieu - Pitaubaguizibo, Between Lakes River 4, 16, 18, 65, 69

Robin - Kui'kueskas, Whistler 63

Roach - (Coxcomb) 64, 66, 73-74, 81, 128, 145

Round basket - Pedeguigek Abazenoda 6

Ruches - Beehives (French) 46

Ruffed Grouse - Pakesso 1, 5, 7, 13-15, 18, 60-61, 64, 92, 159

Saco River, Maine - Msoakutegw, Standing Dead Trees in River 25

Sacred Council - Pônbatami Podauazin 76

Sakso Sackett - Husband of Lowiz 9, 13

Salmon - Mskuamagw: Red Fish 43

Salom - 'Saint Jerome' with an Algonkin accent 145, 150-151, 154-155, 159-161, 166-167, 175

Saint Francis River - Alsigôtekw (Clam Camp River) 157

Saint Jean - 65

Saint Lawrence River - (also as *Fleuve St. Laurent*) 4, 65, 71, 129, 133

Sauvage - Forest (from Sylvan) Person 23-24, 75, 79, 83-85, 93, 110

Scatacôok - Mohican for Still Water (place) 78

Schuylers - Dutch 'patroon' family who collaborated with English 79

Scouts - Nopaosauinnoak (Walk Far Persons) 52, 77-78, 85, 91, 102, 109, 147

Scurvy - *Scorbut* 8, 106

Seed - Oskanimen (Bone - Berry) 43

Seeds, Tobacco - Odamô kikaimenal 43

Seigneury - Estate 18, 65

Semitic - 63

September - Skamonkas, Maize harvesting Moon 19, 50, 52

Sermon - Harangue (archaic term used for a speech or sermon) 20

Shawnee - Suônni (Southern person) 35, 106, 124, 126-128, 147, 163

Sippar - Bird City, city of ancient Sumer 63

Sitchin, Zacharia - 63, 156

Sketching - Gôa'gôa'daôikhimek 4

Skunk - Segôgw 53, 59-60, 62, 68

Skunk's Smell - Segôgimôguezo 53

Small Pox - Maskihlôgan, *l'Vérole* 72

Sleeping Person - Bear Clan Member, Ogauinno 61, 156

Snapping Turtle - Aligedaid 53, 60, 62, 68-69, 169

Soliôn - Abenaki accented 'Juliette' 147, 152, 154, 155, 157, 158-159

Snowshoes - Ô'gemak 1, 7, 10, 44, 113-114, 133

Songbirds - Sipsak 63

Sorel - Québec town at confluence of St. Lawrence & Richelieu Rivers 46

Spear - Astahigan (Stabbing Instrument) 73, 77, 80, 133

Spies - Nadauahak (another expression denoting scouts) 77

Spiritual Medicine Way - Medauliui 57

Spirit - Manitou 75-76, 87, 104, 109, 111, 146, 149, 158-159, 164, 168, 175

Spiritually Powerful Chiefs - (Spirit-Medicine Chiefs) Medaului Sôgemôk 61-62, 68, 75

Spring - Siguak 61, 104, 108, 120, 150, 176

Squash - Wasawa (modern spelling) Ô'asaua (traditional pronunciation) 2, 134

Squirrel - Mikoa (*specifically* Red Squirrel, *may* be used for squirrels in general) 30, 66, 88, 112, 118, 146

Squirrels, Gray - Msaniguak 66, 88, 159

Staghorn Sumac Trees - Zalônak: the name for *Saranac Lake* and River is derived from the Abenaki term 175

Strangers - Auanock (Europeans) 56, 70, 72, 75, 104, 108, 110, 114, 124, 126, 140, 147, 150, 157

Strong Bough - Alsanid Psaôdkueno, A'lon's nephew 21, 26, 29, 58

Strong, Brave - Kagini 68, 85, 173

Succotash - (from Narragansett Msickquatash) 61, 65, 68-69

Sumerian - (Reference to ancient Sumer) 63

Summer - Niben 45, 47-48, 54, 59, 69, 76

Summer Land - Nibenaki (South) 64, 116, 118

Sunflower - 51

Sunday - Sanda (Sunday with an Abenaki accent) 75

Sweet grass - Mskikoiz 5, 52

Tabaldak - The Master: Great Spirit or God 29, 156

Taconics - Taconic Mountains, from Taughkaughnick (Mohican dialect), "Forested Mountains place" 72, 78, 92, 126-128, 163

Tame Beasts - Nidazoak (Cows, livestock in general) 56

Tantaquidgeon, Gladys - 20th century learned herbal researcher and Mohegan Nation Medicine Woman 175

Tellinger, Michael - 63

They Who went Away - Sokuakiiak: Abenaki division whose ancient territory was the Connecticut River watershed from present-day White River Jct., VT (more or less) to the Northfield, MA area 54, 57

Those That Fly - Lidooak 28, 63

Thunder - Padôgi 62, 65, 67, 113, 115-117, 159

Thunderbird - Padôgilidoo 49

Thunderers - Padôgiak 62, 64, 75

Ticonderoga - Peninsula of, 102

Tobacco - Odamô 2-3, 24, 49-50, 62-63, 71, 84, 103, 150, 153, 158, 165, 167, 169, 172, 175

Tobacco's pouch - Odamôinoda 2, 149, 153, 165, 171

Toboggan - 4, 6, 8, 10-11, 20-21, 24, 171

Tomahawk - Alni-tmahigan, Ordinary-transverse cutting instrument (hatchet) 7-8, 106, 177-178

Tracks - Lômptok 35, 76, 78-80

Traditionalist, traditions - 57-58, 67-68, 74, 86, 113-114, 133-134, 145, 158, 173

Trapping - 9, 74

Tree Toad - Ahalôdauasid (the Climber) 88

Trillium, Red - Mkuô-bamegua Sippen 104

Turkey(s) - Nahama, nahamak 7, 92, 121-128, 130, 133, 147, 150, 160

Turpentine - 65

Turtle - Mikinakw 27, 53, 60-61, 76, 169, 176

Voyageurs - 4, 26, 165

Wampanoag - 54, 56-57

War Club - Baskhôdebahigan (Head Breaker) 73

Warriors - Migakauinnoak (meaning Fighting Men) 25, 71-74, 78, 81, 83-87, 89, 91-93, 94, 99, 121, 127-131, 134, 145

Warm Breeze - Asauanlômso 53

Wasp - Ôauilômua 5, 50

Wasp's Sugar (Honey) - Wauiilômwaizogal 5

Water - Nepi (Fresh Water) 12, 52-53, 58, 68-69, 72, 89, 91, 93, 107, 109, 165, 178

Waterfall - Penidzahla: Where water falls. A waterfall 52, 207

Welcoming Song - Kolibiyôn Lintouôgan 22

Weetamoo - Ôu'itamw 54

Westfield, MA - Ôauanokoo, Woronoco 9, 26

Whistling Swan - Ôiguahlo 160, 166

Whitefish Nation - Atticameguesak 161

Whiteman's Way - Plac'môniui 3

Wife (also Husband, meaning Spouse) - Nisuiididsi 20

Wild Animals - Auasaak 19, 52-53, 63, 68, 75, 92, 110-113, 115-119, 124-125, 138, 148, 159, 170

Wilderness - Pisouakamigw 25, 63, 68, 75, 105, 109, 110, 128, 171

Wild Leeks Land, - Ôinozki (Winooski) 25-26

Wild Leeks Place - Ôinozek 147, 149

William of Orange - 70

Windows - Dauzôganal, Cut Openings 65, 67

Winooski River - Ôinozki Tegw (Ôinozkitegw: Onion-Land River) 25-26, 107, 167

Winter - Pebon, 38, 53, 58, 87, 98, 106, 108-110, 114, 116, 118-119, 176

Winter Food - Pebonmizouôgan 38

Wintergreen - Gôa'gôa'gouizak (Repetitive-edged, *dentate* leaves) 7, 10, 175

Wise Woman - Ôeoandamsko, Cloud Eagle's wife 27, 31-36, 39-40, 43, 53-58, 60, 62- 63, 67-71, 74, 75, 87, 101, 103, 140, 143-144, 149, 168-175

Woman of Spiritual Power - Medaulinnoskua 36, 168-169

Women - New Gallic-inspired word: - P'hanemak 9, 13-14, 17, 61, 66, 152, 157

Women (Old, authentic Abenaki word) - Cousoudelak: may indicate Necessary Persons 13

Wonder-tale Stories - Atookuakun Ôdsemouôganal 49, 111, 114-115, 119, 134, 138

Wood - Auazon: Fuel wood or otherwise useful wood. Also Abazi (meaning Tree) 29

Woodcock - Naguibaguihla: Under-Leaf Bird 160

Woodchucks - Agaskuok 67, 146

Wood Creek - 76, 102, 161, 166

Wooden Spoon - Amkuôn 21, 27, 65

Woodpeckers - Knockers, Nôbasasak 64

Young Courteous Girl - Ôski Olakamigesku'sizo - Wise Woman's name when a girl 55, 162

ABOUT the Author: At right, in typical frontier - era Abenaki warrior regalia, flintlock kueni paskhigan, long gun, in hand at the foot of a penidsahla (waterfall), coming down off Woodbury Mountain is author and artist E. George 'Peskunck' Larrabee, of Woodbury, VT.

Peskunck has been writing and illustrating for historical, muzzle loading, and outdoor sports journals for many years, beginning, in the late 1960s, with book and product reviews in *Muzzle Blasts,* the monthly journal of the National Muzzle Loading Rifle Association. Born and raised in Western Massachusetts, where he early engaged in hunting, fishing, and camping, he attended art and printing schools in New York City. Returning to New England, and in 1975, commissioned to execute an American Revolution Bicentennial Series for *Muzzle Blasts,* by 1979 he was invited to become a staff writer for *Muzzleloader* magazine (Gallatin, TN) and in that same year was invited on board the monthly *Black Powder Times,* Washington State, as Historical Editor, serving until 1998. Having equipped himself previously, on May 10, 1975, he participated as one of Ethan Allen's "Bennington Mobb" with Green Mountain Boys direct descendants in the 200th anniversary reenactment of the seizure of Fort Ticonderoga "under Colonel Allen." Later he became a member of the recreated Herrick's Rangers of the Vermont Militia and has also held membership in the NMLRA-chartered Ethan Allen Long Rifles Muzzle Loading Club. A family tradition concerning a paternal 19th century Native great-grandmother, whose places of origin were "Canada, Vermont, and Champlain, New York" (putting her, geographically, in the "Western Abenaki ball park," so to speak) contributed to his early '70s activism in support of the culturally resurrecting Native Rights movement. Motivated to learn the Algonquian dialects of his native region, he increasingly turned his participation in colonial era-imitating reenactments into developing the "persona" of an Abenaki warrior, complete with an in-depth knowledge of the language. "Even without the Indian ancestry on my father's side," he says that he would have striven to know the Algonquian meanings of such names as Massachusetts and Connecticut, &c. Recognized for his efforts on behalf of Native American rights, he was taken into the Abenaki-Sokuakiiak Nation of Missisquoi in a sweat lodge ceremony in 1990. He serves today as a member of the Tribal Council of the (Missisquoi and Koasak- allied) Totem'ua Siômo -- Clan of the Hawk. --

Certificate of Achievement

This is to certify that the bearer _____, a resident of (town) _____, State (or Province) _____, on this date of ___/___/___, has completed reading

A Visit with Chief Grey Lock,

has thoroughly studied the Abenaki words and phrases therein, and… may now be considered, by these presents, as being *familiar* with the Abenaki Indian language.

This citation is hereby awarded in recognition of this outstanding achievement.

E. George 'Peskunck' Larrabee

Signed by the Author: E. George 'Peskunck' Larrabee

www.ingramcontent.com/pod-product-compliance
Lightning Source LLC
Chambersburg PA
CBHW082038230426
43670CB00016B/2702